From Word to Land

AMERICAN CULTURE
Herausgegeben von Norbert Finzsch, Bettina Friedl,
Hans-Peter Rodenberg und Joseph C. Schöpp

Band 5

PETER LANG
Frankfurt am Main · Berlin · Bern · Bruxelles · New York · Oxford · Wien

Maike Kolbeck

From Word to Land

Early English Reports from North America
as Worldmaking Texts

PETER LANG
Internationaler Verlag der Wissenschaften

Bibliographic Information published by the Deutsche Nationalbibliothek
The Deutsche Nationalbibliothek lists this publication in the Deutsche Nationalbibliografie; detailed bibliographic data is available in the internet at <http://www.d-nb.de>.

Zugl.: Hamburg, Univ., Diss., 2007

Cover illustration:
Copper engraving
"The Arrival of the Englishmen in Virginia",
(Engraving by Theodor de Bry, 1590).
Copyright:
akg-images gmbh

D 18
ISSN 1615-567X
ISBN 978-3-631-57364-8
© Peter Lang GmbH
Internationaler Verlag der Wissenschaften
Frankfurt am Main 2008
All rights reserved.

All parts of this publication are protected by copyright. Any utilisation outside the strict limits of the copyright law, without the permission of the publisher, is forbidden and liable to prosecution. This applies in particular to reproductions, translations, microfilming, and storage and processing in electronic retrieval systems.

Printed in Germany 1 2 3 4 5 7

www.peterlang.de

Acknowledgements

Writing this book would not have been possible without the help of those that have accompanied me throughout my academic career and beyond. First of all I would like to thank my academic teacher, Professor Bettina Friedl. Much of the joy and dedication I was able to put into this work is due to the academic guidance and inspiration with which she accompanied this project.

Also, I would like to thank the Johanna and Fritz Buch Gedächtnis Stiftung, Hamburg for generously supporting the publication of this book.

Finally, I am deeply grateful to my parents, Dorothea and Herbert Limpert, my sister, Dr. Anna Silke Limpert, and my husband, Professor Felix Kolbeck for their love, support, and cheer.

Table of Contents

Choice and Treatment of Primary Sources 1
1. Introduction: A New World in Words 3
2. Travel Narratives: Definition and Literary Status 17
   2.1. What Is a Travel Narrative? Towards a Definition 17
   2.2. Formal Criteria 18
   2.3. Travel Narratives and 'Literariness' 21
   2.4. Conventions of Reception 23
   2.5. Author and Narrator, Voice, and Making Fact into Fiction 24
   2.6. Conclusion: Definition of Travel Narrative 25
3. A Short History of Travel and Its Narrative 27
4. Describing a New World with Words from the Old 33
   4.1. Narration and Description in Travel Narratives 33
   4.2. Travel Writing and Narrative Discourse 33
   4.3. Perception and Language 35
   4.4. Description, Naming, and Judgment 37
   4.5. Description, Worldmaking, and Truth in Early American Travel Narratives 40
5. Cultural and Historical Background 43
   5.1. Imagination and Geographical Exploration 43
   5.2. The East and the West in European Imagination 44
6. Early American Travel Narratives as Worldmaking Texts: Narratives of First Contacts 51
   6.1. Models and Precursors 51
      6.1.1. Richard Eden's *Decades of the Newe Worlde, or West India* (1555) 51
      6.1.2. Richard Hakluyt's *Divers Voyages* (1582) 56
      6.1.3. Instructions for Travelers on Voyages of Discovery and Exploration 60
      6.1.4. The First Collection of Narratives of Early English Voyages: Richard Hakluyt's *Principal Navigations* 62
   6.2. Newfoundland 63
      6.2.1. The Frobisher Voyages 63
      6.2.2. Gilbert's Voyage to Newfoundland: Edward Hayes. *A Report of the Voyage [...] by Sir Humphrey Gilbert* 66
   6.3. Prelude to Colonies: The Roanoke Voyages 68

6.3.1.	The 1584 Voyage under Amadas and Barlowe	68
6.3.2.	Arthur Barlowe. *The First Voyage Made to the Coastes of America*	69
6.3.3.	The Roanoke Voyages and Propaganda Writing	71
6.3.4.	The 1585 Voyage: Grenville's Expedition	73
6.3.5.	Thomas Hariot. *A Briefe and True Report of the New Found Land of Viginia*	73
6.3.6.	Ralph Lane. *An Account of the Particularities of the Imployments of the English Men [...] in Virginia*	78
6.3.7.	John White. *The Fourth Voyage Made to Virginia, with Three Shippes, in the Yeere 1587*	82
6.3.8.	John White. *The Fifth Voyage of Master John White into the West Indies and Parts of America Called Virginia, in the Yeere 1590*	83
6.4.	Early Voyages to New England, 1602-1614	85
6.4.1.	John Brereton. *A Briefe and True Relation of the Discoverie of the North Part of Virginia*	85
6.4.2.	Martin Pring. *A Voyage set out from the Citie of Bristoll [...] for the discoverie of the North part of Virginia*	88
6.4.3.	James Rosier. *A True Relation of the Most Prosperous Voyage*	90
6.4.4.	John Smith. *A Description of New England, Or, The Observations, and Discoveries, of Captain John Smith [...]*	92
7.	Narratives of Exploration and First Settlements	97
7.1.	Jamestown	97
7.1.1.	George Percy. *A Discourse of the Plantation of the Southern Colonie in Virginia*	97
7.1.2.	John Smith. *A True Relation of Such Occurrences and Accidents of Noate as Hath Hapned in Virginia*	99
7.1.3.	John Smith. *A Map of Virginia. With a Description of the Countrey, the Commodities, People, Government and Religion*	103
7.1.4.	Robert Johnson. *Nova Britannia: Offering Most Excellent Fruites by Planting in Virginia. Exciting All such as Are Well Affected to Further the Same*	107
7.1.5.	William Strachey. *A True Reportory of the Wracke and Redemption of Sir Thomas Gates Knight*	109
7.1.6.	William Strachey. *The Historie of Travell into Virginia Britania*	111
7.1.7.	Robert Johnson. *The New Life of Virginea*	117
7.1.8.	Ralph Hamor. *A True Discourse of the Present State of Virginia*	119
7.1.9.	Edward Waterhouse. *A Declaration of the State of the Colony in Virginia*	126

7.1.10.	Richard Frethorne. *Letter from Virginia*	129
7.1.11.	Jamestown: Epilogue	131
7.2.	Newfoundland, Four Decades after the Frobisher Voyages	132
7.2.1.	Richard Whitbourne. *A Discourse and Discovery of New-Found- Land*	132
7.2.2.	George Calvert. *Letter to King Charles I*	133
7.3.	New England, 1620-1674	134
7.3.1	Edward Winslow. *Good Newes from New England. A True Relation of Things very Remarkable at the Plantation of Plimoth in New England*	135
7.3.2.	*Francis Higginson to His Friends in England*	139
7.3.3.	William Wood. *New England's Prospect*	143
7.3.4.	John Josselyn. *An Account of Two Voyages to New-England*	147
7.4.	Maryland	150
7.4.1.	George Alsop. *A Character of the Province of Maryland*	150
7.5.	New York, 1670-1695	152
7.5.1.	John Miller. *A Description of the Province and City of New York*	152
7.5.2.	Daniel Denton. *A Brief Description of New-York: Formerly Called New-Netherlands*	154
7.6.	The Carolinas	156
7.6.1.	Letters by Edward Bland and Francis Yeardley	156
7.6.2.	Thomas Ashe. *Carolina, Or a Description of the Present State of that Country*	157
7.6.3.	John Lawson. A New Voyage to Carolina	158
8.	Conclusion	163
Appendix		177
9.	List of Works Cited	183
9.1.	Primary Sources	183
9.2.	Secondary Sources	189

Truth, far from being a solemn and severe master,
is a docile and obedient servant.
Nelson Goodman, *Ways of Worldmaking*

Choice and Treatment of Primary Sources

This thesis is an anaylsis of early travel narratives about North America as "worldmaking" texts of their time because they were among the principal sources of knowledge about the New World. The choice of sources for this thesis was accordingly limited to texts which were either published or at least circulated in manuscript during the time frame chosen for this study, beginning with the Frobisher voyages of the 1570s and ending with John Lawson's description of the Carolinas in 1701. Narratives like William Strachey's *Historie of Travell* were not published until the nineteenth century, but circulated in manuscript among members of the Virginia Company and therefore merited inclusion in this study.

The extant body of sources is considerable, especially regarding those narratives which may be termed promotional. Choices had to be made; some narratives may be found missing whereas others may not seem to belong into this selection at first sight. Under the common title of travel narratives, the selection includes early reports of discovery and exploration of regions which today are part of the United States of America, together with some narratives of voyages to Newfoundland. I chose to focus on selected regions instead of trying to cover narratives of all colonies, and limited the choice of texts to narratives of the early decades of English contact with a respective North American region. Furthermore, the sources were chosen to reflect some central common traits in description and narration of New World encounters which the majority, but not all, early English reports from North America share.

Many of the texts were included in contemporary editions by the younger Richard Hakluyt or his successor, Samuel Purchas. Thus, these narratives were available to an audience interested in America. Whereas Hakluyt did only little editing work, Purchas in some cases shortened texts or even conferred judgment onto some. Because the focus of this thesis is on a text as it was accessible to the public, I chose to study texts in the forms in which they were published.

Most of the texts selected for this study are available today in modern collections, such as David B. Quinn's *Roanoke Voyages*, Emory Elliott's *Letters from New England*, or *Sailors' Narratives Along the New England Coast* by George Parker Winship. In drawing on such modern collections as well as the facsimile editions of Hakluyt's *Divers Voyages*, or the *Principal Navigations* edited by David B. Quinn and Raleigh A. Skelton, and in some cases on microfilms of original texts, I was faced with the problem of very heterogeneous editing practices. The extent to which spelling and grammar have been modernized varies accordingly. Therefore I decided to modernize spelling and grammar in all source texts for the sake of uniformity except for titles of texts and for some grammatical structures which do not impede a modern reader's understanding yet reflect an author's individual style of expression. The names of people and places have been unified as well, as in the case of Sir Walter Ralegh (also spelled Raleigh), Thomas Hariot (also spelled Harriot), or Plymouth (alternatively spelled Plimouth or Plimmoth).

For the sake of convenient readability, I have chosen to treat the travelers, authors/narrators, indigenous inhabitants and other persons mentioned in this thesis in the male grammatical form only.

1. Introduction: A New World in Words

> For it is a certain maxim, [that] no man sees what
> things are, that knows not what they ought to be.[1]

When Columbus wrote the first account of the New World he had discovered for Europe, he produced the first widely disseminated European narrative of the New World, inaugurating a long tradition of writing a hemisphere into being for a European audience. Although he had chanced upon a hemisphere hitherto more or less unknown to Europe, he had known what he would find before leaving Spain: the Eastern shores of Asia. Thus, he came equipped with a set of expectations mirrored in his writings. This was, by no means, unusual; the imagination of many Europeans had long been entertained by myths and lore about faraway worlds and peoples which shaped frames of reference about what to expect. 1492 brought, for Europe, the discovery of a New World, but not a new genre of (travel) writing or new *topoi*; both had long been established before Columbus. However, he had to add to the narrative and descriptive techniques of an established genre the close description of New World phenomena in order to make America intelligible and his discoveries credible for Europeans at home. The emphasis on empiricism, embodied in the observing eyewitness, the catalogue, the detailed description, but also the limits of these techniques are features which characterized early reports of the New World.

After a long delay in overseas colonial ventures, the English nation not only entered the race for American possessions, but the people involved in these activities also began producing a considerable body of narratives in which information about America was distributed throughout England and first culminated in the younger Richard Hakluyt's compilation, the *Principal Navigations*. If, as in the words of Edmundo O'Gorman, America was invented rather than discovered, the narratives of voyages of discovery and exploration were the medium through which much of this invention took place. These travel narratives of the sixteenth and seventeenth century constitute an intersection of historiography, literature, ethnography, and political propaganda. They are the central texts which assembled and propagated knowledge of the New World. Also, they were highly influential and politicized narratives which consequently played a central role in the conceptualization of the New World in the European imagination, as Myra Jehlen points out in an essay on early American literature: "By the end of the colonial period, a literature of colonization [had] not only inscribed but helped forge the

---

[1] Quoted after: Ernst H. Gombrich. *Art and Illusion. A Study in the Psychology of Pictorial Representation.* Oxford: Phaidon, 1978: 10.

identification of the Europeans with the continent. The word [had] been made land."[2]

Finding and Founding America, a seminar dedicated to the study of early narratives about North America held by Professor Bettina Friedl at Hamburg University in the winter semester 1998/1999, had introduced me to some of the narratives chosen here and the topics of historical fact and historical narrative. It also sparked a strong interest in early American literature as a key to later national literary beginnings and mythmaking. The topic of this thesis is derived from that lasting fascination with the fact/fiction question, the role early narratives about North America played in the European conceptualization of the newly discovered geographical entity, and their function in an evolving European discourse of overseas expansion.

In the early stages of developing this thesis, I read through a large body of sources and came across certain recurrent themes, images, and even complete phrases which directed my attention to one characteristic of early English narratives of North America: their often striking uniformity in descriptive passages, regardless of the decade or region of origin. Many English descriptions of North America seem downright composed in the sense a piece of music is composed in order to be coherent and achieve a particular effect on an audience. Intertextuality can only partly explain that uniformity, or rather constructedness which often seemed to ignore empirical evidence. It seemed that the descriptive passages of many English narratives about North America were a peculiar blend of eyewitness observation and standardized rhetoric which apparently had little to do with reality. This paradox becomes particularly clear when descriptions praising America's abundant nature and healthy climate are paired with narrative passages reporting hunger and death by sicknesses and starvation.

These preliminary observations led me to pose the following hypothesis: The reality of early English experience in North America often seemed to have fallen so short of the travelers' (and their financial backers') expectations that descriptive stereotypes reiterating an earthly Eden or immense material riches were composed to keep up an image in writing which appeared elusive in reality. Furthermore, the European tradition of legends about faraway or mythical lands seemed to have left a strong mark on early descriptions of the New World.

Consequently, I decided to analyze a substantial body of English narratives of first contacts with and first settlements in North America with regard to their descriptive content and possible contradictions in descriptive and narrative passages. The objective of this thesis is to study how, and to what effect, the word "ha[d]

---

[2] Myra Jehlen. "The Literature of Colonization." In: *Cambridge History of American Literature*. Ed. Sacvan Bercovitch. Cambridge: Cambridge University Press, 1994: 13f.

been made land" and how these narratives employed language to create knowledge, history, and thus reality. The methodical approach of this thesis is to offer a survey of such narratives focusing on their techniques of describing North America to Europeans. To this end, I selected a body of sources written by Englishmen and accessible at their time to an English (and often European) reading public. Furthermore, I concentrated on the image of North America and its constituent parts as well as contradictory evidence in narrative passages. Narratives are grouped chronologically and regionally, with a division into narratives of first contacts and narratives of first settlements. All of them may be termed travel narratives because they report travelers' experiences in early North America, with the added special challenges and literary features discovery and exploration entailed.

Even though modern scholarship in the fields of literary history, history, or anthropology has devoted a considerable amount of attention to this body of sources, only a few of them have entered the canon of early American literature, whereas others have remained fairly obscure throughout the centuries. Perry Miller summed up one main reason for this obscurity with regard to texts of early Virginia, but his verdict is applicable to many narratives about early North America: Much of it, according to Miller and historians of his age, was "propaganda, much of dubious accuracy, a large part merely rhetoric."[3] Indeed, many of these narratives are neither very appealing aesthetically nor do they tell much that had not been said before in some other way by some other traveler. But it is precisely this uniformity in descriptive passages and these striking contradictions when descriptive and narrative passages are read in comparison which make early English reports about North America valuable sources when dealing with the question of how, why, and to what effect America was reported back to Europe in this way.

The body of texts narrating Europeans' experiences of travel in early North America has been approached in various ways, and by members of various disciplines. Positioned on the borders between literature, historiography, or ethnography, no single conclusive survey of research on this topic is possible in this thesis. The body of scholarly writing dealing with early reports about North America is vast, and shall not be discussed here in any entirety. Instead, I will single out some apporaches by historians, literary historians, and American cultural historians to discuss some of the many possible ways of working with this heterogeneous body of sources.

For historians, texts like Smith's *True Relation* or Winslow's *Good Newes from New England* constitute important sources of information about early life in North America; ethnographers consider Thomas Hariot's *Briefe and True Report*

---

[3] Perry Miller. *Errand Into the Wilderness*. Cambridge, MA and London: Belknap Press, Twelfth Printing, 1996: 100.

an invaluable source on the coastal Algonkian tribes which, with the spreading of European settlements on the Eastern seaboard, soon ceased to exist in the state in which Hariot described them. Anthropologists draw upon such narratives to gain better insight into the (European) observers' "mental baggage" they carried to the New World, revealing European societies' mental prefigurations of other peoples and lands, as for example in Margaret T. Hogden's study *Early Anthropology in the Sixteenth and Seventeenth Centuries*.[4]

Historians of American literature, as reflected in many anthologies, sometimes see its beginnings in John Smith's *True Relation*, "the harbinger of our nation's literature"[5], or in Arthur Barlowe's or Thomas Hariot's narratives of the Roanoke colony. Concerning Smith's narratives, William Spengemann writes that

> certain general resemblances between the America Smith imagined and the one we have inherited have inclined generations of Americans to regard him, rather than Gabriel Archer or Edward Wingfield, as a forefather, and his letter [the *True Relation*], rather than one of theirs, as the beginning of American literature.[6]

However, only a small selection of the texts is usually included in anthologies of American literature. This reflects a decades-long difficulty scholars have had with the hybrid genre of travel narratives. Due to their peculiar status between pragmatic writing, fiction, historiography, and ethnography, together with questions concerning their literary value, travel narratives have only recently been recognized as valuable material for study by various academic fields. This is reflected in the recently published *Cambridge Companion to Travel Writing*.[7] Furthermore, their status as sources written (most often) by Englishmen centuries before the actual founding of the United States of America makes it difficult to rank them as early American literature, yet these narratives also differ greatly from English reports of travel to other regions of the world.

---

[4] Margaret T. Hogden. *Early Anthropology in the Sixteenth and Seventeenth Centuries*. Philadelphia: University of Pennsylvania Press, 1964.
[5] Sharon Rogers Brown. *American Travel Narratives as a Literary Genre From 1542 to 1832*. Lewiston, NY: Mellen, 1993: 24. For a very different assessment of Smith's *General Historie* as a "chronicle of uncertainty", see Myra Jehlen. "History Before the Fact; or, Captain John Smith's Unfinished Symphony." *Critical Inquiry* 19 (1993), 677-692: 692.
[6] William Spengemann. *A New World of Words: Redefining Early American Literature*. New Haven, CT: Yale University Press, 1994: 63. Edward Maria Wingfield and Gabriel Archer wrote reports which cast a more realistic, and much less heroic, light on the early settlement of Jamestown.
[7] Peter Hulme and Tim Youngs, eds. *The Cambridge Companion to Travel Writing*. Cambridge: Cambridge University Press, 2002.

Historians of the "meaning" of America, concerned with American beginnings, focused, like Perry Miller, mostly on Puritan writings to work "that interminable field which may be called the meaning of America."[8] Miller set the stage for the predominance of New England Puritan writings as the "true" beginnings of American culture and history which have only lately been reassessed. For Miller, the Puritan migration was a "beginning of a beginning" since it afforded a "coherence with which [he] could coherently begin." This priority of New England over the earlier English settlements in North Carolina and Virginia suggested that Jamestown, let alone the early experiences at Roanoke, did not offer such a coherent beginning. The reasons are manifold. Figures like John Smith, who has engendered heated discussions concerning his authority, authorial integrity, and questions of fact and fiction, have been adopted by popular culture as suitable "first Americans" but have left scholars divided over the value of their written records. Furthermore, people like the scientist Thomas Hariot excepted, many authors of early English experiences were soldiers (Ralph Lane) or sailors (John Brereton), and their often matter-of-fact narratives were at some disadvantage as "literature" and intellectual heritage when compared to the highly learned styles of William Bradford or John Winthrop, for example.

Miller also preferred New England Puritan writing to Virginia's chronological priority because of the latter's propaganda features, "a large part [being] merely rhetoric, [...] possessing value only for documentation."[9] The solution, for Miller, of this "quality" problem of early narratives was to focus on writings generated in England yet concerned with the Virginian venture with the result that "religion [in English writings concerned with Virginia] seems the compelling, or at least, the pervading force."[10] The majority of reports from early Virginia contradict this assessment, as will be shown in the course of this study. Another important reason for the prominent role of Puritan New England writings in early American literature is summed up by Richard Dunn in an essay on Seventeenth-Century English Historians of America: "The self-righteousness of the New England chroniclers and the self-criticism of the Virginia chroniclers [...] help explain why most Americans ever since have found it easier to respond emotionally to Plymouth Rock than to Jamestown, despite the latter's priority."[11]

Today, the questions of literary quality and coherent beginnings have largely given way to modern literary analysis and interdisciplinary approaches, resulting

---

[8] Perry Miller. *Errand Into the Wilderness*: ix.
[9] ibid.: 100.
[10] ibid.: 101.
[11] Richard S. Dunn. "Seventeenth-Century English Historians of America." In: *Seventeenth-Century America. Essays in Colonial History*, ed. James Morton Smith. Westport, CT: Greenwood Press, 1959, 195-225: 196f.

in a new assessment of the value of such early narratives of European experience in North America for their own sake, without the "help" of English narratives only associated with a venture. Modern cultural historians focus, for example, on early American travel narratives as central components of an emerging English national discourse. Americanists often read early travel narratives like Smith's as the forerunners of an American literature due to "the presence of shared themes and the narrative features of the genre [which] establishes the place of travel narratives in the larger American tradition."[12] In *American Travel Narratives as a Literary Genre*, Sharon Rogers Brown studies narratives by John Smith, John Lawson or Sarah Kemble Knight, among others, as the first narratives about America in which their writers

> share the excitement, optimism and perseverance that Americans seem to have always expressed when writing about travel in their own land. [...] They have characteristics which make them a distinctly American genre, one which embraces in its style, form and content the American character. John Smith's determination enabling him to survive his first winter in the New World [...] reflect[s] an American spirit of survival.[13]

Brown echoes earlier views of scholars like Richard Slotkin who considered "narratives of the Indian wars of New England" as the "first significant genre of New World writing and formed the literary basis of the first American mythology."[14]

In *Colonial Writing and the New World*, Thomas Scanlan dismisses the utilization of early English narratives of discovery and exploration in North America as forerunners of a genuinely American literature. Instead, he reads these narratives as allegorical transfigurations of (English) national desires: "Colonial writing [...] tells two stories: It narrates events in the colony, while referring to the desires of the [colonizing] nation. [...] The authors of these colonial texts [...] do require their readers to draw a connection between the two apparently distinct narratives of colonial adventure and national advancement."[15] Likewise, Mary Fuller's readings of early English reports of voyages to North America in *Voyages in Print* are intended to yield "a revised understanding of England's early contact with America"; this effort builds on Peter Hulme's observation in *Colonial Encounters* that the "obsessive documentation of the early English voyages and colonies" attested

---

[12] Sharon Rogers Brown. *American Travel Narratives as a Literary Genre From 1542 to 1832. The Art of a Perpetual Journey*. Lewiston, NY: Mellen, 1993: 8f.
[13] ibid.: 9, 22.
[14] Richard Slotkin. *Regeneration Through Violence: The Mythology of the American Frontier, 1600-1860*. Middletown, CT: Wesleyan University Press, 1973: 56.
[15] Thomas Scanlan. *Colonial Writing and the New World, 1583-1671: Allegories of Desire*. Cambridge: Cambridge University Press, 1999: 3, 14.

to "a self-conscious effort to create a continuous epic myth of origin for the emerging imperial nation."[16]

While it is quite a stretch to call John Smith or Thomas Hariot and their writings "American", I nevertheless suggest that early English reports from North America were more than just central tools in English national and imperial discourse, as for example Thomas Scanlan claims. I also disagree with Sharon Rogers Brown that early travel narratives like Smith's display a genuinely "American character", not only because of distorted chronology, but also because the alleged success stories of survival in an alien environment often turn out, as will be shown in the course of this study, to be much rather stories of futility. Furthermore, a look at only the anthologized "usual suspects" of early American travel narratives, often John Smith, Winthrop's *Model of Christian Charity* (because it was written *en route* to America), or Bradford's narrative of the 1620 voyage to and arrival at the American shore, strongly distorts the picture: "For the most part, writers of American travel narratives present a positive view of the homeland [i.e. America]. At the start, they expressed the colonial attitude that the New World would be a 'City on a Hill', a model for Europe to follow."[17]

This quote shows the dangers inherent in grouping such narratives into a distinctly "American" genre. Early American Puritan writing was much more concerned with the inner life of man than with the outside world of America, and John Smith's writings should not be discussed without the context of late medieval chivalric romance as a European cultural heritage of this literary "American hero." Most important of all, the "positive view of the homeland" was, as this study will show, usually derived less from actual experience than from Old World literary models of describing an earthly paradise or a classical *locus amoenus*. Once America proved to be a less than paradisaic environment for European settlers, narrative strategies of defense or evasion had to be developed to uphold an image in writing which America often failed to sustain in reality.

A fruitful approach to these early American travel narratives, then, is probably best to be developed with regard to their peculiar situation in a European, but at the same time New World context. They established new knowledge; they created "facts" when they described the New World, its inhabitants, its flora and fauna, its present promises, past, and future potential, as J.H. Elliott points out in the closing chapter of the essay collection *America in European Consciousness*:

---

[16] Mary C. Fuller. *Voyages in Print: English Travel to America, 1576-1624*. Cambridge: Cambridge University Press, 1995: 12, 1.
[17] Sharon Rogers Brown, *American Travel Narratives*: 30.

The past, present, and future of America were all shaped to make it conform as closely as possible to European hopes, aspirations, and requirements. In this sense, America was from the beginning more directly the 'invention' of Europe, to use the phraseology of Edmundo O'Gorman than were either Africa or Asia. [...] America, after all, was both destroyed and created by Europe.[18]

In an extensive study of early travel narratives about North America, Wayne Franklin suggests a combination of the historian's and the literary scholar's approach in order to make "the American travelers [...] reveal their own minds as well as the cognitive character of their culture." Franklin analyzes the "long chronicle of blunted awareness, of slow recognition, of crucial facts never adequately understood" and focuses on the formulae of expression with which early travelers in North America put events into language.[19]

His approach has been a useful start for my own study although my focus is different: Unlike Franklin, I will not study the narratives chosen here for what they reveal about their writers' minds or their cognitive culture. I will read early reports about North America as "worldmaking texts" in Nelson Goodman's sense, as creating knowledge while at the same time laboring to accommodate American reality into European imagination. I will neither consider the role of these narratives in an English national and imperial context as in the case of Scanlan or Fuller, nor will I consider, like Brown, narratives like Smith's, Hariot's, or Winslow's as the first "harbingers" of American literature. Instead, I will study a fairly broad (yet far from comprehensive) selection of early narratives by Englishmen which were published and/or accessible in England and took part in the difficult conceptualization of America in European minds. The focus is on the conventionality, uniformity and iconography of America which these early reports displayed, and the reasons for such consciously composed images in descriptions opposed to often contrary evidence in narrative parts. These contradictions, as well as Miller's "rhetoric" and "propaganda" in early English reports about North America have, if at all, so far been considered as proof of diminished literary value and historical reliability. In this thesis, I will focus on these central features of the sources because they are the key to understanding the role of these narratives as events fixed, and occasionally fictionalized, in written language.

Language, for the discoverer Columbus as much as for explorers and settlers following in his wake, was the main cultural tool by which a multitude of radi-

---

[18] John H. Elliott. "Final Reflections." In: *America in European Consciousness, 1493-1750*, ed. Karen Ordahl Kupperman. Chapel Hill, NC: University of North Carolina Press, 1995, 391-408: 396f.
[19] Wayne Franklin. *Discoverers, Explorers, Settlers: The Diligent Writers of Early America.* Chicago: University of Chicago Press, 1978: 16f.

cally new phenomena could be ordered, categorized and transmitted to those at home. The frequent acts of (re)naming by Columbus filled in gaps where European language fell short of adequately categorizing the new: "To the first island which I found I gave the name San Salvador, in remembrance of His heavenly majesty, who marvelously has given all this; the Indians call it Guanahani."[20] By naming places, peoples, and things, these were introduced into European categories of order and judgment. In this process, established images and expectations provided a framework from which terminology was derived, most famously the term "Indian", and onto which new geographical and ethnographical knowledge could be projected, thus adding fact to fiction, and vice versa.

A European audience transferred age-old hopes and expectations onto the new geographical entity – material riches, spiritual refuge, land to relieve Europe of its crowds – and thus inaugurated an era of unique tension between fulfillment and failure that was to characterize much of European action in early America and the narratives it generated. This power to literally "create" a new hemisphere for a European audience and its various interests was recognized early on by those involved in the compilation and dissemination of knowledge about America. The English compiler of travel narratives succeeding Richard Hakluyt, Samuel Purchas, perceived his work in this sense: "By speech we utter our minds once [...] but by writing man seems immortal."[21] Those represented, it seems, were occasionally aware of the magic powers of writing as well. When John Smith, a captive of Algonkin chief Powhatan's tribe, sent Indian messengers with written orders to Jamestown, the effect of the piece of paper made the Indians believe "that he [Smith] could either divine or the paper could speak."[22] Jesuit Relations from Nouvelle France, later Canada, report much the same reaction of Native Americans towards writing: "I cannot express the admiration displayed by the natives for the little note I had sent [...]. They said that that little paper had spoken to my brother and had told him all the words I had uttered to them here, and that we were greater than all mankind."[23]

Reports *dis-covered* for a European audience what, if understood literally, was already expected to exist, only out of sight and the reach of empirical knowl-

---

[20] Christopher Columbus. "Letter to Lord Raphael Sanchez on his first voyage." In: *Early American Writing*. Ed. Giles B. Gunn. New York: Penguin, 1994: 26.
[21] Samuel Purchas, *Hakluytus Postumus*. Rpt. Glasgow: MacLehose, 1916: 486.
[22] John Smith. "The General History of Virginia, New England, And the Summer Isles." Ed. Philip Barbour. *The Complete Works of Captain John Smith*. Chapel Hill and London: University of North Carolina Press, 1986: 149. Hereafter cited as Barbour, *Works of John Smith*.
[23] James Axtell. "The Power of Print in the Eastern Woodlands." *William and Mary Quarterly*, 3rd ser., 44/2 (1987): 301-9: 302. Axtell sees a connection between reading, mind-reading, and shamanism which helps explain why Native Americans attributed supernatural powers to reading and writing.

edge as yet. Nevertheless, early reports from North America remained heavily influenced by medieval lore about faraway mythical places. The supposed geographical locations of mythical cities (Ralegh's *Manoa*, for instance, or Lane's *Chaunis Temoatan*, the *El Dorados* of central and North America) gradually moved farther West into the interior with European explorers penetrating the American continent and failing to find them. At the same time, writers of such reports had to reckon with a limited ability of their European audience as to what could be considered credible: "Travelers may lie by authority because none can control them. [...] What I speak is the very truth."[24]

Even though truth claims by traveler-writers like Wood were based on their being eyewitnesses, what they reported was nevertheless heavily subjective. The process of reporting depended entirely on what the traveler had seen or was able to see, and what he failed to see or understand. Furthermore, it depended on an individual's skills of expression when describing new phenomena. Often, an explorer felt unable to express what he saw, and thus the "unspeakable" *topos* is a frequent feature in early New World reports. The eminent sixteenth-century Spanish chronicler of the West Indies, Gonzalo Fernandez de Oviedo said of a strange plant he felt he failed to describe adequately in his *Historia General y Natural de las Indias*: "It needs to be painted by the hand of a Berruguete or some other excellent painter like him, or by Leonardo da Vinci."[25] Likewise, comparisons with known phenomena and superlatives were only second-rate rhetorical methods to describe phenomena for which Europeans had no words. Jean Ribaut, in his 1562 *Discoverie of Terra Florida*, still called America "West India" and accordingly was intrigued by (supposed) riches first associated with the East and then, increasingly after Columbus, with the West. The narrator catalogued the natural wildlife but had to end eventually because he felt he could not adequately convey the quality and quantity of American flora and fauna: "Also there be cornies and hares; silk worms in marvelous numbers, a great deal fairer and better, than be our silk worms. To be honest, *it is a thing unspeakable* to consider the things that be seen here, and shall be found more and more, in this incomparable land."[26] (italics mine)

---

[24] William Wood. *New England's Prospect*. Ed. Alden T. Vaughan. Amherst, MA: University of Massachusetts Press, 1977: 19f.
[25] Quoted after: Jay A. Levenson. *Circa 1492: History and Art*. In: Jay A. Levenson, ed. *Circa 1492*. New Haven and London: Yale University Press, 1991: 19.
[26] Jean Ribaut. "The Discoverie of Terra Florida." Transl. Thomas Hacket. In: Richard Hakluyt, comp. *Divers Voyages* [London 1582]. Facsimile Reprint. Amsterdam: Da Capo Press, 1967: 87f.

INTRODUCTION: A NEW WORLD IN WORDS

Such *topoi* of inexpressibility show the limits of European language in descriptions of the New World.[27] Language is based on, and at the same time determined and limited by, the lifeworld and social environment of its speakers, and influences both of these in turn. The same is true for description, classification, and judgment. As Montaigne wrote in his essay *Of the Canniballes*, "men call that barbarism which is not common to them. As indeed we have no other aim of truth and reason than the example and idea of the opinions and customs of the country we live in."[28] Not only did Europeans carry with them images and expectations of what their destination was to be like when they traveled to the Americas. Their narratives of early America also reflect both the limits of Old World language and faculties of perception in describing the new, and the strong influence the imagination had on what people sought, found, or thought to have found.

Nelson Goodman calls this cognitive and linguistic process of categorizing new phenomena by familiar language *Ways of Worldmaking* and describes the limits of perception, language, and memory: "Our capacity for overlooking is virtually unlimited, and what we do take in usually consists of significant fragments and clues that need massive supplementation."[29] What we do perceive depends on whether we find any frame of reference or familiarity of it in our own lifeworld: "Discovery often amounts [...] not to arrival at a proposition [...] but to finding a fit. [...] If worlds are as much made as found, so also knowing is as much remaking as reporting. [...] Recognizing patterns is very much a matter of inventing and imposing them. Comprehension and creation go on together."[30] The "massive supplementation" was usually based on myths and lore and then, increasingly, on previous reports about the New World. Thus, a peculiar mixture of observation, myth, intertextuality and hearsay characterizes these narratives which functioned as a representational, and thus worldmaking, technology.[31]

Some of the most prominent people who in their own time failed to *make* history could still make history for posterity by *writing* it. Captain John Smith, whose actions on the colonial stage came to an end sooner than he might have had wished for, nevertheless promoted his image of America, and to a lasting effect. His early maps of Virginia and New England were widely used; so were his narra-

---

[27] I would like to borrow a fitting definition of the term topos from Caroline B. Brettell: "Topoi represent a rhetorical baggage carried by the traveller [in the form of] commonly held notions about people, places, or things." Caroline B. Brettell. "Introduction: Travel Literature, Ethnography, and Ethnohistory." *Ethnohistory* 33(2): 127-138: 128.
[28] Michel de Montaigne. "Of the Canniballes." Transl. John Florio (1603). In: Andrew Hadfield, ed. *Amazons, Savages and Machiavels (1530-1630)*. Oxford: Oxford University Press, 2001: 287.
[29] Nelson Goodman. *Ways of Worldmaking*. Indianapolis: Hackett, 1978: 14.
[30] ibid.: 22.
[31] The terms "worldmaking" and "worldmaker" are derived from Nelson Goodman's *Ways of Worldmaking*.

tives which circulated widely during his lifetime. Today they are part of the canon for students and scholars of early American literature and a staple in US history books.[32] Another example is a prominent New Englander: William Bradford, towards the end of his life, sought an America of the mind instead of an actual America which fell increasingly short of the ideal refuge of pure religion he had envisioned it to be. His *History of Plymouth Plantation*, however, is, like Smith's texts, a fixture in any history of early America, and his title as Pilgrim "Father"[33] pays tribute to his life but perhaps even more to the enduring influence of his narrative definition of early America. Narratives like Smith's and Bradford's are the victorious participants in a competition of voices over defining America's past, present and future through a discourse of knowledge and power.

The first part of this study lays the groundwork for an analysis of the "worldmaking" functions of early English reports about North America. A brief discussion of travel narratives, the question of their literariness, and a definition of travel literature as it is applied in this study open the theoretical part. Chapter three offers a short survey of the history of travel and its narrative and positions early reports from the New World in this larger context. In chapter four, I discuss narration and description with regard to the worldmaking power of language and its role in describing a New World with words from the old. Chapter five rounds off the theoretical part with a survey of the cultural and historical background to early English voyages to North America in order to assess the role of the imagination in geographical exploration and its narratives.

The second part of this study is a survey of early English narratives about North America. On the basis of the theoretical chapters, I will study the narrative and descriptive parts of the texts concentrating on the image of North America which the texts present individually as well as a body of texts. A special focus will be put on the descriptive techniques and their functions in each text, as well as on recurring images, terminology, and narrative strategies in the whole body of sources with regard to the central hypothesis of this study.

In order to assess the knowledge of the New World which was available to Englishmen before the first English voyages of discovery and exploration, the text analysis begins with some prominent narratives in English collections of continen-

---

[32] "In 1610, wounded and half-dead, Captain John Smith lay huddled below decks of a ship bound from Jamestown Colony back to England. After three years in the New World, his short term as president of America's first permanent settlement was already over. He would never see Virginia again, but *by 1610 Smith had already carved one future notch in US history textbooks*." (italics mine) http://seacoastnh.com/arts/please111899.html, Dec., 2005. Movies like Disney's *Pocahontas* (1995) or Terence Malick's *The New World* (2005) testify to the lasting fascination and popular appeal of this figure on the early American stage.
[33] Like, for example, in the title of Alexander Young's *Chronicles of the Pilgrim Fathers*. Boston, 1841.

tal European travel narratives about North America. French or Spanish reports in Richard Eden's *Decades* or Richard Hakluyt's *Divers Voyages* had already established many features of the English New World narratives, such as rumors of gold and silver, descriptions of an earthly paradise, noble or ignoble savages, cannibals, and also descriptive strategies which would soon become stereotypical.[34] A large part of English reports from North America can be classed as promotional tracts. They will be assessed for their value as propaganda and, as a "reality check", read against some other, non-propagandistic accounts in private letters. Although the degree of circulation of the latter texts is difficult to assess, some have been included here to shed light on "official" narratives of colonial success.

The conclusion will be devoted to answering the central questions of this study: Which constituent parts of description can be found in most of the narratives, and where were they rerived from? Why were such stereotypical passages of description used in the face of frequent narrative passages dealing with futility and death? How did "official" texts promote their usually positive image in the face of hardships and failure, and what light can narratives intended for private use shed on these acts of propaganda? Close readings of a body of travel narratives from and about North America will help answer these questions and trace the changing pattern of ascribing meaning to this new-found land and the degree to which travel reports contributed to America's eventual story of itself, to "making" a New World with Old World words.

---

[34] Cannibalism is an especially interesting aspect of New World Otherness and has engendered discussion as to historical truth and its role in intercultural encounter and representation. Cf. Peter Hulme et al., eds. *Cannibalism and the Colonial World*. Hulme reads cannibalism as the mark of greatest cultural difference and a projection of European fantasies rather than actual practice. Some narratives show that acts of cannibalism were far from reserved for "savage" people; Richard Hakluyt recorded in the *Principal Navigations* "A Voyage of Master Hore and Divers Other Gentlemen to Newfound Land, and Cape Breton" (1536), which tells of cannibalism among English sailors stranded and almost starving on the American shore.

2. Travel Narratives: Definition and Literary Status

> I have passed my life in reading the accounts that travelers give, and I have not met with two that have given the same idea of the same people.
> Jean-Jacques Rousseau

2.1. What Is a Travel Narrative? Towards a Definition

The first part of the term, travel, may be generally described as "a broadly defined practice featuring human movement through culturally conceived space, normally undertaken with at least some expectation of an eventual return to the place of origin."[35] Such a definition allows for the inclusion of discoverers, explorers, sailors, wandering missionaries, and also settlers who travel through their New World as possible authors of travel narratives. In fact, the aspect of travel through "culturally conceived space" is important as the new space of America was radically different culturally from what Europeans were initially able to conceive, understand, and report, and thus often lacked a set of established linguistic practices to order and describe New World phenomena. I would like to add to the definition of travel and traveler the aspect of voluntary travel. In the course of this thesis, I will limit the choice of texts to those which were written by people who traveled voluntarily. This necessarily excludes, for example, captivity narratives like Mary Rowlandson's. I have also extended the definition to people who came to North America with the intention to stay but wrote narratives of their early experiences of travel to and within North America, like for example Francis Higginson. As travel through a space conceived not just as culturally different, but often as absolutely alien, early American travel narratives do share features with European travel narratives, e.g. about the *Grand Tour*, but are at the same time set apart by the discovery/exploration aspect. This is why I use the terms discovery and exploration report/narrative as synonyms for early American travel reports in this study. Narrative, according to Gérard Genette,

> may be defined simply as the representation of a real or fictitious event or series of events by language, and more especially by written language. [...] Every narrative includes two types of representation, although they are fused and always in varying proportions: representations of actions and events, which constitute

---

[35] Helen Gilbert, Anna Johnston, eds. *In Transit. Travel, Text, Empire*. Introduction. New York: Peter Lang, 2002: 5.

the narration properly speaking, and representations of objects or people, which make up the act of what we today call 'description'.[36]

Such a general definition of narrative is easily applicable to travel accounts, too, but does not yet help much to set the genre apart from others.

2.2. Formal Criteria

Regarding formal criteria, a general definition might center around the topic of a real voyage, undertaken by its author.[37] This would, on a general level, also include writers of travel guides and say nothing about the question of literary status. It is more useful to start with the content of narratives involving travel. A distinction can be made between purely fictional accounts of travels and travel narratives which argumentatively support truth claims concerning their content. A novel may take a journey as its motif or as the shifting setting of the action. However, an audience will most likely be able to discern the motif as such and recognize that the voyage itself is not the core of a story. Whether accounts of travel are true or not is acknowledged as obsolete in this case, as is the search for verifiable information on places or peoples as subordinate to story or *personae*. Thus, a distinction between fictional and factional content of a narrative can help to distinguish travel narratives from novels. Fictionality, however, is not a principle *per se* and is occasionally difficult to discern, especially if it is not possible to verify truth claims. It should therefore be connected with conventions of literary reception because a work of art and its possible interpretations depend on the cultural community for and within which it has been produced. An audience will most likely read a fictional text involving travel as fiction due to various signals, while travel narratives about real voyages may be read for their entertainment value, but also for information on their principal objects, a land or region described, also signaled by narrative devices. Still, travel narratives can manage to trespass the boundary between fact and fiction and deceive audiences for quite some time, as in the case of Mandeville's *Travels*.

Two more formal criteria may help to distinguish travel narratives from other, purely fictional text forms involving travel. A travel narrative takes a voyage as its center and thus usually contains only so much, beginning with a departure or preparations for a voyage and ending roughly with the return of the traveler. Chronology, accordingly, is a central structuring element. Descriptions in travel

---

[36] Gérard Genette. "Boundaries of Narrative." *New Literary History*, Vol. III, No.1 (1976), 1-13: 1, 5.
[37] Compare the definition below from Barbara Korte.

narratives will be recognized as true or at least possible by an audience. Consequently, travel narratives are recognized as sources of information and knowledge and are used accordingly, notwithstanding their entertainment value. This is a feature which sets travel narratives apart from travel fiction. Travel narratives about the New World, which were often titled "history", "relation", or "report", were an integral part of public European discourse on the Americas. While travel narratives often intended to convey scientific observation, e. g. in the case of Hariot's *Briefe and True Report*, they were also often written with a very specific intention in mind, usually propagating a colonizing venture. A history of a voyage or a relation of some exploratory voyage signaled by their respective titles that they contained empirically gathered information and were meant to be accessible to the public or at least written with a distinct audience in mind, as Caroline B. Brettell points out in an essay on travel literature: "The point of reference in the travel account is the readership, members of the traveler's own culture."[38] The report or relation was a very common form of such public discourse and combined a chronological narrative of movement and action with geographic and ethnographic observation. A preface often consisted of a tribute to a patron whose position added further weight to the narrative's truth claims, and an address to the reader, usually containing a justification both for traveling and writing the narrative at hand.

Examples of a different, more private discourse on the Americas can be found in letters or diaries. However, many of these texts were rewritten for publication or circulated in letter form among friends and family. Francis Higginson, for example, hints at the great interest of those back home in England who were eager to learn more about America. Consequently, he introduces his account of the ocean crossing, dated July 24, 1629, as a letter of events "faithfully recorded according to the very truth for the satisfaction of very many my loving friends who have earnestly requested to be truly certified in these things."[39] Truth claims, along with a usually fairly strict chronological order and digressions into close descriptions of flora, fauna, or social customs of foreign peoples, are central formal criteria by which a sixteenth- or seventeenth-century English New World travel narrative can be identified.

A second criterion is mentioned in Joseph Strelka's definition of travel narratives and refers to the question of artistic style. This approach is useful in telling

---

[38] Caroline B. Brettell. "Introduction: Travel Literature, Ethnography, and Ethnohistory." *Ethnohistory* 33(2), 127-138: 133.
[39] Francis Higginson to His Friends in England. July 24, 1629. In: Everett Emerson, ed. *Letters from New England. The Massachusetts Bay Colony, 1629-1638.* Amherst, MA: University of Massachusetts Press, 1976: 12.

purely informative texts, such as travel guides or captains' logs, from literary travel narratives. According to Strelka, literary merit is based on the "internalization [Verinnerlichung] of reality by subjective creation [which] prevails over an objective accumulation of facts and a pure rendering of knowledge [my translation]."[40] While we may place travel guides and other pragmatic texts involving travel at the factual/pragmatic end of a line and fictional travel accounts on the other, "literary" end, travel narratives share, as has been demonstrated, some features of both these groups but can be distinguished from either one by the degree of artistic (re)creation of a voyage on the one end and by higher degrees of verisimilitude on the other end of this line.

Travel narratives, therefore, hold a median position between pragmatic texts involving travel and fictional *belles lettres* containing accounts of travels, combining literary and pragmatic features. Barbara Korte defines travel narrative as an account of a real journey undertaken by its author and narrated at least partially in the narrative mode, usually by a first-person narrator. Beyond such basic features, however, she admits that it is difficult to separate a literary (i.e. fictional, as in the case of a "Reiseroman" which uses travel as a motif) from a non-literary travel account (based on an actual journey) and, more generally, to tell fact from fiction because there exist numerous overlappings of fictional and nonfictional prose, resulting in a "hybrid character" of the travel narrative.[41] Joseph Strelka's definition, then, centers around degrees of artistic arrangement and may help to distinguish travel narratives from travel guides. It would, for example, most likely exclude promotional tracts which would have to be situated on the border between literary and non-literary narratives since they were often commissioned to be written as fundraising propaganda. The function of such reports was not unlike today's travel guides. However, they often contained a strongly subjective stance, and even though they were rarely elaborately styled, they cannot be ranked as factual accounts either. A definition might at best be developed between these positions. A travel narrative, then, is the account of an actual journey, voluntarily undertaken by its author and written down either during a voyage, within a short time after a return, or retrospectively. It is either ordered chronologically or structured by categories (geographical, military or naturalist observations) instead of

---

[40] Joseph Strelka. "Der literarische Reisebericht." In: *Prosakunst ohne Erzählen: Die Gattung der nicht-fiktionalen Kunstprosa*. Ed. Klaus Weissenberger. Tübingen: Niemeyer, 1985, 169-183: 175. "In jenen Fällen, in denen an Stelle der objektiven Faktenakkumulation und der reinen Wissensvermittlung die Verinnerlichung der Wirklichkeit durch subjektive Gestaltungsform [...] in 'essayistischer Weise' als wesensbestimmend in den Vordergrund tritt, handelt es sich zweifellos um literarische Werke."
[41] Barbara Korte. "Der Reisebericht aus anglistischer Sicht: Stand, Tendenzen und Desiderate seiner literaturwissenschaftlichen Erforschung." *Zeitschrift für Anglistik und Amerikanistik* 42 (1994), 364-387: 364.

chronology. It is set apart from travel guides, ship's logs, and other forms of purely pragmatic intention by an internalization of the experience within the traveling subject and varying degrees of fictionalization when written down retrospectively. The latter aspect shows the common denominator of travel narratives and fictional literature.

2.3. Travel Narratives and 'Literariness'

New World travel narratives usually took a form and title which suggested that their function was primarily pragmatic. They were captains' logs, diaries of explorers, reports written during or after a voyage to report to the sponsors of a voyage; they also came in the form of informative letters, written home to officials, friends or family members. Often, they intended, as their titles suggest, to tell the "history" of a voyage or, more generally, the "history" of a specific region or colony. They were usually structured chronologically like diaries or log books. Another model for travel narratives was developed specifically for information purposes aimed at diplomatic, trade, or military personnel: Travelers were requested to note the geographical situation, climate, harbors, military strength, number of cities and inhabitants of a given place. Since many early travelers were not exactly experts at the fine arts of writing but rather men of action – sailors, merchants, surveyors, military captains – , their narratives were for a long time excluded from the canon of literature proper for their lack of "literariness" and their primarily pragmatic character. Also, the peculiar status of travel narratives as factual reports, suspected of telling lies when embellishing or inventing, and lacking literary merit when not inventing but recording facts, put this complex genre on the margins of literature. Ethnologists and historians have paid closer attention to these texts ever since because they are often the only historical sources of knowledge, which has to be reconstructed on their basis. In these fields of research, too, travel narratives labored under reduced credibility and could be highly distorting when taken at face value. The prominent story of Pocahontas and John Smith (John Rolfe being little more than an extra in this story) as a fairy tale of colonial romance and a utopia of interracial harmony shows that such stories, once they make it into history, often proliferate in a way that may even take them to the silver screen but, at the same time, very far away from historical "truth".

Modern literary scholarship, however, has developed a more comprehensive definition of literature to include such seemingly pragmatic writings as early American travel narratives. What is more, with the opening up of literary criticism to fields such as gender studies, colonialism, or cultural history, travel narratives are now recognized as a rich field of research. Barbara Korte sums up this development in an essay on the future of travel narrative criticism: "Not until a literary scholarship oriented towards cultural semiotics began to be interested in mentalities, perception and representation of national otherness, images of foreign lands, and intercultural aspects, did travel narratives emerge as valuable objects of study in the 1970s."[42] Also, modern scholarship has begun to appreciate the legacy of early American travel narratives as the first reports on the Americas which left a deep impression on all accounts of the New World that were to follow.[43] Early American travel literature is central to studying the discourses of power, race, or gender, and also of creating and perpetuating historical realities. In the recently published *Cambridge Companion to Travel Writing*, Peter Hulme summarizes this complex character of travel literature and its wide reach into related fields of study:

> The subjects of race, colonialism, and gender cut across any single discipline, and within the academy evidence of the centrality of travel is the spread of its study across several fields. Interest in the rôle of travel and exploration literature in contributing to and reflecting the colonial past has been joined by a growing sophistication of textual readings based on an understanding of the operation of narrative conventions and by an acceptance that claims to truth and objectivity are not always reliable.[44]

Regarding its topic, a travel narrative is both pragmatic writing in respect of recording real events for information purposes (e.g. concerning history, navigation, trade, or ethnography), and at the same time assumes literary status by subjectively recording, (re)arranging and interpreting facts, including descriptions of setting, or establishing a subjective narrative voice. Travel narratives about early America are a special group within the genre because they constitute the earliest body of writing in and about America. An assessment of the artistic value of early American travel narratives should not be separated from the circumstances of its genesis and reception: Because the American environment often ravished its

---

[42] Barbara Korte. "Der Reisebericht. Der Reisebericht aus anglistischer Sicht: Stand, Tendenzen und Desiderate seiner literaturwissenschaftlichen Erforschung." *Zeitschrift für Anglistik und Amerikanistik*, 42 (1994), 364-372: 3. "Erst eine kultursemiotisch orientierte Literaturwissenschaft sieht seit den siebziger Jahren in Reiseberichten einen lohnenden Gegenstand für Untersuchungen, die sich mit Mentalitäten, mit der Wahrnehmung und der Darstellung nationaler Andersartigkeit, mit der Imagologie fremder Länder oder mit Problemen der Interkulturalität befassen."
[43] Evelyn Page, for example, has accordingly termed her survey of pre-colonial writing on the Americas "American Genesis" and analyzes motifs and structures of narrative which were, and remain to be, core features of American literature. Evelyn Page. *American Genesis. Pre-Colonial Writing in the North*. Boston: Gambit, 1973.
[44] Peter Hulme and Tim Youngs, eds. *The Cambridge Companion to Travel Writing*. Cambridge: Cambridge University Press, 2002: 9.

European beholder at first sight, yet later proved hostile and harsh during first experiences of settlement, American nature has often been indelibly imprinted in the little polished, matter-of-fact style of prose. However, these characteristic features also paid some tribute to the conventions of reception in Europe.

2.4. Conventions of Reception

Conventions of reception play a large part in the question of how fact relates to fiction in travel narratives. The famous example of Mandeville's *Travels*, long taken at face value, and the real experiences of Marco Polo, for a long time considered a fraud, make it clear that the distinction between fact (in travel narratives) and fiction (accounts of travels in novels, for example) often depends on the readership and its expectations about a text. The first reports of the New World had to struggle for trustworthiness because what they told not only seemed absolutely marvelous, but occasionally contradicted what Western Europe had for centuries taken as fixed categories of geographic and ethnologic knowledge. Therefore, travel narratives deployed various strategies of authentification. The emphasis which was based on the eyewitness report frequently occurs in early texts of discovery and exploration and may serve to differentiate them from fictional literature which *per definitionem* is not expected to deliver truth claims. With the beginning of the Age of Discoveries, travel narratives were recognized as sources of knowledge and were often the basis of new encyclopaedia on the world and its peoples. For this reason, credibility ranked high on the scale. Samuel Purchas introduced his collection of travel and exploration narratives, meant as a compendium of scientific information, by saying, "what a world [...] travelers have by their own eyes observed [...] is here [...] delivered, not by one preferring methodically to deliver the history of nature according to rules of art, nor philosophically to discuss and dispute; but as in way of discourse, by each traveler relating what is the kind he has seen."[45]

The shift from adhering to traditional knowledge, based on conjecture and analogy, to gathering of empirical information is a major feature in early New World reports. Conventions of reception were influenced by this development, resulting again in various strategies of authentification or a supposedly neutral narrative voice; titles like *The Historie of Travell* (Strachey) or *A Briefe and True Report* (Hariot) suggest that what is told is true and transmitted for information purposes. There are, once again, two points of reference on opposite ends, now of a thematic trajectory which determines formal criteria of vision and writing: On

---

[45] Quoted after: Peter Hulme. "Introduction." In: Peter Hulme and Tim Youngs, eds. *The Cambridge Companion to Travel Writing*. Cambridge: Cambridge University Press, 2002: 4.

the one hand, the traveler's attention focuses on what he expects to see based on common knowledge of his own culture. This includes, for example, *topoi*, "rhetorical baggage carried by the traveler" and most likely by his audience as well.[46] On the other hand, a travel narrative's frame of reference is the audience it is written for, be it private or public. Thus, the text had to balance new knowledge with what a society was able and willing to consider credible.

> The sea captains and sailors who undertook overseas voyages [...] were not willful frauds, attempting in folly to gull their homebound fellows. They were members of the European community; they drew upon a stock of ideas common to all. [...] Their minds, like the minds of their forefathers, had been nourished on a commonly cherished blend of fact, legend, and fable. When abroad, their eyes saw no more than their minds, shaped at home, were prepared to accept.[47]

2.5. Author and Narrator, Voice, and Making Fact into Fiction

Probably the most important aspects of establishing the literary status of travel narratives concern the author-narrator question, the question of voice, and the process of writing. Non-literary travel writing usually employs a neutral narrator who presents facts but little else, as in the case of travel guides or log books. It is neither necessary nor fruitful in any way to distinguish between the author and the narrating voice. The establishment of such a non-intrusive narrator, consequently, may result in a scientific text (of ethnography or geography), but usually not in a text which would be recognized as literary. In the case of narratives like Columbus', for example, it is known that the author is identical with the person who traveled.

Nevertheless, a distinction ought to be made in narratives of discovery, exploration and travel between author and narrator, as is proper for literary artifacts, because such travel accounts are always re-"creations" of a past experience. The journey may represent itself as a "shapeless, endlessly shifting accumulation of experience."[48] Its narrative, however, is a planned, intentionally and sometimes artistically created piece of work. It is subject to the same need for coherence as other literary narratives. A travel narrative may be classified as literature, therefore, if the authentic travel experience is fictionalized by consciously reconstruct-

---

[46] Caroline B. Brettell. "Introduction: Travel Literature, Ethnography, and Ethnohistory." In: *Ethnohistory*, Vol. 33, No. 2 (May 1986), 127-138: 128.
[47] Margaret T. Hogden. *Early Anthropology in the 16th and 17th Centuries*. Philadelphia: University of Pennsylvania Press, 1964: 184.
[48] Jonathan Raban. *Coasting*. London: Picador, 1987: 246.

ing it in the process of writing. The narrative voice is staged with a certain effect intended, be it persuasive, apologetic, or informative. It is manipulated because the narrating persona is no longer identical with the traveling persona: "When writing down the experiences of authentic travel, they are reconstructed and thereby fictionalized in the process."[49] The decades-old debate over the person and narratives of John Smith, for example, in part centered on the history versus fiction question.

2.6. Conclusion: Definition of Travel Narrative

To sum up, a travel narrative can be described as a written report of a temporary departure by an individual to another location which in turn is conceived as culturally different from the place of departure. The traveling individual relates not only the story or rather the events of the voyage but also supplies relevant, yet subjectively chosen information on its setting via descriptive passages. What is more, in the process of fixing a real journey in writing, the traveler re-creates and thus fictionalizes the experience by establishing a narrative voice, arranging the "shapeless accumulation of experience" into a subjectively coherent narrative, often with specific effects on an audience in mind.

A special aspect in the definition of travel narratives is the general relation of fact and fiction in the travel experience. Due to the strong influence of expected features of the New World and a frequent failure at adequate perception and comprehension, there is a certain amount of imagination involved in these narratives. Thus, early travel narratives about North America share central features with fictional prose beyond narrative voice or artistic effect: They tell a story, describe its setting(s), and they occasionally tell more than the truth – or less, depending on an author's intention, indebtedness to traditional lore, and faculties of perception. Last, but not least, New World travel narratives were also confined by their audience and what it could, and would, accept as credible.

---

[49] Barbara Korte. "Der englische Reisebericht": 16. "Eine authentische Reiseerfahrung wird beim Reise-Schreiben [...] rekonstruiert und dadurch fiktionalisiert."

3. A Short History of Travel and Its Narrative

Travel is almost as old as mankind, mobility the original *conditio humana*; sedentary life is a much younger development. When wandering hunters and gatherers became sedentary, however, travel entered the stage of human experience as a (temporary) departure from the known sphere of home into the unknown. Travel in ancient times had much to do with fate or necessary movement; penitents like Oedipus left their homes to wander the world in search of forgiveness for their sins, and his guilt was visible to everyone by his aimless wanderings.

The Middle Ages saw a considerable shift in these ancient definitions of travel. The first non-utilitarian travelers probably were pilgrims who took upon them long and hazardous journeys to holy places like Santiago de Compostela, Lourdes, Rome, or the Holy Land. Since this kind of travel involved people from all social groups and brought them in repeated contact with strangers, foreign lands and new ideas, even pilgrimages carried, from early on, the stigma of dubious motives and results: Spiritual salvation could, it was claimed, be profitably gained on an inward journey just as well, but without the danger of dissolution and moral corruption which traveling might entail.

Towards the end of the Middle Ages, other reasons for traveling gained importance: Trade, military enterprises and exploration led people into ever greater distances from their homeland, and it is a human wish not to go unprepared, but to look for information on the destination, the way there, safety or diet instructions before embarking on a voyage. An increasing amount of written information about previously accomplished voyages to the fringes of European civilization became available for all who wanted or had to travel. Thus, writing and travel have always been connected; some of the most prominent tales in classical times relate stories of travel, and the Biblical tradition is rich in examples of narratives of travel as well. Some of these narratives, such as the *Aeneid* or the *Exodus*, have served as frames of reference and intertexts for later travel writers, as for example the *Exodus* for some of the most prominent New England Puritan writings. The journey to America, the hoped-for spiritual asylum, was often framed in a rhetoric derived from the Biblical text.

Despite such authoritative models, however, the attitude of societies towards travelers has always been ambivalent. Travel could broaden the mind by extending the individual's and society's knowledge about other lands and cultures, but it could also result in fundamental changes of character or even dissolution. William Strachey, a visitor to the early Jamestown colony, mused on the origins of American indigenous peoples in his *Historie of Travell*. He suggested that their seemingly barbarian and heathen ways were a result of having traveled far away from the cultural heartland of Christianity and "knowledge of the eternal [...] truth."[50] Furthermore, before it became possible for larger numbers of people to travel, the tales of returned travelers could hardly be verified, and were thus often suspected of being made up or at least fancifully enhanced. Ulysses' ambivalent character – "powerful yet cunning" – is "perhaps the appropriate archetype for the traveler, and by extension for the travel writer."[51] It is remarkable in this context that of the two most widely known travel narratives of the later Middle Ages, Marco Polo's and Mandeville's, the former - and largely true - was accused of being a fabrication, while the latter, though wholly made up, was taken at face value for a long time. Regardless of that, however, both texts saw wide circulation and translations into numerous languages, demonstrating the early popularity of the genre.

With the Age of Discoveries, travel writing achieved a new prominence among representatives of pragmatic writing because the act of discovery was incomplete if it was not made known to the public by a report.[52] In the Renaissance, travel reports were no longer privately used to confer knowledge and advice to would-be travelers. Instead, they were often compiled into publicly accessible compendia of all existing knowledge of other lands. After the first great voyages of discovery in Columbus' wake had subsided, the newly acquired empirical knowledge was worked into compendia by scholars who sought to systematicize the current state of knowledge about the world existing in various forms of texts. Consequently, these collections rendered old and new travel reports and often fabrications like Mandeville's along with the latest "true" reports of eyewitnesses, as in the case of Richard Hakluyt's *Divers Voyages*: The 1582 edition lists "the names of certain late travelers [...] which also for the most part have written of their own travels and voyages." This includes Mandeville and also lists him among "certain late writers of geography."

With increasing travel to faraway lands, the sixteenth century saw a rise in demand for reports and material on distant worlds, including America. As a result, travel writers were valued as principal sources of new knowledge and accordingly their texts were collected. The fact that names like Mandeville's appear and frequent recourses to Pliny's natural history occur shows that Europeans were, despite all empiricism, still deeply indebted to traditional sources of knowledge and, more importantly, classical or scriptural authority. Some well-known examples of such collections were Francanzano da Montalboddo's *Paesi nuovamente retrovati*

---

[50] William Strachey. *The Historie of Travell into Virginia Britania*. Ed. Louis B. Wright and Virginia Freund. London: Hakluyt Society, 1953: 55.
[51] Peter Hulme and Tim Youngs. "Introduction." In: Hulme and Young, eds. *The Cambridge Companion to Travel Writing*. Cambridge: Cambridge University Press, 2002: 2.
[52] "To discover" means more than to see for the first time; it also means to make known, most of all by writing.

(1507), Pietro (or Peter) Martyr D'Anghiera's *De Orbe Novo*, later translated in parts into English by Richard Eden (*Decades of the Newe Worlde*, 1555), *Delle Navigationi et Viaggi* (Venice 1550, 1556, 1559) compiled by Giovanni Battista Ramusio as well as the *Divers Voyages* (London 1582) and the *Principal Navigations* (London 1589) compiled by Richard Hakluyt and continued at the beginning of the seventeenth century by Samuel Purchas. At the end of the sixteenth century, the Frankfurt engraver Theodor de Bry published a lavishly illustrated multi-volume edition of New World narratives, which was translated into the major European languages (and also Latin) and established knowledge of the New World within Europe in words and pictures.

Compilers like Richard Hakluyt, Theodor De Bry, and Samuel Purchas made the first-person narrative of experience the basis for a travel writer's authority. New demands of veracity were put on authors whose experiences could be, at least theoretically, verified in an age of increased accessibility and travel to the lands in question. Thus, passages emphasizing visual testimony abound in early travel reports. However, especially the earliest ones from the New World faced the problem of how to report what was not only radically different from everything known but also lay beyond the traveler's verbal capacities: "If we compare [Guiana's magnificence] to that of Peru, and but read the report of Francisco Lopez and others, it will seem more than credible."[53] The New World could thus not be narrated convincingly without describing its phenomena as closely as Old World language and the traveler-writer's perception would allow. Word of mouth or reports from other travelers helped establish additional credibility, and New World abundance or alleged riches could best be conveyed through comparison and superlatives: "I have been assured by such of the Spaniards as have seen Manoa the Imperial City of Guiana [...] that for the greatness, for the riches, and for the excellent seat, it far exceeds any of the world."[54]

If there were no Spanish witnesses at hand to support English hopes of riches, natives were quoted as authorities, too, and such passages usually reveal how faulty the communication process was by frequent hints at signs instead of words: During an exploration voyage along the coast of Florida, the French explorer Jean Ribaut reported that the natives showed them "by signs that they had in the land gold and silver and copper."[55] Mary B. Campbell sums up such techniques of transmitting what could not be described with Old World words and faculties of

---

[53] Sir Walter Ralegh. *The Discovery of [...] Guiana*. In: *Early American Writing*. Ed. Giles B. Gunn. New York: Penguin, 1994: 66.
[54] ibid.: 66.
[55] Jean Ribaut. "The Discovery of Terra Florida". In: Richard Hakluyt. *Divers Voyages*. Facsimile reprint: 90.

perception and therefore either needed further authorization by foreign sources or by describing as closely as possible what was there, as in the case of Ralegh's Guiana:

> This wasteland [Guiana] to which neither Marco Polo nor Virgil nor the Bible can prepare the way, is Ralegh's matter [in *The Discoverie*]. The paradox of the superabundant wasteland, confronted by an inadequate vocabulary, gives rise at last to the art of close description and establishes narrative as the necessary structure of the travel 'relation'. The narrator's *experience* is the only object of which his knowledge can be comprehensive and to which his language can be equal. It is with this experience that he fills the wilderness and his relation.[56]

Although documentation of observed experience was the appropriate narrative form, travel narratives remained highly personal and thus subjective, the author's attitude towards a region and his (or his patron's) intentions central features of any text.[57] There were, however, various strategies of authentication: The author could attempt to impress his readers by the weight of his own personality, that of his patron, or the recipient of the dedication; he could quote authorities, indigenous people or other European travelers, as the quote from Ralegh demonstrates, or he could resort to a plain, unassuming and deliberately realistic style, the *genus humile* of classical rhetoric.[58] In other cases, quoting foreign sources, like Spanish or native ones, supplied European observation of New World phenomena with additional authority. These characteristics have rendered travel narratives highly problematic source texts for the historian, yet for literary as well as cultural studies, the subjectivity involved in travel narratives and its efforts at representations of own and foreign cultures can much rather be regarded as an asset.

Traveling does not only convey information about the world, but also about the traveler and his lens, his (or her) inherited set of cultural preconceptions and pre-judgments through which a traveler-writer views the Other. This mechanism of assimilating the Other characterizes not only the traveling individuals but also the culture they belong to. Travel reports function as a key to individual as well as

---

[56] Mary B. Campbell. *The Witness and the Other World*. Ithaca, NY: Cornell University Press, 1988: 228.

[57] Mary B. Campbell sheds interesting light on Columbus' writing: "When Columbus imposed on his 'new heaven and new earth' [...] the generic egotism and greed of romance, he also opened up the travel account to a subjectivity and narrativity new to the form and essential to its later masterpieces. The autobiographical and experiential bent and the ample sensitivity of the modern genre bear the stain upon them of original sin: It was in the self-love of conquering heroes that the travel memoir was born." *The Witness and the Other World*: 209.

[58] Cf. Montaigne's testimony about New World peoples, most credibly described by a "plain and artless man". Justin Stagl. *A History of Curiosity: The Theory of Travel, 1550-1800*. Chur: Harwood Academic Publishers, 1995: 51.

collective patterns of conceptualization and discourses of power which discoverers, explorers and colonists brought with them on their journeys to the New World. The texts they wrote permit an insight into these pre-judgments and possible reassessments during or after encounters with the New World. In this process, the human mind employs techniques of making alike what it recognizes as new and different from what it has known before. The integration of new knowledge into individual as well as collective canons of knowledge is a complex process often contaminated by the human capacity for imagination. What we read in early travel reports, then, are impressions of the New World tainted by traditional concepts of how the world and other peoples were perceived and understood to be. This explains why categories of identification inherited from classical antiquity as well as the Bible were instantly used to cope with the new. Only gradually did European travelers learn to describe what they saw instead of drawing analogies with what they had hitherto known.

4. Describing a New World with Words from the Old

4.1. Narration and Description in Travel Narratives

Early travel narratives about the New World are made up largely by two components: the narration of events, of action, and the description of the setting of events and various New World phenomena. This is a central feature which travel narratives share with fictional discourse, and it offers a valuable field of literary analysis of travel narratives. Several questions ought to be asked about this twofold structure in order to make these texts accessible as literary artifacts. First, I will draw on Hayden White's analysis of historical narrative discourse to identify central characteristics of narrative technique which historical and travel writing share and which also open up travel narratives to aspects of literary and cultural criticism. Next, the functions of description in New World travel narratives will be assessed based on questions of perception and language. This will facilitate understanding of allegedly factual representations in descriptions of New World phenomena and help identify the functions of narration and description in "worldmaking" English travel narratives of early America.

4.2. Travel Writing and Narrative Discourse

On a basic level, narration can be understood as a technique of fashioning a sequence of actions in time into a coherent story, involving personae, events, setting, and action. Applied to the "hybrid genre" of travel narratives, which claim to recount truthfully actual journeys and their incidents, narrative cannot be understood as an innocent rendering of what happened, and what happened next, and why. Rather, early travel narratives about encounters with the New World and its peoples were produced in a complex web of types of discourse imported from Europe and used to make sense of an encounter which often riddled its protagonists more than it enlightened them. Thus, the need for structures of human understanding, for accepted patterns of meaning-making was especially important. A journey could not be told without setting it in a frame of narrative discourse recognizable to a European audience at home. In a traveler's encounter with the New World, the facts – or what he may have perceived as facts – may have been there, but causality and coherence most often were not. Thus, a narrative had to be fashioned from a disparate array of observations, actions and reciprocal actions, all of which were frequently based on misinterpretation. The raw material a traveler was confronted with thus resembles the data of the historian, and looking at how historical narrative discourse is generated will shed some light on the way a discourse of the New World was generated in travel reports and how it functioned as social practice.

Hayden White has argued that historical narratives do not simply tell a sequence of facts; neither do they render causalities inherent in the facts. Instead, he argues that in order to make a coherent story out of value-neutral, disparate data, historians apply much the same cultural patterns, archetypes, or structural concepts as literary narrative discourse does to create a coherent narrative. Therefore, White's definition of narrative can be applied to travel narratives as well: "Narrative is not merely a neutral discursive form that may or may not be used to represent real events [...] but rather entails ontological and epistemic choices with distinct ideological and even specifically political implications." Narrative discourse is no neutral medium for the representation of events, but "the very stuff of a mythical view of reality." [59] It thus shapes historical facts, as well as facts of New World journeys, both of which might be incomprehensible in unprocessed, i.e. unnarrated form, into "story types that we conventionally use to endow the events of our lives with culturally sanctioned meanings." Such a narrative "mediates between the events reported in it on the one side and pregeneric plot structures conventionally used in our culture to endow unfamiliar events and situations with meaning, on the other."[60] The pronoun *our* is important in this context, for it is always the writer's specific culture and its familiar "pregeneric plot structures" which account for the meaning in which narrative structure can frame facts and events. This, it should be noted, was by no means limited to Europeans telling of their first encounters with the New World. It seems much rather to be a universal human activity of dealing with incomprehensible phenomena.

Reports by Thomas Hariot and William Strachey suggest that among various North American Indian tribes, tales of the arrival of white gods from the East was part of their folklore and thus an available narrative frame in which the first encounters with Europeans could be put, and which offered a way of making meaning of such first encounters.[61] Likewise, European travelers could shape their experiences in early America into their respective "pregeneric plot structures" of finding an earthly Eden, Salomon's fabled Ophir, or redeeming heathen tribes. The heritage of stories about mythical lands, their riches, distant and often monstrous peoples on the one hand and the Biblical and classical tradition on the other hand have to be regarded as the main repository from which frames of reference or plot structures were derived. Narrative discourse about early travels to and in

---

[59] Hayden White. "The Content of the Form." In: *The Content of the Form: Narrative Discourse and Historical Representation*. Baltimore: Johns Hopkins University Press, 1987: ix.
[60] Hayden White. *Tropics of Discourse. Essays in Cultural Criticism*. Baltimore: Johns Hopkins Press, 1984: 88.
[61] Cf. the chapters on Strachey and Hariot.

the New World, therefore, is best accessed not so much via the truth value it contains (or does not) or a search for accurate chronicles. Travel narratives should be studied much rather under the aspect of how the disparate and often frustratingly incoherent facts of New World encounters could be shaped into a coherent narrative which managed to make some sense not only to the traveler, but also to members of his society at home. The expectation that Indians were "treacherous", for example, is mentioned frequently, and also in the complete absence of any falsehood – a sign that Europeans did not know how to deal with people whose behaviour seemed frustratingly inconsistent.[62] Some Europeans, it seems, were able to look beyond a stereotype. Peter Arundel wrote in 1623, one year after the so-called Virginia massacre: "We ourselves have taught them how to be treacherous by our false dealings."[63]

4.3. Perception and Language

In order to portray the setting in which encounters between Europeans and indigenous peoples took place, it had to be described. Often, the impressions of New World phenomena were so numerous that the catalogue became a popular form of describing an alien environment for merchants, investors, military personnel, scholars, or would-be settlers. The form itself may seem innocent, yet a closer look will reveal that language, and descriptions made up of it, are never neutral: "In one sense, description is formal, citational, systematic even in its clashes. In another sense [...] it is a reading of perception."[64] In his collection of essays, *Tropics of Discourse*, Hayden White assesses historical narratives and their predeterminative tendencies grounded in language: "All descriptions of phenomena are already interpretations of its structure, and [...] the linguistic mode in which the original description (or taxonomy) of the field is cast will implicitly rule out certain modes of representation [...] and tacitly sanction others."[65]

The same observation, however, is true of description in early reports from North America as well: The language in which description is cast is never value-neutral. Description, much more than narration, exerts a subtle influence on the

---

[62] Cf. Karen Ordahl Kupperman. "English Perceptions of Treachery, 1583-1640: The Case of the American 'Savages'." *Historical Journal* XX (1977): 263-287.
[63] Quoted after Alden T. Vaughan. "'Expulsion of the Savages': English Policy and the Virginia Massacre of 1622." *William and Mary Quarterly*, 3rd ser., 35 (1978): 72. The Virginia "massacre" was the result of an attack by Indian tribes on the English settlements around Jamestown in 1622.
[64] Jeffrey Kittay. "Introduction." In: Jeffrey Kittay, ed. *Towards a Theory of Description*. Yale French Studies, 61 (1980): ix.
[65] Hayden White. *Tropics of Discourse. Essays in Cultural Criticism*. Baltimore: Johns Hopkins Press, 1984: 128.

audience's imagination which produces images of the New World perpetuated in reports, but almost always without a possibility of verification. An audience, therefore, had to rely on narrative and descriptive representation of the New World in order to form a mental concept of it. Narrative passages inform audiences about *what happened* – which usually entails a subjective point of view easily recognized by an audience. The point of view plays an important role here, for even when a narrator tries to be as non-intrusive as possible, common conventions of narrative signal an individual voice behind such passages. Descriptive passages, however, are usually judged to be information derived primarily from the senses, especially the sense of sight: "Description attempts to represent, at least in a first stage, the manifest, that which is either present or meant to seem so, and the manifest tends to take the form of a visual display."[66] A subjective, distorting factor may not necessarily be implied here at first. What is there, or "meant to seem so", is there to see for every eyewitness. Perception, however, is no neutral concept. Rather, it depends on an *a priori* existing frame of reference within which perceived phenomena can be arranged, structured, and named. Accordingly, Nelson Goodman states a case against "perception without conception": "Talk of unstructured content or an unconceptualized given or a substratum without properties is self-defeating; for the talk imposes structure, conceptualizes, ascribes properties. [...] We can have words without a world but no world without words or other symbols."[67]

Once an eyewitness sits down to describe what he has seen, language enters the process. Putting perceptive impressions into words is already an interpretation of the phenomena, for usually a choice of alternative words has to be made to produce a coherent narrative. "There is no value-neutral mode of emplotment. [...] Not only all interpretation, but also all language is politically contaminated."[68] Even the words of a simple man, whom Michel de Montaigne regarded as the most credible narrator of a voyage because he was thought to be incapable of embellishments or lies, do not warrant a truthful narrative, for even "ordinary language [...] has its own forms of terminological determinism, represented by the figures of speech without which discourse itself is impossible."[69] Language and perception went hand in hand with another powerful influence on men's minds in early New World travel writing: the imagination and the inherited European lore by which it was shaped. Men returning from overseas voyages and writing about their experiences

---

[66] Jeffrey Kittay, "Descriptive Limits." In: Kittay, *Description*: 227.
[67] Nelson Goodman, *Ways of Worldmaking*: 6.
[68] Hayden White, *Tropics of Discourse*: 129.
[69] ibd.: 134.

were members of the European community; they drew upon a stock of ideas common to all. [...] Their minds, like the minds of their forefathers, had been nourished on a commonly cherished blend of fact, legend, and fable. When abroad, their eyes saw no more than their minds, shaped at home, were prepared to accept.[70]

4.4. Description, Naming, and Judgment

One of the most striking examples of how language can never be value neutral is the naming of indigenous peoples Europeans met in the Americas as "Indians". Given common knowledge of Asia in his time, Columbus had a certain set of expectations of the people he encountered. Asia was, as detailed in the chapter on the historical background of New World exploration, imagined as a realm of vast riches and highly developed civilizations. Consequently, Columbus was disappointed that he found no "great cities" which were taken as an acknowledged sign of civilization in contrast to smaller nomadic societal entities. Furthermore, civilized societies were expected to care for gold, silver and other precious commodities as well as for arts and sciences. He soon discovered that not all "Indians" were alike. He found some to be friendly (Arawaks), others to be brutal and bellicose (Caribs). Given the fact that he assumed them to be "Indians", the Native Americans may have fallen painfully short of what he expected "Indians" to be like.

The term "savage", applied very early on to indigenous peoples as well, carries another, distinct set of connotations with it. This term, more than any other, not only designates a specific condition of uncivilized life, but derives most of its evocative power from its dialectical antithesis, the civilized man. This term, according to Hayden White in an essay on the "Forms of Wildness", does "not so much refer to a specific thing, place, or condition as it does dictate a particular attitude governing a relationship between a lived reality and some area of problematical existence that cannot be accomodated easily to conventional conceptions of the normal or familiar." White calls the technique of negative definition (we may not know our cultural identity, but we are very likely to know how we do not want to be) "the technique of ostensive self-definition by negation, and it is certainly much more generally practised [...] than any other form of cultural definition."[71] Partakers in early voyages also termed the native inhabitants the "naturals".[72] Nevertheless, of course, naturals were far from civilized, and thus a pa-

---

[70] Margaret T. Hogden. *Early Anthropology in the Sixteenth and Seventeenth Centuries*: 184.
[71] Hayden White, *Tropics of Discourse*: 151f.
[72] Ralph Hamor. *A True Discourse of the Present State of Virginia* [London, 1615]. New York: Da Capo Press, 1971: 16.

tronizing attitude accompanies even this term which at first may look innocent enough.

The images, concepts and judgments which descriptions evoke are, as demonstrated in the cases mentioned above, "conceived in an ideological area defined by the axis of myth and that of a value system. Literary descriptions remain quite opaque and meaningless to those unaware of the 'story behind them', *and* the cultural values they embody. Thence the pressing need for interpretations."[73] Description, as a consequence, is meaningless until received in a culture from whose value system the elements of a description are derived. This also entails that, had Native Americans been able to read a description by, say, Columbus, they might not have been able to make much of it because they lacked the cultural frame of reference necessary for judgment of the objects described. Once received in the intended social group, description must necessarily evoke judgment because it is not value-neutral. Observations of native nakedness for example or promiscuity, as well as eating raw flesh, may at first sight look like interesting and valuable ethnographic data. For sixteenth-century Europeans, however, these three features were the strongest testimony of savagism and ranked at the far end of the scale of human evolution. The way Europeans, especially those who stayed at home and read or heard such reports, reacted to the New World was fundamentally shaped by the descriptions which eyewitnesses (however fallible) reported home about the land and its peoples.

Thus, along with the necessity to differentiate between a participant in a voyage and the narrator of its story, we need to differentiate between what is witnessed and what is described, for "to describe is never to describe a reality, but to prove one's rhetorical know-how, to prove one's book-learning. [...] It is a textual praxis, both coded and aimed, opening onto concrete, practical activities."[74] Furthermore, it should be noted that description can be "a working between texts"[75] in as far as rewriting other reports or the conscious application of rhetorical models is concerned. Intertextuality is a central constituent in early American travel reports. Thomas Hariot or John Smith, for example, were repeatedly quoted as authorities and their texts quoted at length, often verbatim as in Strachey's *Historie of Travell*. The numerous applications of the Golden Age *topos* in descriptions – and judgments - of indigenous nakedness are further examples of such intertextual characteristics. Often, too, a certain intention behind description is to be expected, as in a catalogue of merchantable commodities. Hariot's *Briefe and True Report* contains such a chapter and thereby introduces American plants, animals, and

---

[73] Michel Beaujour. "Some Paradoxes of Description." In: Kittay, *Description*: 33.
[74] Philippe Hamon. "Rhetorical Status of the Descriptive." In: Kittay, *Description*: 6.
[75] ibid.

minerals not only to categories of knowledge by naming them, but also to commercial use; American flora and fauna is thus very early on cast into a language of profit and possible exploitation.

What is more, the potential autonomy of descriptive passages may result in effects wholly unintentional because "description can open up to possibilities, explore, include what somehow does not belong, what is inessential, but that accidence is essential, is essence."[76] Such "essential accidence" reveals much about what a traveler perceived (or failed to), and how he was able to conceptualize it in writing. As a textual practice within a narrative, it may seem like an unwarranted digression, away from the narrative structure and into the realms of the audience's fancy. Philippe Hamon, in his discussion of classical (i.e. normative) rhetorical discourse on description, claims it "appear[ed] as a threatening area" because it might result in "useless detail", "excess of luxury", or even "skip[ped] the reader" and thus forfeited his or her attention – or diverted it from report to imagination. As a result, description "might be that place in the text where the generative power of language might show itself most clearly and as quite unmanageable."[77] Therefore, when studying descriptive passages in early American travel narratives, the "generative power of language" in descriptions of the New World may make a text speak more than it knows and unearth hidden dichotomies of rhetoric, as for example when passages describing America's abundant nature are juxtaposed with narrative passages about a colony on the brink of starvation.

Judging by the evidence found in early American travel narratives, a European consensus seems to have existed which engendered expectations (and subsequently, inferences or even claims of the same) of indigenous nakedness, cannibalism, but also of a state of prelapsarian innocence. Many travel narratives catered to this pool of European expectations. Here we can draw a distinction between factual narratives, whose descriptive parts are subject to the limits of verisimilitude described above, and fiction, whose descriptive passages are not confined to such an *effet de réel*. Travel narratives, to avoid the age-old and widespread accusation of telling lies, have to remain credible if these texts want to achieve their aims – to inform, to persuade, or to describe for scientific purposes. But with regard to the expectations which the Americas engendered in travelers and their audience, the question of truth and credibility becomes more complicated. Truth should not be understood as a neutral and scientific concept when dealing with early American travel narratives. Even though many travelers attempted to describe closely what they saw or perceived, there still had to be some

---

[76] Jeffrey Kittay. "Introduction." In: Kittay, *Description*: ix.
[77] Philippe Hamon. "Rhetorical Status of the Descriptive." In: Kittay, *Description*: 25.

kind of reference point, as Margaret Hogden explains in a study on early anthropology:

> If improvement were to be made in current canons of description, in which epithets were sometimes the only content, some stable touchstone of comparison had to be found. With this in mind, it seemed clear that the only known and useful standard was that of Europe. [...] On the whole, however, it was the failure to find similitudes, due to what were taken to be radical divergences from the European norm, which often attracted most attention; and it was then that the negative mode of attack was invoked. [Europocentrism's] function as a criterion of description was inverted [now]. Instead of serving conceptually as a means of bringing alien cultures into some degree of rapport with that of Europe, it emphasized their cleavage and separation. In some uses, it segregated and classified as barbarians any people who failed to fit into the European scheme of things. In others, the denial of likeness was endowed with historical implications. By virtue of undeclared assumptions, the cultures thus submitted to negative description were assumed to be in an aboriginal, a natural, or a prelapsarian condition of either purity and goodness or corruption and lawlessness.[78]

4.5. Description, Worldmaking, and Truth in Early American Travel Narratives

In the essay collection on description quoted above, Michel Beaujour introduces his topic of paradoxes of description by asking, "what could appear more natural than the 'picturing in words' of a *garden*", and adds, "provided we possess some commonplace ideas of what a *garden is*", an act "so simple that the reader already is enjoying mental images of plants and vegetables"[79] even before the description begins (italics in the quote). In the case of early travel narratives, there may possibly not have been such a commonplace idea of what an Indian village is, or some exotic plant or animal early discoverers or explorers chanced upon. Description in early travel narratives about the New World often could not draw upon a set of fixed images in the mind of the reader, but was faced with the task of describing phenomena for which Old World language had no adequate words, let alone precise names. Nevertheless, New World phenomena had to be structured and named in some way in order to be assimilable and "tellable" in exploration reports at all. On the other hand, if reports were taken to be credible, they created in the imagination of their audience a world its members had not seen, and presumably never would. Accordingly, Nelson Goodman poses the question:

---

[78] Margaret Hogden, *Early Anthropology*: 193, 196.
[79] Michel Beaujour. "Some Paradoxes of Description." In: Kittay, *Description*: 27f.

What are the criteria for success in making a world? [...] A version is taken to be true when it offends no unyielding beliefs and none of its own precepts. Among beliefs unyielding at a given time may be long-lived reflections of laws of logic, short-lived reflections of recent observations, and other convictions and prejudices ingrained with varying degrees of firmness. Among precepts, for example, may be choices among alternative frames of reference, weightings, and derivational bases.[80]

When considering the impact of New World accounts on the European imagination, we have to keep these limits in mind which were put on "versions" of the world. This mechanism may, for example, be responsible for the "blunted impact" news of the New World is occasionally said to have had.[81] But whatever passed such limits of acceptability can be viewed as "the constitution of America in European minds as a verbal construct, an artifact."[82] Occasionally, the writers "encounter the boundaries of [their] familiar language, and of the culture implicit in it." In the reports from early colonial America, language "comes to exert a subtle influence on how life in the colony is conceptualized", and how an image of the colony, but also the continent, takes shape in the minds of those who had not been there; language becomes a "vehicle of political and intellectual control."[83] By rendering New World experience in Old World words, the strange and often incomprehensibly alien hemisphere was domesticated by naming, describing, and thus making it assimilable to human faculties of understanding, but at the cost of losing objectivity. Clifford Geertz describes this process:

> What we call our data are really our own constructions of other people's constructions of what they and their compatriots are up to. [Descriptions of other peoples] must be cast in terms of the constructions we imagine [other peoples] to place upon what they live through, the formulae they use to define what happens to them. Anthropological writings themselves are interpretations, and second and third order ones to boot. They are, thus, fictions, in the sense that they are 'something made'.[84]

---

[80] Nelson Goodman, *Ways of Worldmaking*: 17.
[81] John H. Elliott. "Renaissance Europe and America: A Blunted Impact?" In: *First Images of America. The Impact of the New World on the Old*, ed. Fredi Chiappelli. Berkeley, CA: University of California Press, 1976. Vol. I, 11-26.
[82] Wayne Franklin, *Discoverers, Explorers, Settlers*: xi.
[83] ibid.: 4.
[84] Clifford Geertz. *The Interpretation of Culture. Selected Essays*. New York: Basic Books, 1973: 9ff.

This process is not only a feature of anthropological writing but also of early American travel narratives. They are Englishmen's interpretations of what they perceived and experienced in America, and they are also fictions, "something made" to a considerable degree. This process of making fact into fiction by interpretation and writing will be analyzed in the second part of this thesis. But before that, another central determinant in Europeans' mental equipment for construction and interpretation in Geertz's sense remains to be considered: the European cultural and historical background of exploration.

5. Cultural and Historical Background

5.1. Imagination and Geographical Exploration

> The admiral [Columbus] says that the sacred theologians and learned philosophers were right in saying that the earthly paradise is at the end of the East [...] so those lands which he had now discovered are, he says, the end of the East.[85]

When Columbus set sail to reach Asia on a westerly course, he most likely knew where he was going and what he expected to find upon landfall. He allegedly carried letters from the Spanish sovereigns to the Great Khan and was, it seems, well acquainted not only with the "sacred theologians" and "learned philosophers" but had also read the tales of John de Mandeville. When explorers and travelers viewed the New World, it seems as if the products of cognitive faculties were contaminated with images which existed in the mind before a journey was actually begun:

> Imagination [...] must be viewed as critical for the processes of geographical exploration by which unknown lands are brought within the horizons of human experience. Imagination becomes a behavioral factor in geographical discovery as courses of action are laid out according to preconceived images; later decisions based on field observations may be distorted by these images. The results [...] are modified by reports written and interpreted in the light of persistent illusions and by attempts made to fit new information into partly erroneous systems and frameworks.[86]

The human mind had been prepared for worlds beyond the known realm since antiquity. Philosophers like Strabo transferred geographical knowledge about the familiar world onto unfamiliar or yet unknown areas, a universal technique of

---

[85] Columbus believes he is exploring in or near the earthly paradise, Feb 21st entry 1493. Quoted after Mary B. Campbell. *The Witness and the Other World*: 202. Columbus is, according to Campbell, also the first to stumble upon the not yet "dressed and kept" Garden Eden analogy – his Garden is not peopled but merely decorated by Indians. "The issue of dressing and keeping a Paradise is a complex rendering of the contradictory images of garden and wilderness." This dichotomy was to reappear frequently in later descriptions of – or should we say ascriptions to – the New World. "A garden is an image of nature cultivated and formalized, but Eden is also an image of leisure." Mary B. Campbell. *The Witness and the Other World*: 203.

[86] John L. Allen. "Lands of Myth, Waters of Wonder: The Place of the Imagination in the History of Geographical Exploration." In: *Geographies of the Mind. Essays in Historical Geosophy*. Ed. David Lowenthal and Martyn J. Bowden. New York: Oxford University Press, 1976, 41-61: 43.

conceptualizing the unknown until better data were available.[87] This process, for example, accounts for puzzling misjudgments about the climate of Newfoundland, whose first explorers considered it very suitable for colonization, or early promoters of Virginia who expected the new colony to bring forth agricultural produce which flourished in the same latitude on other continents but continually failed to prosper in America. In both cases, inferences about the new were made based on extending knowledge of the familiar world (Europe) onto the unfamiliar until an often painful and costly reassessment could be made empirically. Hope, desire, or ambition colored the geographical imagination; in terms of quick gain or agricultural produce to be expected from the Americas, it was primarily Asia, the locale of vast riches and highly developed civilizations, which influenced Europeans' hopes and ambitions regarding the New World.

5.2. The East and the West in European Imagination

Until the European discovery of the continent at the end of the Atlantic Ocean, the East exerted a strong influence on the European imagination. Close to the Christian heartland yet far enough away from European civilization, the East was the location of symbolical extremes: the place, according to the tales of Jean de Mandeville, of earthly Paradise, the incredibly rich kingdom of the fabled Christian king Prester John, but also the apocalyptic tribes of Gog and Magog which would bring ultimate destruction at the day of doom. Thus, in the European imagination spatial distance was often associated with supernatural distance, rendering the East heavily laden with symbolic associations. Along with marvelous riches on the one hand and terrible hazards on the other (especially in forms of huge or poisonous beasts), the East also engendered associations of extraordinary men with extraordinary achievements and supernatural powers, such as Prester John, famed king and Christian priest. The most famous reports by travelers to the East were the narratives of Marco Polo and Mandeville. Marco Polo, on his deathbed, is reported to have said he had only reported as much as he thought his contemporaries were able to believe.

Whereas the East embodied mankind's paradisaical origins as well as its final destruction and thus combined great civilizations, wonders and riches with fearsome tribes and monsters, the West engendered much more positive associations like the Islands of the Blessed. These used to wander across empty spaces of the

---

[87] See, for example, James S. Romm. *The Edges of the Earth in Ancient Thought. Geography, Exploration, and Fiction.* Princeton, NJ: Princeton University Press, 1992; Henri Baudet. *Paradise on Earth. Some Thoughts on European Images of Non-European Man.* Transl. Elizabeth Wentholt. New Haven and London: Yale University Press, 1965.

Atlantic according to the cartographic conventions of the times; myths of enchanted and enchanting islands were derived from Greek mythology or medieval legend, such as the tale of the Irish abbot St. Brendan. He allegedly journeyed among enchanted islands to the west of Ireland and chanced upon the paradisaical saints' land of promise which was still placed on some maps as late as 1755.[88] Spanish folklore knew of the Seven Bishops who had fled Moorish Spain and built seven Christian Cities in the West. Early empiricism of geographical science up to Columbus' voyage began only tentatively to move away from the medieval tradition of world mapping which relied heavily on biblical, classical and medieval lore. The *Catalan Atlas*, produced around 1375 on Majorca, represented the most up-to-date knowledge of the world - and what Europe believed to exist beyond its borders: The legendary *Insula de Brazil* appears as it did in medieval maps of the North Atlantic; the Islands of the Blessed made people believe theirs was the locus of the earthly Paradise, and Prester John is mentioned in the accompanying text as a ruler in North Africa.[89]

Little more than one hundred years later, the Portuguese had already been active in the Atlantic, exploring the African West coast. In that time, Hartmann Schedel's *liber chronicarum* (Nuremberg 1493), a survey of the history of the world from creation to 1493, was one of the most widely distributed books of the fifteenth century with more than 1200 extant copies; it contains an account of the fabulous races of mankind, citing as its authority Pliny, Saint Augustine and Isidore of Seville. At the same time, Columbus sailed to the Americas and failed to find Pliny's monstrous races, yet found people living quite well in the "torrid zone" for centuries believed to be uninhabitable. Columbus' letter *de insulis inventis*, written on the homeward journey in 1493, described the New World more or less in the explorer's own words instead of using terminology derived from classical authorities. It confirmed that the natives went naked "as their mothers bore them;" Columbus also noted that he had found neither "great cities", which he expected due to tales of Asia's great civilizations, cities and riches; nor had he chanced upon the human monstrosities so popular in folklore and expected to live in those distant lands Columbus had traveled to.

When the kingdom of Prester John could not be located in Asia and, later, in North Africa, it was expected to lie somewhere in the New World; ultimately, the search for Prester John "died out in the New World along the mighty Orinoco, about which Columbus had expressed the hope that this might be the River of

---

[88] Cf. Mary Helms, *Ulysses' Sail*: 218.
[89] All quoted after Jean Michel Massing. "Observations and Beliefs: The World of the Catalan Atlas." In: Jay A. Levenson, ed. *Circa 1492. Art in the Age of Exploration*. National Gallery of Art Exhibition Catalogue. National Gallery of Art: Washington, DC, 1991: 27-34.

Paradise flowing from Prester John's realm."[90] The strong and ambiguous connection between myth, imagination and geographical discovery, however, continued for centuries:

> The power of imagination over experience in the expansion and consolidation of geographical knowledge is exemplified also by the persistence of myths that constantly retreat into still unknown territory. [...] The reports of explorers who failed to find [mythical cities or peoples] had not removed the myth from geographical lore but had only transferred it in space.[91]

Accordingly, many explorers of early North America searched for a Northern El Dorado, the Northwest Passage, or the South Sea which was for a long time expected to be located beyond the Appalachian mountains. Thus, during the first two centuries after the Americas appeared in writing before the eyes of Europeans, medieval lore, conjectures regarding America's climate, peoples, and history based on traditional authorities like Pliny or St. Augustine, and new knowledge gathered on voyages of exploration created a curious mixture of fact and fiction which is mirrored in early New World reports. The search for the Seven Cities of Cibola, for example, became a preoccupation of Western explorers until there was no more uncharted space left towards the West where they could be found. English readers could learn from Thomas Hacket's translation of Jean Ribaut's 1562 Florida voyage that Cibola was not far off:

> As we now demanded of [the natives] concerning the city of *Sevola*, whereof some have written not to be far from thence [i.e. Florida], and to be situate[d] within the land, and toward the sea called the South Sea. They showed us by signs that which we understood well enough, that they might go thither with their boats (by rivers) in twenty days.[92]

The English translator John Florio quotes, in the preface to his translation of Cartier's narratives, Giovanni Ramusio who first translated the French text into Italian: "This learned man's judgment concerning the planting of colonies" is the authoritative basis for claiming as true the exploring voyages commissioned by Antonio de Mendoza. This "Viceroy of Mexico, willing to put in execution, sent forth his captains both by sea and by land upon the Northwest of *Nuova Spagna*, and discovered the kingdom of the seven cities about Cibola." Cibola (allegedly) discovered, the kingdom of Saguenay "which abounds with gold and other metals,

---

[90] John Allen, "Waters of Wonder": 54.
[91] ibd.: 53f.
[92] Jean Ribault. "The Discoverie of Terra Florida". In: Richard Hakluyt, *Divers Voyages*: 88.

as in the second relation [of Cartier] is to be seen"[93] almost dis-covered by the French – it was high time, therefore, for the English to enter the American stage. Information about North America, especially regarding climate and geography, remained for a long time

> subject to the interpretations, modifications, and inventions of those faculties of the human mind that are collectively called the imagination. [...] To say that geographical information is available as the result of exploration is not to say that a region is known empirically. [...] If empirical and nonempirical lore about a region differ before exploration, empirical and nonempirical lore will differ following the exploration as well. Disjunctions between the actual and imagined lore nearly always exist and are responsible for much of the subjectivity in the writing and interpretation of exploratory accounts. The difficulty of assimilating exploratory accounts into the general store of knowledge results from problems of fitting the new information into recognized geographical frameworks. If an explorer returns with information that contradicts or subverts strong and generally accepted concepts, his data may have little immediate effect in creating more accurate regional images.[94]

It took much longer than Vespucci, who is credited with realizing that the Americas were no part of Asia, for Europe to endow the new continents with their appropriate meanings. Until then, strategies of assimilation of otherness had long been established and were hard to break with. European cosmography grappled with the efforts of absorbing and defining these newly recognized distant places of the West, "a culturally unique task which, in effect, required not only the recognition but the creation of a new spatially and perhaps temporally supernatural domain in the geographical-cosmological periphery of the European cosmos."[95] Europeans ascribed to that new continent a time frame different from Europe's. The West essentially was without time if understood as biblical time since the Fall; native inhabitants seemed to mirror earlier stages of European development, as is shown for example by John White's watercolors based on his North American experience and the pictures of "ancient Picts" to render parallels between such different stages of mankind's evolution. Thus, it is not surprising that Europeans were often wont to assume a patronizing attitude towards the natives and to regard it as a noble task to lead them out of their ancient ways into the times of early

---

[93] Jacques Cartier. "A shorte and briefe narration of the two Navigations and Discoveries to the Northwest partes called Newe France: First translated out of French into Italian [by Ramusio], and now turned into English by John Florio" [1580]. In: Richard Hakluyt, *Divers Voyages*. Facsimile Reprint: 126f.
[94] John Allen, "Lands of Myth, Waters of Wonder": 52.
[95] Mary Helms, *Ulysses' Sail*: 219f.

modern European Christianity – an argument especially reiterated in promotional tracts. Settling "those vast and unpeopled countries, [...] being devoid of all civil inhabitants" became another staple in many English New World narratives which portrayed the continent as a *vacuum domicilium* reserved for the English.[96]

Compared to Spanish America, even though the Northern continent seemed to yield little riches apart from codfish and timber, its seeming emptiness was in time to become its peculiar promise to Europeans. Christianizing those natives that Europeans encountered remained high on the agenda of English colonial officials; what, according to John Smith, could be "more agreeable to God, than to seek to convert those poor savages to know Christ, and humanity, whose labors with discretion will triple requite thy charge and pains?"[97] Yet the same man admitted freely that he was "not so simple to think that ever any motive than wealth will ever erect there a Commonwealth; or draw company from their ease and humors at home."[98] This peculiar mixture of religious and economic motives, at times judged promising, at other times futile, was mirrored by another polarity of ascriptions. As the native inhabitants were regarded either as noble savages or as brutish beasts, so descriptions of the country could range from "Earth's only Paradise" (Thomas Drayton) to a "hideous and desolate wilderness" (William Bradford). Thus, over time, North America was partly discovered as it was and partly invented in the way writers wished or perceived it to be.

Even before the first English voyages of exploration were sent out after the Cabots, America had been established in the European imagination through narratives portraying the New World on a scale ranging from a newfound Eden to a desolate wilderness. Images of the New World like those conveyed in Martyr's golden age analogy played a central role in the European imagination. Yet the first actual experiences of Europeans with indigenous peoples and, in the case of the Northern continent, occasionally forbidding climatic conditions very unlike those of an earthly paradise added a darker hue to the initially glossy images. By the beginning of the sixteenth century, the first reports of explorations of the North American coast by Englishmen were occasionally less than optimistic because the land fell increasingly short of expectations engendered by narratives like Laudonnière's *Florida*. From early voyages to the Northern regions of the North American continent, the image of a barren wilderness, hostile natives and harsh climate emerged. "I believe that this land was the land God gave to Cain," wrote Jacques

---

[96] William Bradford. *Of Plymouth Plantation, 1620-1647.* Ed. Samuel Eliot Morison. New York: The Modern Library, 1967: 25.
[97] John Smith. "A Description of New England." In: Philip L. Barbour, ed. *Works of John Smith*: 346.
[98] ibid.: 346.

Cartier of the Labrador coast.[99] A member of Frobisher's 1577 Northwest expedition remarked: "In place of odoriferous and fragrant smells of sweet gums, and pleasant notes of musical birds, we tasted the most boisterous boreal blasts mixed with snow and hail in the months of June and July."[100]

This was even more puzzling and frustrating to the explorers as the climate of America was usually expected to correspond to the respective climates in the same latitude on other continents. This assumption extended to comparable natural products concerning flora and fauna, but also precious metals, which helps to explain why early promoters of the Northern regions expected that North America would yield minerals, silk, wine, or pearls, as did other regions around the globe on the same latitudes: Although the effort to establish a colony at Sagadahoc in Maine failed, Sir Ferdinando Gorges argued that "New England's latitude was in the center of the temperate zone, the golden mean, and therefore comparable to Constantinople, and Rome, [...] Italy, and France, the Gardens of Europe."[101]

The parts more to the South of today's United States were deemed far more attractive and easier to reconcile with classical images of pastoral idyll: Giovanni da Verrazzano named part of the coast "Achadia" because it reminded him of the Arcadian landscapes described by Virgil or, more recently, Jacopo Sannazaro.[102] More than a century later, descriptions of Virginia echoed this golden age image: Michael Drayton wrote of Virginia where "the golden age / Still Nature's laws doth give." And even though Virginia failed to produce the expected wines, silkworms or olive trees, all of which flourished in European or Asian regions of the same latitude, the climate seemed much more inviting for settlement than the regions farther north. Also, first reports of contact with the natives were often promising and seemed to support earlier descriptions like that of David Ingram, who told of the generally friendly and tractable nature of the Indians. Accordingly, when the first English set foot on Roanoke island, the reports of Hariot and Barlowe, for example, echoed the original, idyllic vision of natural peoples who lived in a prelapsarian state, with Virginian nature as the adequate backdrop of an earthly Eden. However, three years after the "Virginia Massacre" in 1622, Samuel Purchas wrote of the Virginia Indians that they were "bad people, having little of

---

[99] "The First Relation of James Cartier of the New Land Called New Fraunce, Newly discovered in the yeere of our Lorde, 1534." Transl. John Florio. Quoted after Richard Hakluyt, *Divers Voyages*: 135.
[100] Christopher Hall's narrative, quoted after Hakluyt's *Principal Navigations*, 1589 edition. Facsimile Reprint, ed. David B. Quinn and Raleigh A. Skelton. Cambridge: Hakluyt Society, 1965: 623.
[101] Quoted after Karen Ordahl Kupperman. "The Puzzle of the American Climate in the Early Colonial Period." *American Historical Review* 87 (1985), 1262-1289: 1272.
[102] Hugh Honour. *The New Golden Land*. London: Lane, 17.

humanity but shape, ignorant of civility, or arts, or religion: more brutish than the beasts they hunt, more wild and unmanly than that unmanned wild country, which they range rather than inhabit."[103]

In the *Decades* by Peter Martyr, the New World very early underwent a subtle fictionalization into a mythicized Golden Age, whose indigenous peoples lived "in the golden world of which the old writers speak so much: wherein men lived simply and innocently [...] content only to satisfy nature, without further vexation for knowledge of things to come."[104] Later narratives would oscillate between the indebtedness to such literary models of New World reports and the reality of an often frustratingly forbidding American environment. Consequently, many of the English travel narratives of early America described an America that was almost as much fiction as it was fact. The second part of this thesis is dedicated to the question of how, and to what effect, such narratives brought home news and information about North America and functioned as worldmaking texts.

---

[103] Samuel Purchas. *Purchas His Pilgrimes*, XIX, 231. Quoted after: Gary B. Nash, "The Image of the Indian in the Southern Colonial Mind." *William and Mary Quarterly*, 3rd ser., 29 (1972): 223. Purchas echoes a central notion of Western thought that human civil life can only take place within settled communities, the *civitas* of antiquity. Nomadism was the given antithesis to civilized life.
[104] Peter Martyr. *Decades*, transl. Richard Eden, 1555. Quoted after J. H. Elliott, *The Old World and the New*: 26.

6. Early American Travel Narratives as Worldmaking Texts: Narratives of First Contacts

For the first English travelers to North America, a considerable body of sources of information existed, drawn from continental European discovery and exploration reports. These precursors to English voyages are likely to have shaped the expectations of English travelers; they also offered narrative models and in particular established some of the central techniques of description later employed in English narratives. Some of these collections will be presented here together with official English instructions for travelers issued for a projected reconnaissance voyage to North America in the 1580s. Both the early continental reports as well as the instructions help to situate the first English reports in this European historical and literary context.

6.1. Models and Precursors

6.1.1. Richard Eden's *Decades of the Newe Worlde, or West India* (1555)

Richard Eden's English translation of parts of Peter Martyr's *Decades* and excerpts from Sebastian Münster's *Cosmographia*[105] introduced the English, in 1555, not only to narratives of Spanish voyages of discoveries, but also to the strategies of representation and meaning-making that were to influence English New World travel narratives. Eden's work clearly demonstrates that travel and colonial writing[106] were highly political genres. Eden's translation of parts of Peter Martyr's *Decades* emphasizes the English need for counteracting Spanish expansion on the American continents and taking up colonial possessions in the West as well. While Eden's work introduced the English public to new knowledge and new realities concerning the New World and thus had, in pragmatic respects, a primarily informative character, the book also inaugurated a long tradition of promotional narratives intended to encourage support for colonial ventures. Writing about discoveries was the method of choice:

---

[105] *The First Three English Books on America. Being Chiefly Translations, Compilations, &c., by Richard Eden*. Ed. Edward Arber. Rptd. New York: Kraus Reprint Co., 1971. Texts are chiefly taken from Peter Martyr, Sebastian Münster's *Cosmography* and Sebastian Cabot.
[106] I would like to understand the term colonial writing in this study, following Peter Hulme's definition in *Colonial Encounters*, as texts relating to or promoting overseas colonies, consisting of settlements of people from the mother country in another country. The term colonialism is closely related to this group of writing often involved with representing the Other, yet bears stronger connotations in terms of asymmetrical power relations.

> Governors, lieutenants, captains, admirals, and pilots [have] by their painful travels [...] not only subdued these lands and seas, but have also with like diligence committed the order thereof to writing. [...] This new world is now so much frequented, the ocean now so well known, and the commodities so great.[107]

Eden quotes the Spanish exploits as virtuous examples and seeks to call Englishmen to action, too:

> How much more then shall we think these men worthy [of] just commendations who in their merciful wars against these naked people have so used themselves toward them in exchange for benefits of victory, that greater commodity has thereof ensued to the vanquished than the victors. They have taken nothing from them but such as they themselves were well willing to part with, and accounted as superfluities, as gold, pearls, precious stones and such other. [...] But some will say [that the Spanish] possess and inhabit their regions and use them [i.e. the natives] as bondmen and tributaries, where before they were free. They inhabit their regions indeed: Yet so that by their diligence and better manuring [of] the same they may now better sustain both than one before.[108]

This double argument of "merciful wars" and an empty, unkept and thus wasted land was to be reiterated in English promotional tracts. Even though, after the reign of Mary, the English cultivated the then opportune Black Legend of Spanish cruelties in the New World, the arguments Eden put into the mouths of Spanish colonizers were freely adopted by the English and used whenever they suited the narrative and argumentative needs, as for example in Robert Johnson's tract *Nova Britannia* in 1609: The English are not willing

> to look on whilst so huge and spacious countries (the fourth part of the world) and the greatest and wealthiest part of all the rest should remain a wilderness, subject (for the most part) but to wild beasts and fowls of the air, and to savage people, which have no Christian nor civil use of any thing. [...]

The narrator refutes Spain's claims to North America and dates England's claims to 13 July, 1584 [Roanoke, see the appended timeline], reinforced by the first settlements, the 1587 colony under John White, who "left them there to inhabit to this day", even though the narrator obscurely hints at the failed colony.[109]

---

[107] Richard Eden, *Decades*; quoted after Hadfield, *Amazons*, p.17.
[108] Quoted after Andrew Hadfield, *Amazons, Savages, Machiavels*: 18.
[109] Robert Johnson. "Nova Britannia". In: David B. Quinn. *New American World. A Documentary History of North America to 1612*, 5 vols. New York: Arno Press and Hector Bye, 1979: 235-237.

Although Eden's book claimed that this New World was now "so well known and the oceans so well traveled", the compilation nevertheless contained much classic and medieval lore which had at least partly been lore of the East and was gradually moved into the newly discovered Western hemisphere, featuring marvelous riches, fabulous creatures and savages noble and ignoble. The first book, for instance, contains the legend of Prester John and his superbly rich Christian empire. In accordance with later descriptions of foreign lands, this text sets the stage for narratives of abundantly rich countries, gold and silver for the taking, strange beasts, human monstrosities, and the like. It is thus an interesting backdrop linking medieval legend, with its search for remote Christian allies, rumors of precious metals and strange creatures, to early modern voyages of discovery and exploration. In fact, the description of Prester John's realm seems to be a repository for all kinds of rumors that had been circulating about distant lands from antiquity onwards. The empire is immensely rich in gold and silver; its flora and fauna comprises pygmies and sagittarii "the which being from the middle upward like men and from the middle downward [are] they like the [lower] part of a horse;"[110] the mythical Phoenix lives there; the fountain of youth keeps inhabitants young and healthy;[111] and some of Pliny's monstrous races, such as the dog-headed men, appear.

Excerpts from Sebastian Münster's *Cosmography* make up the second book and are supposed to show the "diligent reader [...] the good success and reward of noble and honest enterprises, by the which not only worldly riches are obtained, but also God is glorified, and the Christian faith enlarged."[112] A report of Vespucci's first voyage introduces the audience to strange indigenous peoples who seem to be a conglomerate of all that had been reported about different West Indian tribes until then: They are gentle, well-built, hardy, clean and friendly; however, they are immoral, having all women in common but no institution of marriage; furthermore, they only know communal possession and no trade: "They use no kind of merchandise or buying or selling, being content only with that which nature has left them." They do not care for "gold, pearls, precious stones, jewels, and such other things", although they have them and seem to know where to obtain such goods. A feature not at all in line with the friendly, innocently natural state described before is the fact that they are cannibals: "They eat no kind of flesh except man's flesh" which they take in wars, the latter never being fought

---

The first attempts at settlement at Roanoke ended in the loss of several groups of colonists; Roanoke later became known as the "Lost Colony" (see the timeline in the appendix).
[110] Richard Eden, *Decades:* xxxiii.
[111] ibid.: xxxiv.
[112] ibid.: 3.

over possessions or riches but only in cases of retribution. Apart from such composite pictures, the reports of Vespucci's voyages are interspersed with hints at friendly tribes and "gold everywhere." The other stage props of New World description are already in place, too: The variety of fruit is "innumerable", the land is *"fair* and *fruitful*, having many *pleasant* woods". Trade with the natives is excessively profitable, the Europeans "receiving for one bell five hundred pearls."[113] The terms in italics can be found in almost every English New World report; it is remarkable that *fair, fruitful* and especially *pleasant* are rather nondescript terms.

The third book is a translation of parts of Martyr's *Decades*. At the beginning, the voyages of Columbus are narrated, complete with the geographical conjectures of the time, based on antiquity and Scripture. After "discovering" and sailing along Juana ("otherwise called Cuba"), "he [Columbus] affirmed that he had found the island of Ophir, whither Salomon's ships sailed for gold. But the description of the cosmographers well considered, it seems that both these, and the other islands adjoining, are the Islands of Antilia." This passage shows the mechanism of categorizing new entities based on traditional knowledge; the New World somehow had to fit in with European geographical knowledge, and thus Columbus' act of discovery and Martyr's learned injunctions of what had been found are less acts of "discovery" than of "finding a fit."[114]

The New World, not at all new when regarded as possible locales of Ophir or Antilia, was as much found as it was "made" by what European discoverers and stay-at-home cosmographers declared it to be, and the weight of the eyewitness's and the scholar's authority helped to carry these definitions across decades. Even after the said islands of the Caribbean were recognized as actually "new" to European knowledge and not to be Ophir or Antilia, only the names changed, but many of the ascriptions made during the first contact stayed intact: Friendly natives who marveled at the newcomers, accorded them god-like status, brought them quantities of gold and contented themselves with trifles continued the image of lands of mythical riches even when refined geographical knowledge had placed them on the real map of the Americas. The following quote exemplifies the methods by which Columbus, and after him Martyr, made conjectures about where, and what, the newfound islands were. Parrots had been described to Europeans before, in this case in Pliny's *Natural History*, which had placed these animals somewhere in India. Accordingly, parrots serve, for Columbus, to prove that he is sailing somewhere close to Asia, because these animals are "like them of India [...] as Pliny describes them." And

---

[113] Richard Eden, *Decades*: 37f.
[114] Nelson Goodman, *Ways of Worldmaking*: 2.

albeit the opinion of Christopher Columbus (who affirms these islands to be part of India) does not in all points agree with the judgment of ancient writers as touching the bigness of the sphere [...] yet the popiniaies [i.e. parrots] and many other things brought from thence, do declare that these islands resemble somewhat of India, either being near unto it, or else of the same nature; for Aristotle [...] and likewise Seneca, with diverse other authors not ignorant in cosmography, do affirm that India is no long tract by sea.[115]

At another place, beautiful young (and naked) women dance for the Spanish discoverers, so that "they supposed that they had seen those most beautiful *Dryades*, or the native nymphs or fairies of the fountains whereof the antiquites speak so much."[116] This method was to be repeated until there was too much new knowledge that could not be made to fit anymore and forced Europeans to revise their geographical and ethnographical knowledge, this time including a hemisphere about which the ancients had not said anything. From now on, knowledge was increasingly based on experience, and this turn away from citing classical sources as authorities on new lands and peoples towards relying on close description of the eyewitness report marks the beginning of early modern travel writing. Subtitles of travel reports spoke of "a new and experimentall discoverie"[117] and emphasized the empirical, and thus authoritative character, of the eyewitness report. Francis Yeardley, son of Virginia governor Sir George Yeardley, reported that "South Virginia or Carolina [was] experimentally rich in precious metals," even though nothing specific, especially no gold or silver, came of his exploratory voyage.[118]

The process, however, was a slow one; even a century after Columbus, many European discoverers showed themselves still deeply indebted to geographical lore, even in the face of adverse facts. Often, if the eyewitness was not able to describe convincingly what he saw, analogies served to enable fellow Europeans to imagine the New World better.

This method of description by using analogy – often ending in New World superlatives - appears frequently in the earliest reports of voyages of discovery, as in this quote from Eden's translation of Martyr: "Let us therefore without shamefastness compare the island of Hispaniola to Italy, sometime the head and queen of the whole world. For if we consider the quantity [of natural resources], it shall

---

[115] Richard Eden, *Decades*: 67.
[116] ibid.: 83.
[117] John Underhill. *Newes from America. Or, a New and Experimentall Discoverie of New England* [London, 1638]. New York: Da Capo Press, 1971.
[118] Francis Yeardley. "Letter to John Ferrar Esq." In: Alexander S. Salley, Jr. *Narratives of Early Carolina*. New York: Barnes and Noble, 1911, rpt. 1967: 25.

be found little less, and much more fruitful.[...] It is surely much more blessed and fortunate than Italy."[119] Describing new phenomena by using analogies of known ones was a central element in reports from early North America. Usually, however, America was described using the comparative ("much more fruitful than", "much more blessed than") or, even more often, the superlative: Francis Yeardley found Carolina to be "most fertile"; John Lawson said of Carolina compared to other regions, "none that I ever saw exceeds it."[120]

Richard Eden's translation of various European discovery and exploration narratives exemplifies the traditional strategies of gaining and perpetuating knowledge first based on conjecture, with recourse to ancient authorities, Scripture, or legend. With increasing experience, close observation replaced such recourses and afforded the narratives a new authority, but descriptions had to be supported by analogies of Old World phenomena. Superlatives lent additional force to new phenomena, and these strategies of creating knowledge and of representing the New World to the Old were firmly in place, together with ubiquitous hints at gold and other minerals or some human monstrosities, before the English entered the stage of American discovery, exploration, and colonization. Richard Eden's compilation can be considered as a sourcebook of knowledge of the Americas which was accessible to Englishmen in the second half of the sixteenth century, and strongly inspired the myths, themes and narrative strategies which the English discoverers and explorers brought with them to North America.

6.1.2. Richard Hakluyt's *Divers Voyages* (1582)

The first accounts of voyages by Englishmen or under English command which reached a reading public in England were assembled in the first edition of the younger Richard Hakluyt's *Divers Voyages* of 1582. He continued a European discourse on the New World by translating and editing narratives of French and Spanish voyages which may be regarded as narrative models for English reports published in Hakluyt's second compilation, the *Principal Navigations*. In the *Divers Voyages*, the central topics, *topoi* and narrative strategies of later English New World reports were already in place, for example the claim that North America was a *vacuum domicilium* awaiting the European civilizing hand. In the *Epistle Dedicatorie*, the narrator quotes a talk with an old "Portingale" on matters of navigation and exploring the Americas. The Portuguese wonders that the vast realm of North America, except Florida, was still "unplanted by Christians" and

---

[119] Richard Eden, *Decades*: 167.
[120] Francis Yeardley, "Letter": 25. John Lawson, *A New Voyage to Carolina*: 52, 55. Cf. the chapter on the Carolinas.

suggests settling there and "reducing those gentile people to Christianity." The narrator goes on to say that "we might not only for the present time take possession of that good land, but also in short space by God's grace find out that short and easy passage by the Northwest, which we have hitherto so long desired, and whereof we have many good and more than probable conjectures."[121] The noble task of settling a vast and empty realm, converting the heathens, and also finding a Northwest passage to Asia were to remain central motifs of later English voyages to North America.

John Verazzano's voyage, in the *Divers Voyages* entitled *The Discoverie of Norumbega*, adds the paradisaic hue that was to pervade many first encounters with native societies to the point of almost verbal repetition. Verazzano reported that the natives he encountered on the voyage were

> well featured in their limbs, of mean stature and commonly somewhat bigger than we, [...] not strong of body yet sharp witted, nimble and great runners, as far as we could learn by experience, and in those qualities they are like to the people of the East parts of the world, and especially to them of the uttermost parts of China.[122]

Later descriptions of New World natives were to use the same terminology. Comparing American natives to peoples of the East was a convenient method of describing American indigenous societies and people to Europeans at home. It should be noted here that the comparisons, as also in the following quote, establish a fairly positive image due to the referred people of the East: China, Egypt or Syria were locales of heathen, yet civilized populations, renowned for riches, desired commodities, and highly developed cultures dating back to antiquity. Verazzano reported that "we were enforced to return to our ship, leaving this land to our great discontentment, for the great commodity and pleasantness thereof which we suppose is not without some riches, all the hills showing mineral matters in them." The term "pleasant" and its grammatical variants would become a staple in New World promotional literature, as would be the enumeration of commodities and assumptions concerning mineral riches.

The indigenous women of an island close by, according to Verazzano, dress "themselves like the women of Egypt and Syria, these are of the elder sort; and when they are married they wear diverse toys, according to the usage of the people of the East as well men as women."[123] Comparisons of American indigenous peoples with more or less well-known peoples of the East cast Indians in a posi-

---

[121] Richard Hakluyt, *Divers Voyages*: 6.
[122] ibid.: 47.
[123] ibid.: 52ff.

tive light of the noble savage: heathen yet naturally favored and in an innocent state of nature echoing golden age *topoi*. Comparisons with peoples of the East, though, were not the only alternative. In circumstances of strained relations between natives and Europeans or when negative comparisons were needed to serve a narrative's purpose, Indians were often compared to other uncivilized peoples [according to central European tastes of the time, that is] like the Irish, the Turks, or Lapplanders. Then, Indians were entered into the category of ignoble savages, and apart from being heathens and idolaters, cannibalism, polygamy, and treacherous and cruel warfare were standard characteristics.

Another central feature of early New World reports, the attempt to describe what a traveler saw either by comparison, often with superlatives reserved for American items, or by seemingly endless enumeration, was already firmly in place in the *Divers Voyages*. Often, when there were no more words (or sheets of paper) to adequately describe America, narrators would resort to the "it is a thing unspeakable to narrate..." *topos*. Jean Ribaut's *The Discoverie of Terra Florida* (1562), translated by Thomas Hacket, catalogues the natural wildlife, but the narator has to end because he cannot adequately convey the quality and quantity of American flora and fauna:

> Also there be cornies and hares; silk worms in marvelous numbers, a great deal fairer and better, than [...] our silk worms. To be honest, it is a thing unspeakable to consider the things that be seen here, and shall be found more and more, in this incomparable land, which never yet broken with plough irons, brings forth all things according to first nature.[124]

The precursors to English early American travel narratives already exhibit several strategies of describing the New World with words from the Old: Description by using analogies, or description by comparison, often paired with American superlatives; copious use of the fairly nondescript term "pleasant"; and, most interestingly, the failure of description like Ribaut's "unspeakable" richness of American flora and fauna.

Apart from these recurring strategies (or failures of) description, some other themes emerge in texts compiled in the *Divers Voyages* which reappear frequently in later English reports of North America: The question of mineral riches, particularly gold and silver, seems to have been an issue no text could afford to leave out. Ribaut's natives "showed unto us by signs that they had in the land gold and silver and copper."[125] As a conclusion, Ribaut reports the situation of the land:

---

[124] Richard Hakluyt, *Divers Voyages:* 87f.
[125] ibid.: 90.

A good climate healthful, and a good temperature, marvelous[ly] pleasant, the people good, of a good and amiable nature, which willingly will obey; yea, content to serve those that shall with gentleness and humanity go about to allure them, as it is needful for those that be sent thither thereafter to so do, [...] to the end that they may ask and learn of them where they take their gold, copper, and turquoises, and other things yet unknown to us. [...] For if any rude or rigorous means should be used towards this [sic] people, they would flee hither and thither through the woods and forests, and abandon their habitations and countries. [...] There we saw the fairest and the greatest vines with grapes accordingly, and young trees, and small woods, very well smelling, that ever we [had] seen: whereby it appears to be the pleasantest and most commodious dwelling of all the world.[126]

Pleasant climate and abundantly fertile land, supposed riches, and amiable natives who might easily be won for Christendom and European civilization are the quintessential ingredients to be found in most later narratives of discovery and exploration in North America. David Ingram, an Englishman whose largely fantastic narrative was included in the first edition of the *Principal Navigations*, told of North American Indian tribes which were so rich in silver that they covered their roofs with it. Kings wore huge rubies as insignia of their status and lost all of their power if robbed of these. The better sort of people were carried "by men in a sumptuous chair of silver or chrystal, garnished with divers sorts of precious stones." Also, many settlements abounded in pearls "as big as beans"; people wore bracelets of gold and silver. "The people in those countries are professed enemies of the cannibals, or man-eaters; the cannibals do most inhabit between Norumbega and Bariniah; they have teeth like dogs' teeth, and thereby you may know them." Finally, apart from listing possibly true and possibly fancy creatures and plants, Ingram testifies that the natives of the land towards the North had signified to him that ships pass to the North of the country, which was taken as proof of an existing Northwest passage. [127]

Although David Ingram's relation was omitted in the later editions of the *Principal Navigations* due to credibility problems, much of his America's fantastic hue remained with New World reports for a considerable time. Rivers were almost habitually described as glittering with sparkles of gold, and commending the soil's marvelous fertility was almost never omitted. Nevertheless, a more empirical approach to travel writing and reporting took shape as instructions to dis-

---

[126] Richard Hakluyt, *Divers Voyages*: 92f.
[127] *The Principal Navigations, Voiages and Discoveries of the English Nation*. First edition, 1589. Facsimile Reprint, ed. David B. Quinn and Raleigh A. Skelton. Cambridge: Hakluyt Society, 1965: 557-559.

coverers and explorers were issued to ensure a systematic ordering of New World impressions.

6.1.3. Instructions for Travelers on Voyages of Discovery and Exploration

The instructions for voyages of reconnaissance to North America in 1582 or 1583[128] are an early example, usually associated with the activities of Sir George Peckham in 1582/1583. The first part is missing. A reference to "Norramberge" (Norumbega) and Cape Breton hints at a planned New England voyage. This set of instructions details what aspects future explorers are expected to note and report home: They were expected to explore "springs together with their diversities in color or taste noting distinctly the particular place where every such thing shall be found to be set down both in the journal and drawn plots (maps or sketches)." This extended to islands, their size and geographical situation; kinds of fish and shellfish; beasts and especially the differences between them and their European correlates; "their [i.e. the natives'] manner of taking birds, fowl, fish and beasts in those countries." The engravings which accompanied Thomas Hariot's *Briefe and True Report* edition by Theodor de Bry are entitled, "their manner of making their boats" or "their manner of fishing in Virginia", following these instructions almost verbatim. Furthermore, the kinds of earth were to be described and assayed with special attention to fertility or barrenness; trees, fruits and gums, herbs and apothecary plants, naval stores, "their manner of planting and manuring the earth"; the "statures, conditions, apparel and manner of food, which of them be men eaters, with the things that they in every particular place shall most esteem either of their own country commodities or of ours" are to be reported. Attention to military strength, political units, diversity of native languages, with the request that someone bring an English dictionary and add native terms to the respective English ones; observations of rivers, bays, and harbors, places convenient to make salt are further aspects to be considered. The captain is requested to "let the master never go without [...] writing tables and one always to attend him with pen, ink and paper." Furthermore, fishing banks are to be noted. "Also in your discovery search every river that is navigable so far as you may pass with your pinnaces and boats and learn of the inhabitants how much farther every river shall extend itself."[129]

These instructions resemble those for continental European travelers. Guidebooks developed and set forth categories and methods of inquiry by which a trav-

[128] In: David B. Quinn, ed. *New American World*. Vol. 3: 240-245.
[129] ibid.: 240f.

eler might not only make sense of a multitude of new impressions but also make his voyage profitable for those at home, including officials and military personnel, while at the same time relieving the traveler of the stereotypical accusation of lingering around uselessly. Instructions for overseas explorers supplied travelers with a whole set of categories, too, according to which they might come to grips with startlingly new phenomena. Interestingly, the instructions do not ask the traveler so much to search for fundamental difference, but for likeness: "Also draw and set down [...] where you shall find anything worth the noting either like our things in Europe or differing from them in any manner or way. Noting always the differences in color or quantity although they be of one sort, as the new land's herring is far bigger then ours being both of one kind." [130]

With such precise instructions, including the tools, writing and drawing materials to be taken on daily trips, an explorer most likely set out well equipped to order the New World and its phenomena and thus make it assimilable to the Old World canon of knowledge. The early descriptions of North America, derived from Eden's and Hakluyt's Spanish and French sources, are replete with *topoi*, terminology and narrative conventions of description. Combined with instructions for travelers to the New World, they form a narrative program of travel reports about North America most later texts were to follow. There were, however, also cautionary pieces of advice which suggest that, from the earliest voyages of exploration onwards, violence was always to be reckoned with in encounters with indigenous populations: In instructions of the London Company to the first settlers under Captain Newport in 1606, settlers are urged that they

> must in no case suffer any of the natural people of the country to inhabit between you and the seacoast for you cannot carry yourselves so towards them but they will grow discontented with your habitation and be ready to guide and assist any nation that shall come to invade you and if you neglect this you neglect your safety. [...] In all your passages you must have great care not to offend the naturals if you can eschew it", but there are also distinct passages on how to avoid seeming vulnerable to the Indians: "Above all things do not advertise the killing of any of your men. [...] You shall do well also not to let them see or know of your sick men if you have any which may also encourage them to many enterprises. [131]

After landing, the settlers are required to find a navigable deep-water river, and if there appear several rivers likewise suitable, they are expected to "make choice of

---

[130] David B. Quinn, ed. *New American World*: 243.
[131] Quoted after Philip L. Barbour, ed. *The Jamestown Voyages under the First Charter, 1606-1609*. Cambridge: Hakluyt Society, 1969: I, 49-54.

that which bends most towards the Northwest for that way shall you soonest find the other sea." The search for a Northwest passage to Asia was almost as important as finding gold. The settlers are asked to explore the hinterland and "try if they can find any mineral". Last but certainly not least, the leaders of the voyages are asked to write a report themselves *and* make sure no negative reports are sent back to England which might dampen the economic success of future ventures:

> You shall do well to send a perfect relation by Captain Newport of all that is done, of what height you are seated, how far into the land, what commodities you find, what soil, woods [...] and so of all other things else to advertise particularly and to suffer no man to return but by passport from the President and Council nor to write any letter of anything that may discourage others.[132]

Although such instructions ensured a somewhat systematic approach to New World phenomena, the censorship of private communication required of the colonial leaders suggests that disappointed hopes or even grand failures of colonial ventures were part of the picture. Official communication based on such instructions was most likely to be promotional; the propaganda aspect will be discussed in detail in the chapter on the Roanoke Voyages.

6.1.4. The First Collection of Narratives of Early English Voyages: Richard Hakluyt's *Principal Navigations*

After the defeat of the Armada in 1588, it became clear that England was able to partake in the race for maritime exploration and overseas possession hitherto dominated by the Iberian empires. The first voyages had long been made by the time Hakluyt published his compilation, but as yet the narratives of the early voyages circulated largely in manuscript. Apart from the political situation of the time, particularly a renewed rivalry with Spain, the compilation answered the needs of several audiences: It supplied mariners, merchants, military captains and investors in overseas ventures with knowledge on navigation and trade goods and thus provided the most up-to-date body of knowledge in these fields. Furthermore, it catered to a steadily growing interest in prose narratives commenting on current events such as new discoveries and informing an interested public on recent travels and distant lands. The *Principal Navigations* established a political and scientific frame for the genre, but the texts were also unified by a quite distinctive style

---

[132] Philip L. Barbour, ed. *The Jamestown Voyages under the First Charter, 1606-1609.* Cambridge: Hakluyt Society, 1969: I: 49-54.

of prose which made the texts accessible as entertainment, too, as the modern editors Quinn and Skelton point out:

> With the publication of the *Principal Navigations* a new harvest of popular prose writing came into the hands of readers. This was vigorous, racy, exciting, colored with touches of poetic feeling [...] As documents, true statements made at the time, the narratives had the attraction of actuality: their matters had the interest of novelty and constantly changing incident: Their manner was in almost all cases well fitted to the matter.[133]

6.2. Newfoundland

The voyages under the command of Martin Frobisher to Newfoundland were the first fairly well-documented English reconnaissance voyages to the North American shore. The narratives reflect strongly positive expectations prior to the voyages, but the arctic region of the New World obviously failed to conform to the paradisaic images Verazzano or Ribaut had described. Nevertheless, the search for the Northwest passage and for gold led to three consecutive voyages. In the end, they proved rather futile, and the narratives convey much of that disappointment. Richard Whitbourne's report from Newfoundland four decades later[134], however, shows that the idyllic image of fruitful and temperate Northern regions remained intact, at least in writing.

6.2.1. The Frobisher Voyages

Several accounts of Frobisher's three voyages to the arctic regions of North America survive, and they were included in the *Principal Navigations* except the one by George Best. The first voyage in 1576 was chronicled by Christopher Hall and reported friendly relations at first with a few natives which the English met. The stay in Newfoundland, however, ended with five Englishmen lost somewhere at the shore, and the ships' crews suspected they had been abducted or killed by the natives.[135]

---

[133] *The Principal Navigations, Voiages and Discoveries of the English Nation*. First edition, 1589. Facsimile Reprint ed. David B. Quinn and Raleigh A. Skelton. Cambridge: Hakluyt Society, 1965; ix-x.
[134] For a timeline of the voyages and events discussed here, see the appendix.
[135] Christopher Hall. "The First Voyage of Master Martin Frobisher [...]" In: *The Principal Navigations, Voiages and Discoveries of the English Nation*. First edition, 1589. Facsimile Reprint ed. David B. Quinn and Raleigh A. Skelton. Cambridge: Hakluyt Society, 1965: 615-622.

The second voyage a year later took up the search for these men, and accordingly relationships with the natives were marked by mutual distrust. Also, the climatic conditions were less than promising and differed markedly from what Europeans expected from North America: In the middle of summer, "in place of odoriferous fragrant smells of sweet gums and pleasant notes of musical birds, which other countries in more temperate zone[s] do yield, we tasted the most boisterous boreal blasts, mixed with snow and hail, in the month of June and July."[136] It did not help either that skirmishes with the natives ensued just after Frobisher had taken some men ashore, taken possession of the land, and exhorted his men "that by our Christian study and behavior those barbarous people trained up in pagantry and infidelity might be reduced to the knowledge of true religion." The narrator resorts to established categories of savagism and ranks them in the lowest category, a conglomerate of cannibalism, nomadism, and paganism:

> I think them rather anthropophagi, or devourers of man's flesh, than otherwise; for that there is no flesh or fish which they find dead (smell it never so filthy) but they will eat it as they find it without any other dressing. [...] As the country is barren and unfertile, so are they rude and of no capacity to culture the same to any perfection; but are contented by their hunting, fishing and fowling, with raw flesh and warm blood to satisfy their greedy paunches, which is their only glory.[137]

The main intention of this voyage, however, was not an inquiry into the nature of the natives, but the search for a Northwest passage, combined with a hope for access to riches of the Far East. Some hope remained although the fleet failed to find the passage, for the natives "make signs of certain people that wear bright plates of gold in their foreheads and other places of their bodies", probably suggesting geographical closeness to the coasts of Asia. Finding riches, especially gold, was another major goal of Frobisher's arctic voyages, but the gold ore that was taken to Europe proved to be worthless.[138]

The third voyage, undertaken in 1578, was narrated by Thomas Ellis. It was a largely ill-fated enterprise, but it is interesting to note that the English left a small house on the shore in order to acquaint the natives with the English even after

---

[136] Dionyse Settle. "The Second Voyage of Master Martin Frobisher [...]. In: *The Principal Navigations*: 623.
[137] *Principal Navigations*: 629. Thomas Hariot used quite the same sentence to describe some Roanoke colonists over a decade later: They "had little or no care of any other thing but to pamper their bellies [...] after gold and silver was not so soon found." *Briefe and True Report*: 11.
[138] For a study of Frobisher's quest for gold and the ongoing trials and debates in Europe over the Newfoundland gold ore, see Robert McGhee. *The Arctic Voyages of Martin Frobisher*. Seattle: University of Washington Press, 2001.

they had left again for Europe and to make future contact easier and probably more peaceful. In the house, the men left "many kinds of trifles, as pins, points, laces, glasses, combs, babes on horseback and on foot, with innumerable other such fancies and toys; thereby to allure and entice the people to some familiarity against other years."[139] This foreshadowed another such experiment: During the Voyager II mission in the 1970s, disks containing achievements of this world's civilizations were sent into space in order to facilitate peaceful future contacts with extraterrestrial life forms.

The narratives of the Frobisher voyages are remarkable in several respects: The search for gold or the Northwest passage remained central motifs of New World explorations, and Ralph Lane would report later that only if one of these two were found and exploited would voyages to North America and colonization be considered worth the effort. With regard to first encounters, the description of natives seems to fall into either one of two opposed categories with little neutral ground in the middle. If encounters were peaceful and amiable, narrators often resorted to early descriptions of innocent, naked natives living in a paradisaic state. Violent encounters usually triggered the other extreme, that of cruel and treacherous barbarians to be fought because they were deemed beyond reform, and it also often entailed doubts of their humanity in general. Closeness to animals rather than humans, nomadism, cannibalism, and idolatry defined the portrait of the ignoble savage.

All in all, the America of Frobisher's voyages was little more than a geographical obstacle on the way to Asia and its riches. As a consequence, the American landmass itself sparked almost no interest in the English travelers. The land seemed hostile, as did the natives. This, however, changed as soon as trade, colonization, and agricultural exploitation of America became part of the agenda. Even though Sir Humphrey Gilbert had been an early proponent of the Northwest passage, he nevertheless shifted his attention from that single goal of finding the passage to making use of the landmass in his way when he traveled to Newfoundland, and one result of this shift in attention was a description of America very different from the ones of the Frobisher voyages.

---

[139] Thomas Ellis. "The Third and Last Voyage into Meta Incognita [...]." In: *The Principal Navigations*: 634.

6.2.2. Gilbert's Voyage to Newfoundland: Edward Hayes. *A Report of the Voyage [...] by Sir Humphrey Gilbert*

Five years after the last Frobisher voyage, Sir Humphrey Gilbert sailed to Newfoundland. The account of this voyage was written by Edward Hayes and was also included in the *Principal Navigations*. As reasons for the voyage, Hayes cites "our ignorance of the riches and secrets within those lands which unto this day we chiefly know by the travel reports of other nations."[140] Religious motives are mentioned as well to balance the materialistic aims of the enterprise. To establish authority, the narrator "thought good, so far as myself was an eyewitness, to deliver the circumstance and manner of our proceedings in the action."[141] According to the narrator, Gilbert undertook to "plant Christian people and religion in those remote and barbarous nations of America" after having procured from the queen the commission to "inhabit and possess at his choice all remote and heathen lands not in the actual possession of any Christian prince." Gilbert took possession of St. John's harbour in the name of the Queen by having read out a declaration and had "delivered unto him (after the custom of England) a rod and a turf of the same soil."[142]

Thus, the narrator establishes what would become another stereotypical claim of European colonizers: If land was inhabited by "heathens" who, to add to their diminished civil status, did not work the land according to English methods of husbandry, possession of the land could be rightfully taken. It helped, though, that North America was claimed to have been discovered by the Cabots for England.

The compiled reasonings – the discoveries of the Cabots, no previous possession by any "Christian prince", and native tribes of some nomadic character "wasting" the land's potential – were invoked time and again to preclude any discussions of the English right to possess the land. In Gilbert's case, it helped particularly that

> in the South part we found no inhabitants, who by all likelihood have abandoned those coasts, the same being so much frequented by Christians; but in the North [there] are savages altogether harmless. [...] Nature has recompensed that only desert and incommodity of some sharp cold by many benefits,

after which follows a catalogue of flora and fauna useful for habitation or trade:

---

[140] "A Report of the Voyage [...] Attempted in the Year 1583 by Sir Humphrey Gilbert [...] Intended to Discover and to Plant Christian Inhabitants in Places Convenient [...] Written by Edward Hayes..." In the *Principal Navigations*: 679-697: 679.
[141] *Principal Navigations*: 681.
[142] ibid.: 681ff.

We could not observe the hundredth part of creatures in those uninhabited lands; but these mentioned may induce us to glorify the magnificent God, who has superabundantly replenished the earth with creatures serving for the use of man, though man has not used the fifth part of the same [...]. The mountains make show of mineral substance. [...] I will not aver of richer metals [than iron or copper]: albeit by the circumstance following, more than hope may be conceived thereof.[143]

Gilbert's America has all the features that by now may be regarded as staple ingredients in any New World report: tractable or absent natives, natural abundance already viewed not for its own sake but its future economic use, and mountains "making show of" gold and other precious metals. The description of early North America already displays its strong orientation towards a glorious future of converted infidels, cultivated land resulting in material abundance, and rich mines almost everywhere Europeans set foot. It may serve as an ironic note that, on the voyage back, Gilbert drowned when the little vessel he had boarded in Newfoundland sailed into a storm; however, she may also have been over-freighted with goods taken back from America's shore, especially (suspected) gold ore.

Newfoundland and Frobisher's and Gilbert's largely abortive expeditions, however, were soon removed to the back row of English interest in North America when Sir Walter Ralegh began to sponsor a series of voyages to the North American coast. The Roanoke voyages and the colonial experiment at the shore of the Carolinas represent a crucial link between the earlier unsuccessful attempts at planting English colonies in North America and the later experiments at Jamestown which, after much hardship, evolved into permanent settlement. The Roanoke venture itself remained, in the end, an instance of grand failure because the settlers repeatedly disappeared after reinforcements and victuals failed to reach them – the fabled "lost colony" was indeed the second group of people lost, and their fate remains unclear to this day.

Nevertheless, one narrative of these voyages has entered the canon of early American literature and may be regarded as taking part in a "founding myth" of the later United States of America, though much overshadowed by the copious narratives of Puritan settlement in New England. Thomas Hariot's *Briefe and True Report*, together with John White's watercolors and the engravings by Theodor de Bry based on them, introduced the English and also European reading public to yet another grand narrative of a New World paradise, potential racial harmony, and great riches to be gained in the future. And even though the site at Roanoke was eventually abandoned, the narratives and images have become cen-

---

[143] *Principal Navigations*: 689.

tral sources of early American history. The irony should be noted here: What human action could not accomplish at Roanoke, the narratives did. When Hariot's *Briefe and True Report* was published in 1588, three years after it may first have been composed, and told of loving natives, natural bounty and beauty, and numerous "merchantable commodities", the colony of 1587 was already doomed as its sponsors failed to send supplies from England. In 1590, when John White finally managed to sail to Roanoke, he found the settlement abandoned. Hariot's *Briefe and True Report*, together with de Bry's engravings, was published in a multi-volume grand edition in four languages the same year.

The narratives of the early English Newfoundland voyages already exhibit some characteristic features that were to reappear throughout the next decades in narratives of other voyages of discovery and exploration. The narrative passages reveal the quest for gold and/or a Northwest passage as central motivations for the voyages, yet the ventures remained largely futile. A strong prospective rhetoric compensates for a lack of present success, and this was soon employed again as a central narrative strategy of dealing with futility and tragedy, of dealing with the gap between American reality and an ideal America based on inherited notions of easily obtainable riches and natural abundance as well as cultural and technological superiority.

6.3. Prelude to Colonies: The Roanoke Voyages

After the voyages under Frobisher and Gilbert, the 1580s saw a renewed English interest in voyages to North America. Sir Walter Ralegh was the main instigator of the next series of voyages, this time to Roanoke on the Outer Banks of today's North Carolina shore.

6.3.1. The 1584 Voyage under Amadas and Barlowe

On April 27, 1584, two ships under the command of Philip Amadas left the English shore for America. After cruising along the Carolina coast they found an entrance into the Carolina Banks by July 13. After ceremonies of taking possession had been held, the group encountered Indians with whom they traded and also made friendly contacts. The voyage was obviously intended to serve reconnaisance purposes, and the ships reached England again safely by the middle of September the same year.[144] The narrative by Arthur Barlowe is the chief source of

---

[144] For a detailed chronicle of all voyages of the Roanoke venture, see David B. Quinn. *The Roanoke Voyages, 1584-1590. Documents to Illustrate the English Voyages to North America Under*

information about this voyage. Barlowe's text was published by Hakluyt in 1589. As for the background of its author, next to nothing is known, except that he may have traveled in the Mediterranean region and Eastern Europe before going on the voyage to America.[145] His text is addressed to Ralegh as the sponsor of the voyage, and it was obviously designed to work as propaganda for the ensuing voyage of 1585. Much of the information on Indian life and social organization may have been gleaned from the two Indians Manteo and Wanchese whom the English took with them to England.[146]

6.3.2. Arthur Barlowe. *The First Voyage Made to the Coastes of America*

Barlowe's narrative is one of the "classic" texts narrating the discovery of an earthly paradise awaiting the English in North America. Although it is not as well known as Hariot's *Briefe and True Report*, it nevertheless reflects, like the former, the English attitudes towards the natives and the land upon first encounter, as much as the narrative and descriptive stereotypes already in place in New World reports.

The text was, like Hariot's, included in the 1589 *Principal Navigations* and was originally intended as information for Sir Walter Ralegh, the instigator of the Roanoke voyages. "I have presumed to present unto you this brief discourse by which you may judge how profitable this land is likely to succeed" of which "as much by us has been brought to light, as by those small means and number of men we had, could any way have been expected, or hoped for." The intention behind this narrative, then, is largely informative. Nevertheless, Barlowe cannot but apply a rhetoric derived from a literary *locus amoenus* tradition to the newfound land: "The second of July, we found shoal water, which smelled so sweetly, and was so strong a smell, as if we had been in the midst of some delicate garden, abounding with all kind[s] of odoriferous flowers", and two days later they make landfall. The delicate olfactory premonitions described here set the tone for much of the narrative.[147]

After taking possession of the land "according to the ceremonies used in such enterprises" the men set out to view the land. Of everything there is "such plenty

---

the Patent Granted to Walter Raleigh in 1584. London: Hakluyt Society, 1955. Barlowe's narrative: I: 77 ff.
[145] In his narrative of the 1584 voyage, Barlowe refers to Virginia woods as "not such as you find in Bohemia, Moscovia, or Hyrcania." Arthur Barlowe. *The First Voyage Made to the Coastes of America*. In: Quinn, *The Roanoke Voyages*, I: 90.
[146] ibid.: 15f.
[147] ibid.: 92-95.

[...] that I think in all the world the like abundance is not to be found", and Barlowe points out that he has seen considerable parts of the richest areas in Europe which still fall short of what he sees now. The difference, he says, is "incredible to be written."[148] The *topos* of unspeakable difference pervades much of the text. The "green soil of the hills", the "plains", the "tops of high cedars", "valleys replenished with good cedar trees" and "good woods full of deer, conies, hares, and fowl" all make up parts of a *locus amoenus* that seems to have been transferred out of a classical narrative onto American soil. The trees, for example, can only be adequately described, one feels, by saying that they are "far bettering" the cedars of Mediterranean locales famous for them.

The people, according to Barlowe, are "very handsome, and goodly people, and in their behavior as mannerly and civil as any of Europe. [...] We were entertained with all love and kindness. [...] We found the people most gentle, loving, and faithful, void of all guile, and treason, and such as lived after the manner of the golden age." Interestingly, Barlowe mentions guile and treason, showing that the English probably expected such traits in the natives, either informed by Spanish New World narratives or by common prejudice. The absence of such traits must have been notable enough to point this out explicitly, and this occurs at several places during the narrative: "A more kind and loving people there cannot be found in the world as far as we have hitherto had trial."[149]

Barlowe describes the soil and its fertility with the help of superlatives: "The soil is the most plentiful, sweet, fruitful, and wholesome of all the world. [...] They have those oaks that we have, but far greater and better." As if that was not enough praise, Barlowe also states that "the earth brings forth all things in abundance, as in the first creation, without toil and labour." As a result, Barlowe's narrative of the 1584 voyage establishes America as a peaceful, paradisaic place of abundance and ease, where labour is not necessary. In case the earth failed to bring forth what the English needed or wanted, the Indians would supply them, as they did Barlowe and his group, with " fat bucks, conies, hare, fish, the best of the world. [They] sent us diverse kinds of fruit [...] and of their country's corn." [150]

It may not come as a big surprise that the next year, the English did at first not worry too much about how to sustain themselves in America. Narratives such as Barlowe's, with their frequent descriptive passages adorned with superlatives or *topoi* of unspeakable riches, references to the fabled golden age, natural abundance, and catalogues of commodities played a central role in establishing America for the English reader and audience as a new-found Eden and a land of ease. It

---

[148] David B. Quinn, *Roanoke Voyages*: 95.
[149] ibid.: 98, 108, 110.
[150] ibid.: 105-108.

helped, of course, to draw settlers, financial backers, and whatever else was necessary for subsequent voyages of exploration and settlement projects. It also kept Europeans from developing a realistic image of early North America. The discrepancy between such an idyllic image as Barlowe's narrative projected and the real America which fell somewhat short of the ideal, would soon be "narrated away" by focusing on prospective rhetoric ("if only") in the face of present failure.

Since Barlowe's group of explorers stayed in America for only a short time, planting and other labour was not necessary to sustain them. Later groups which attempted to settle soon found out that natives were not always willing to feed the English and that labour was indeed needed to stay alive in this New World paradise. In spite of that, the narratives of later voyages would continue to praise America while paradoxically chronicling instances of famine or native hostility. Therefore, narrative strategies had to be developed to respond to this dichotomy between real and ideal America so central to most early American travel narratives.

6.3.3. The Roanoke Voyages and Propaganda Writing

Narratives like Barlowe's or Hariot's were included in Richard Hakluyt's *Principal Navigations* (first edition: 1589), a compendium which sought to collect all descriptions of the New World among other destinations of interest and thus established a well-respected canon of knowledge. This kind of second-hand information was hardly verifiable by any reader until there were enough narratives of New World voyages to counter-check assumptions and claims made in them. Due to the authority of many authors and their patrons, too, there was little cause to doubt that all the reports were to be taken at face value. Nevertheless, Barlowe's narrative is one of the first in a long effort at propagating an America not so much as it was (if that had been possible at all), but as it was needed to be in order to make it an attractive destination for colonizers and financial backers.

Propaganda, in Jacques Ellul's words, first creates "pseudo-needs through pre-propaganda" and then follows up with "pseudo-satisfactions". Concerning "pre-propaganda" for English voyages of discovery and exploration, a whole complex of reasons for entering the competition for New World possessions existed: the fear of losing the race with Spain, religious motives, and an assumed over-population in England which might lead to social unrest and decay, to name just a few. Promotional tracts sought to supply "pseudo-satisfaction" to these needs by presenting North America as a vast and empty space to be settled and exploited by Englishmen for individual as well as national good. The satisfaction in many respects, however, had to be projected the further into the future the more the present state of America failed to fulfill the role expected of it. According to Ellul, propaganda is especially effective if it profoundly influences the thought-world of individuals who do not have any outside points of reference.[151] This is especially true for early modern travel narratives of North America when the "facts" reported home were often based on conjecture, hearsay, inference, or misunderstandings and could hardly be verified. The English audience had to shape its image of North America based on the pieces of information it had access to, without being able to verify any claims. It makes little sense to search for truth behind what come as facts in propaganda; what counted was whether people believed what was said.[152] However, a distinction should be made between the facts the discoverers and explorers reported, and their interpretations of such facts. The historical background plays a role in what New World reports contained and how they presented their "facts". In the case of Sir Humphrey Gilbert, for example, his Newfoundland voyage was a desperate effort, after many failed attempts, to come up with tangible evidence that New World voyages would eventually be profitable. The same is largely true for the Roanoke voyages. As a consequence, the content of early New World travel narratives is a complex web of facts, interpretation, and intention – or rather, propaganda.

Given that Barlowe's report most likely helped to fund further voyages of exploration, the narrative must be regarded as successful propaganda:

> All effective propaganda is based on [...] fundamental currents [within a society's culture and value system] and expresses them. Only if it rests on the proper collective beliefs will it be understood and accepted. It is part of a complex of civilization, consisting of material elements, beliefs, ideas, and institutions.[153]

In the time frame treated here, various constituents make up this complex of beliefs: The necessity of emulating Spain in its successful exploitation of overseas resources while at the same time despising the ruthless methods, notorious as the "Black Legend"; chances of individual gain alongside patriotic calls for bringing England to the forefront internationally, as well as carrying the Gospel into heathen land; and, last but not least, strong traditions of an earthly Eden, noble savages living in a golden age, exerted a strong influence way beyond the Middle Ages. Barlowe's report, then, is a curious mixture of very up-to-date intentions

---

[151] Jacques Ellul. *Propaganda. The Formation of Men's Attitudes.* New York: Vintage Books, 1973: 17.
[152] Cf. Ellul, *Propaganda*: 57.
[153] ibid.: 39.

and traditional categories of describing the Other, derived from classical antiquity and perpetuated in America again and again. Barlowe's narrative posts America and its peoples at the far end of positive connotations, even though much of the fulfillment remained elusive for a long time.

6.3.4. The 1585 Voyage: Grenville's Expedition

On April 9th, Sir Richard Grenville left Plymouth with a fleet of seven ships and approximately 600 people on board. After some privateering and trading stops in the West Indies, parts of the fleet reached Wococon, an inlet of the Carolina Banks, on June 16. In the following weeks exploring trips were made across Pamlico Sound and to the Indian village of Pomeiooc, which John White sketched along with natives of another village, Secoton. The English established themselves on Roanoke Island, and only a short time after the arrival of the English, the colony's governor Ralph Lane was writing home letters from "the new fort in Virginia", where he remained with a limited number of colonists while Grenville and others of his party had returned home to organize shipping of supplies for the first colony. This, however, was soon forestalled by an embargo on Spanish shipping which delayed the departure of relief ships. In the meantime, the colony was running out of supplies. When Sir Francis Drake called at the colony with his fleet, he offered to help the colonists. They decided to go home with Drake's fleet, ending the first attempt of sustained English settlement on the North American seaboard with a hurried escape.[154]

A comprehensive story of the first colony survives in two narratives, Ralph Lane's *Account*[155] of the colony and Thomas Hariot's famous *A Briefe and True Report of the New Found Land of Virgnia*.

6.3.5. Thomas Hariot. *A Briefe and True Report of the New Found Land of Viginia*

In many respects, the mathematician and navigation expert Thomas Hariot picked up where Arthur Barlowe had left North America in his narrative. Barlowe reported that the soil of Virginia was so fruitful and the flora and fauna so abundant that they " at that time had no leisure to view," and had made this first voyage "as

---

[154] A detailed account of this voyage and the colony is given in David B. Quinn, *Roanoke Voyages*. I: 244 ff.
[155] *An Account of the Particularities of the Employments of the English Men left in Virginia by Sir Richard Grenville Under the Charge of Master Ralph Lane*, first published in Hakluyt's *Principal Navigations*. Quoted after David B. Quinn, *Roanoke Voyages*. Vol. I: 255-294.

far forth as the shortness of the time [they] there continued would afford us to take view of," especially with regards to commodities which might prove this region of America to be a promising arena of future investments.[156] Barlowe's report, however, was also still heavily indebted to the tradition of describing a New World Eden alongside the materialistic and promotional purposes of the narrative. As a narrative of first encounter, it is a short survey glowingly tinged with paradisaic connotations regarding the descriptions of the land and encounters with the natives. It remains a fairly unsystematic report, probably due, above all, to the short time the company spent in Virginia.

Thomas Hariot's stay in Virginia was much longer, lasting about a year; he left with sets of instructions which are now lost but may have resembled the instructions discussed above (cf. chapter 6.1.3.) to ensure that his observations, along with the paintings to be done by John White, were arranged systematically and thus would make North America easily assimilable to European categories of thinking. It is no surprise, then, that the *Briefe and True Report* is ordered primarily according to the use to which American nature might be put in the near future. In this respect the *Briefe and True Report* is an ordered and enlarged sequel of Barlowe's report, but no longer a narrative of enchanted first encounters. It rather focuses on inquiries into the material use of American flora and fauna. America is no longer described by a ravished discoverer. In the *Briefe and True Report*, American nature is, through the central cultural tool of language, ordered, categorized, and introduced into a centrally European rhetoric of economic use. The methods of description and rhetorical strategies of making intelligible what the explorers encountered in America, however, largely remain the same: The search for likeness – deer are "of the ordinary bigness as ours in England, and some less [so]"[157] or the abundance of plants which exceeds the explorer's powers of description, prevails in this text, too.

The reason for writing and publishing this narrative differs from Barlowe's in that the latter was the first report on a region and thus an authoritative narrative, the truth claims of which could hardly be verified or falsified at the time, until the next expedition set out to Virginia a year later. With the growing number of voyagers came enlarged numbers of viewpoints and opinions, and thus Hariot could no longer write the only first-hand and authoritative account of the venture. When the *Briefe and True Report* was first published in 1588 (even though it was presumably written fairly soon after Hariot's return in 1586) Hariot claimed that "there have been diverse and variable reports with some slanderous and shameful

---

[156] In: David B. Quinn, *Roanoke Voyages* I: 91-115: 115.
[157] Thomas Hariot. *Briefe and True Report*. Reprint of the second edition. London, 1893: 29.

speeches bruited abroad by many that returned from thence."[158] The narrator expressly refers to colonists of the 1585-1586 Grenville voyage under the governor Ralph Lane, whose report will be investigated next as to what kind of picture he produced of America for his backers at home. Hariot's narrative, then, is a central propagandistic effort of the Virginia Company to maintain the dominant voice in the worldmaking process of early North America. In the face of multiple and decidedly less favorable descriptions of that voyage, the narrator

> thought it good being one that ha[s] been in the discovery and in dealing with the natural inhabitants specially employed; and having therefore seen and known more that the ordinary [colonists]: to impart so much unto you [i.e. Sir Walter Ralegh, the sponsor of the voyage] of the fruits of our labours, as that you may know how injuriously the enterprise is slandered.[159]

In order to uphold the positive image of Virginia developed in Barlowe's report, Hariot's narrative is based on the authoritative eyewitness ("I thought it good to impart unto you...") as well as on the weight of his patron, Ralegh. Furthermore, Hariot's narrative is a first ordered catalogue of American flora and fauna, together with a description of the natives, their customs, beliefs, and attitudes towards the English. It should be noted, however, that this text remains the central and often the only narrative which is cited as a historical account of the Roanoke voyages and early contact with the coastal tribes. Given the fact that Hariot referred to "diverse and variable reports" about the same venture which have been either lost or largely ignored, it is clear that Hariot's and the Virginia Company's aim to hold onto the power of writing and publishing "worldmaking" descriptions of early North America, this effort was uniquely successful. Hariot's narrative has remained the best known account of the Roanoke voyages until today.

The image of North America, the land, the natives, and Virginia's potential, which it developed before the eyes and in the minds of Europeans, has remained highly influential, even though much of what Hariot had to say about future economic prospects remained in the realm of conjecture. This kind of projective affirmative rhetoric in the face of absent empirical proof pervades the chapters on "commodities". "If [silk grass] be planted [here] and ordered as in Persia, *it cannot in reason be otherwise, but that there will rise in short time great profit* to the dealers therein."[160] (italics mine) The same kind of rhetoric pervades other passages as well: "There will rise as great profit in time to the Virginians" (i.e. English colonists): "We have that experience of the soil, as that there cannot be shown

---

[158] Thomas Hariot. *Briefe and True Report*: 9.
[159] ibid.: 10.
[160] ibid.: 13.

any reason to the contrary, but that it will grow there excellent well."[161] Where own observation or inferences fail, the natives are used as firsthand sources: Of rich supply of furs, "[we] make no doubt by the relation of the people", and farther into the country there are "as they say [...] mountains and rivers that yield also white grains of metal, which is to be deemed silver."[162] Virginia is thus presented as a region of boundless opportunity and fertility, yielding two rich harvests a season and requiring little labour:

> The increase [of wheat] is so much that small labour and pains is needful in respect that must be used for ours [in England]. For this I can assure you that according to the rate we have made proof of, one man may prepare and husband so much ground [...] with less than four and twenty hours labour, as shall yield him victual in a large proportion for a twelve month.[163]

The *Briefe and True Report* is usually noted for its ethnographic value. In fact, Hariot was probably one of the most knowledgeable people of his time concerning the Algonkian tribes, and he also had acquired some proficiency in their language. The narrative reported that the natives "are not to be feared; but that they shall have cause both to fear and love us that shall inhabit with them."[164] Also, they possessed only weak weapons, never settled in big cities, went naked except for a loin cloth of deer skin, and were, "in respect to us [...] a poor people, and for want of skill and judgment in the knowledge and use of our things [they] do esteem our trifles before things of greater value." With respect to their lifeworld, the narrator admits, "they show excellency of wit". Even in religious matters they were inferior to the English, but not without parallels of belief like for example in the immortality of the soul and the existence of heaven and hell, and they seemed to be "brought into great doubts of their own [religion], and no small admiration of ours." The natives marveled exceedingly at the gadgets of "magic technology" of the English, such as "guns, books, writing and reading, spring clocks" and the like.[165]

For all the positive aspects of the encounter on the English side, there are some dark forecasts as to the future of peaceful and mutually fruitful cohabitation. The first sicknesses which the English brought to the American shore seemed to kill natives even at a distance as if shot by "invisible bullets", and the extent of the sickness must have been epidemic even then: "In some towns [there died] about twenty, in some forty, in some sixty, and in one six score, which in truth was very

---

[161] Thomas Hariot. *Briefe and True Report*: 14.
[162] ibid.: 18.
[163] ibid.: 24.
[164] ibid.: 36.
[165] ibid.: 37ff.

many in respect of their numbers."[166] Some natives judged these English to be superior beings, probably gods, entering the country to take it away from the indigenous inhabitants: "Some would likewise seem to prophesy that there were more of our generation yet to come, to kill theirs and take their places, as some thought the purpose was by that which was already done." And truly, the narrator has to admit that the initial purpose of winning the natives with gentleness was crossed by some Englishmen who "towards the end of the year showed themselves too fierce in slaying some of the people in some towns upon causes that on our part might easily enough have been borne withal."[167]

The bottom line of Hariot's description of Virginia and the natives was once again a land of ease, yet apt not only for man's easy sustenance, but also for extensive material gain, all combined with tractable natives who seemed to be in great awe of the English. All of this suggested a future of benign dominance, peaceful cohabitation and individual as well as collective gain at little cost. There is already even a westward glance promising an even more pleasant and richer America awaiting the European explorers once the coastal regions were explored:

> As we made our journeys farther into the main and country, we found the soil to be fatter, the trees greater and to grow thinner. [...] Why may we not look for [gold] in good hope from the inner parts of more and greater plenty, as well as of other things, as of those [parts] which we have already discovered?[168]

Much of what Hariot said about easy living, abundant means of sustenance, and peaceful relations with natives who would "honor, obey, fear, and love" the English has entered a stock canon of early American images, and much of the prospective rhetoric and promises concerning the West of the continent have remained constituent parts of the historical image of the United States until today. Thus, Hariot's *Briefe and True Report* may rightfully be called a worldmaking text, and it is of little importance whether this propagandistic narrative contained facts as they were or facts as they were needed to be. Hariot managed to write early American history in a way that others of the same Roanoke venture did not.

Two little known narratives remain which told a very different story of America but have never been "worldmaking" in the way that Hariot's narrative has. The

---

[166] The eventual success of the English in conquering the natives was greatly helped by diseases which fell on virgin soil among the indigenous inhabitants. In New England, for example, estimates suggest that up to 90 per cent of the native population died of European diseases. One of the first epidemics occurred between 1616 and 1618 and helped "clear" the way for English settlement. Cf. Alfred W. Crosby. "Virgin Soil Epidemics as a Factor in the Aboriginal Depopulation of North America." *William and Mary Quarterly*, 3rd ser., 33 (1976): 289-299.
[167] Thomas Hariot, *Briefe and True Report*: 41f.
[168] ibid.: 44.

first of these two, Ralph Lane's account of the 1585/1586 colony, can be read as a counter narrative of futility in its narrative passages whereas the descriptive passages retain the Garden Eden rhetoric established long ago and repeated in the previous narratives of Barlowe and Hariot. John White's narratives of the 1587-1590 colony established the myth of the "Lost Colony", and the history of the Roanoke voyages ends with a letter by John White to Ralegh expressing deep resignation over the tragic course of events. The literary history of the Roanoke voyages, however, remains dominated by Hariot's *Report* of a bright future of material gain and racial harmony, inaugurating a rhetoric of America which was to dominate for a long time the image Englishmen, and also continental Europeans, nourished based on narratives like Hariot's.

6.3.6. Ralph Lane. *An Account of the Particularities of the Imployments of the English Men [...] in Virginia*

Lane's account of the 1585-1586 colony figures mainly as an apology of Lane's activities; nevertheless, it offers valuable insight into the day-to-day situation of the colony and may be closer to the truth than Hariot's "official" account of the colony. It is possible that a longer, detailed description of the country and the colony's affairs was lost in the hasty departure from Roanoke with Sir Francis Drake's fleet.

The first part is a description of the colony and its seat. The second part explains the reasons for the colony's sudden return with Drake and a "conspiracy of Pemisapan" (the chief of a neighboring tribe). The first passages on the country echo Hariot's and Barlowe's paradisaic accounts: "The territory and soil [of the Chesapeake region] is for pleasantness of seat, for temperature of climate, for fertility of soil, and for the commodity of the sea [...] not to be excelled by any other whatsoever."[169] Lane gives some account of the political structure of the surrounding Indian tribes, mentions corn fields (which would become such an important bone of contention) and the "king of the province" Menatonon: According to Lane, he was, "for a savage, a very grave and wise man" who tells Lane of a tribe, presumably in the Chesapeake region, which possesses pearls in great abundance.[170]

The following part of the narrative, however, does not chronicle a successful quest for this tribe and its pearls, but instead shifts into a rhetoric of lost opportu-

---

[169] Ralph Lane. "Account of the Particularities of the Imployments of the English Men Left in Virginia". In: David B. Quinn. *The Roanoke Voyages*, 255-294: 257. Lane's narrative was, like Barlowe's and Hariot's, included in Hakluyt's *Principal Navigations*.
[170] ibid.: 262.

nity, centering on Grenville's failure to send a relief ship in time: Had this ship with men and victuals come, Lane "would have raised a sconce with a small trench" along the way to this said tribe; at some place he "would have raised a main fort", and so on. A real trip up a river, however, was undertaken for badly needed food, and keeping his colonists alive was the only project Lane could follow: "The hope of recovering more victual from the savages made me and my company as narrowly [...] escape starving in that discovery before our return as ever men did that missed the same."[171]

In connection with the Englishmen's quest for Indian victuals, a "confederacy against us of [several tribes] was altogether and wholly procured by Pemisapan himself", and it remains unclear from the sources available whether Lane regarded the annual retreat of large portions of Indian tribes into the interior to live on hunting game as such a conspiracy to withhold food from the English, or whether Pemisapan and others planned to retreat in order to avoid extortions by the English colony threatened with starvation: "Having passed three days' voyage up the river, we could not meet a man, nor find a grain of corn in any of their towns; [...] considering with myself that we had but two days' victuals left." Lane still had some copper left which he intended to trade for corn, but the Indians had receded too far into the interior. It seems that Pemisapan and his tribe, like others along that river, were no longer willing to put up with Lane's "daily sending to him for supply of victual for my company" and stopped sowing fields in the vicinity of the English settlement.[172] Pemisapan is eventually killed by an Indian who brings his head back to the English.

The "further view of that most goodly river" contrasts starkly with the dreadful situation of the explorers. Still, the men decided to continue the voyage upstream and, "if the worst fell out", to eat the two mastiffs which the English carried along. The main reason, however, was not the beauty of the river, and not even the search for necessary food supplies; it was the rumor that a tribe upstream possessed "a marvelous and most strange mineral. This mine is so notorious amongst them" that all tribes know the name of the place, Chaunis Temoatan. Some hints point to gold; "of this metal the Mangoaks have so great store, by report of all the savages adjoining, that they beautify their houses with great plates of the same; and this to be true I received by report of all the country."[173]

Ralph Lane was obviously taken so much with rumors of precious metals that he, and likewise his men, neglected the more mundane but vital necessities of colonizing, i.e. planting food. The quest for the fabled town of Chaunis Temoatan

---

[171] Ralph Lane, "Account": 263ff.
[172] ibid.: 284.
[173] ibid.: 267ff.

echoes earlier descriptions of some location abounding with gold in the interior of North America; David Ingram reported to have seen such an abundance of silver during his alleged travels from the Rio Grande to Cape Breton: Silver is so common that it is used to make dustbins and nightpots, "all [of] which this Ingram saw [to be] common and usual in some of these countries."[174] Even though Lane may not have known this account – both Lane's and Ingram's were first published in the 1589 *Principal Voyages* -, similar ones may have circulated among those involved in colonizing enterprises.

Lane's voyage towards the Mangoaks and Chaunis Temoatan, however, failed completely, for after two more days of travel, victuals are gone yet the English have not met a single soul until a group of Indians ambush the men. Downcast, Lane asserts that

> there wanted no great good will from the most to the least among us, to have perfected this discovery of the mine: For that the discovery of a good mine [...] or a passage to the South Sea, or some way to it, and nothing else can bring this country in request to be inhabited by our nation. And with the discovery of any of the two above shown, it will be the most sweet and healthful climate, and therwithall the most fertile soil being manured in the world: and then will sassafras, and many other roots and gums there found make good merchandize and lading for shipping, which otherwise of themselves will not be worth the fetching.[175]

It seems as if Lane, unlike many other promoters of colonies, was strongly indebted to the Spanish model of a successful colony, based primarily on bullion rather than agriculture. As a result, the quest for such riches effectively kept the colonists from providing for themselves and sparked discontent among the Indian tribes on which they relied for food. The English followed up some "promises", usually upriver voyages in quest for minerals: "This river [...] promises great things..."; the failure was clothed in terms of "if only": "Thus Sir I have [...] set down what my labour [...] could yield unto you, which might have been performed in some more perfection if..." circumstances had not been as adverse, and relief ships with men and victuals would have reached the colony in time.[176]

It did not help either that some Indians regarded the English as supernatural beings; magic technology like superior weapons helped to instill awe in the natives for some time, as one Indian told his tribe: "He had often told them that we

---

[174] "The Relation of David Ingram." Richard Hakluyt. *The Principal Navigations, Voiages and Discoveries of the English Nation*. First edition, 1589. Facsimile Reprint ed. David B. Quinn and Raleigh A. Skelton. Cambridge: Hakluyt Society, 1965: 559.
[175] Ralph Lane, "Account": 273.
[176] ibid.: 273ff.

were the servants of God and that we were not subject to be destroyed by them [...] and that we, being dead men, were able to do them more hurt than now we could do being alive." Indian conceptions of disease play a part here, too, for some natives believed that the English could strike any foe at a distance, and that the English are "dead men returned into the world again."[177] This passage echoes almost verbally Thomas Hariot's assessment of Indian religion and English superiority; but Lane's account, unlike Hariot's, does not culminate in the glorious future of English settlements in America anymore.

A striking discrepancy between Lane's actions on the American scene and the subsequent European interpretation is shown in a marginal comment possibly added by Hakluyt in the *Principal Navigations*: "The sufficiency of our men to deal against the savages 10 to 100" is added to a passage recounting how the Indians surrounding the English settlement "did immediately put it into practice that they should not for any copper sell us any victuals whatsoever", right after Lane has asserted that "indeed ten of us with our arms prepared were a terror to a hundred of the best sort of them." For all the military power of the English, they are not able to feed themselves until they resort to Indian customs of disbanding into several places to live on ground nuts, fish, and what the earth would provide; a marginal note comments that "the savages live by fishing and hunting till harvest", activities of roaming nomads but not civilized men; nevertheless, Lane has to disband his men "for the famine grew so extreme among us."[178]

America, in Lane's report, is still a beautiful, edenic place, but as soon as man steps onto the American stage, conflict follows, either from strained relationships between the two groups or from hunger and other hardships which add an ironic note to Lane's initial description of a pleasant and fertile country. Hardship and the imminent threat of starvation in a country which had been praised exuberantly for its fertility and ease of man's sustenance by Barlowe, Hariot, and even Lane, mark the core dichotomy between the imagined and the real America in the 1580s. A rhetoric of futility ("if only...") pervades much of the report and thus renders one of the earliest texts of English exploration in North America a testimony of failure rather than success.

---

[177] Ralph Lane, "Account": 278.
[178] ibid.: 282f.

6.3.7. John White. *The Fourth Voyage Made to Virginia, with Three Shippes, in the Yeere 1587*

White's text chronicles the 1587 voyage and the second colony. The fleet arrived on the American mainland on July 16, 1587, and first White and his men looked for "those fifteen Englishmen which Sir Richard Grenville had left there the year before", i.e. those that did not make it on board for the hasty return voyage with Sir Francis Drake's fleet. These men were expected to serve as informants "concerning the state of the country, and savages", yet they were nowhere to be found. At Roanoke, the new colonists found only the bones of one of these men "which the savages had slain long before."[179] This is the first hint at the fact that Englishmen might not be welcome at all and once their numbers were low enough, the natives might wipe them out.

It is striking that White's narrative of the 1587 voyage is completely devoid of descriptive passages and only narrates the incidents from the beginning of the sea voyage to White's return to England in order to procure new supplies. Since White had been in the area before (of his next, the 1590 voyage, he wrote that it was his fifth) and drawn lots of its sights in watercolor, it is possible that White simply had not much new to say, apart from narrating the events.[180] The latter, however, cast an ominous shadow over Indian-English relationships as early as 1587 and are a strong antidote to the first narratives, especially those by Barlowe and Hariot. "A more kind and loving people there cannot be found in the world as far as we have hitherto had trial,"[181] as Arthur Barlowe reported, seemed to be no longer true. The process of differentiation between friendly and hostile natives had begun, and discord, fear of attacks and treachery had been introduced to the narratives. Barlowe's and Hariot's American paradise, in White's account of the 1587 voyage, had undergone a reality check and lost much of its idyllic hue. This is witnessed in the complete absence of descriptive passages which were the readily available narrative *locus* for praise of the New World and a positive outlook, whereas the narrative passages, in the texts of the Frobisher voyages as well as in Lane's and White's, often contradict the glowing descriptions with instances of futility and hardship.

---

[179] John White, "The Fourth Voyage Made to Virginia." In David B. Quinn, *Roanoke Voyages* II, 515-539: 523ff.
[180] There are small but significant hints at identifying White the painter with White the governor of the 1587 colony; compare Quinn, *Roanoke Voyages*, II, 521.
[181] Arthur Barlowe, "Discourse of the First Voyage". In: David B. Quinn, *Roanoke Voyages* I, 91-115: 110.

6.3.8. John White. *The Fifth Voyage of Master John White into the West Indies and Parts of America Called Virginia, in the Yeere 1590*

The 1590 voyage of John White marks the end of several ill-fated attempts at procuring and sending out relief ships for the Roanoke colony, interrupted either by bad weather, tight funds, or political considerations concerning the Spanish Armada. The voyage itself was almost as ill-fated as the previous attempts, for some men drowned in an attempt to row ashore during bad weather, and there was no sign of the colonists apart from the famous letters CROATOAN. White found three of his chests, broken up and the content spoiled with rain and rust: "This could be no other but the deed of the savages our enemies"[182], White wrote, but believed his colonists to be safe at Croatoan. Stormy weather and battered ships prevented the men from searching for the colonists, and in the end the ships were forced to sail for England without having accomplished anything in America. White's second narrative is even shorter and more matter-of-factly than the first and the only descriptive passages it contains center not around America, but White's belongings rotting in the abandoned fort and the leaky English ships.

The narratives of the Roanoke voyages thus fall into two groups: Barlowe's and Hariot's mark the hopeful beginning of English settlements in America, adorned with descriptive passages of the beauty and fertility of the country as well as of the friendliness and childlike admiration the natives seem to harbor for the English. Both, it must be remembered, were "official" narratives because they were commissioned to spark and sustain financial interest in the ventures. Both narratives also portray Virginia as a lush land of ease where nature freely yields whatever man needs for sustenance, or for very little labour. It is no surprise, then, that Lane's report of the same year which Hariot spent in Virginia contrasts so markedly with the *Briefe and True Report*. Lane chronicles the test-driving of a colony of people who may have been wholly unsuitable for the enterprise or spoiled already with glowing "come-hither" reports promising that hard labour would be the last thing required in America. Hariot anticipated some of these conflicts when he wrote, at the beginning of his *Report*, that many colonists

> had little or no care of any other thing but to pamper their bellies [...] after gold and silver was not so soon found"; also, "because there were not to be found any English cities, nor such fair houses [...] nor any soft beds of down or feathers: the country was to them miserable, and their reports thereof according.[183]

---

[182] John White, "Narrative of the 1590 Voyage". In Quinn, *Roanoke Voyages* II, 598-622: 616.
[183] Thomas Hariot, *Briefe and True Report*: 11.

With the first European descriptions of America, a literary model had been established, and both its conventions and the expectations engendered by it were obviously hard to break with.

Apart from these small hints at discontent, however, Hariot's narrative has managed to maintain, with Barlowe's as its precursor, an edenic image of America which would later echo in narratives of Jamestown or even New England – with the same painful reality check and a slow learning process at great costs. This learning process, however, had little influence on the narratives which were produced as official propaganda and which, it must be assumed, achieved the widest degree of circulation and prominence not only in England, but also in continental Europe. Hariot's *Briefe and True Report*, together with John White's watercolors, was included in Theodor de Bry's *America*, which was published in four major European languages. Lane's and White's reports, in contrast, refrained from exuberant praise of a country which, in reality, hardly sustained the Englishmen sent there to plant. They were peculiarly dependent on the natives who, as Hariot suggested, were inferior to the English in almost every respect and who would in due course "honor, love, and obey" the English. It can only be assumed that such a clash of expectations and futile attempts at putting them into practice bred frustration and discontent. The "diverse and variable reports with some slanderous and shameful speeches" which Hariot mentioned may have come out of such frustration over an ideal America that remained elusive and a very real America meaning hardship, hunger, and continual danger of violent clashes with the natives. It is striking that many later narrators would cite the same "scandalous and diverse reports" about an American colony as the reason for writing a travel narrative of North America.

John White's "Lost Colony" has entered the mythology of early Anglo-America; yet apart from it, Lane's and White's rhetoric of futility, of what could have been achieved in America "only if ...", has not prevailed in the face of Barlowe's and Hariot's New World Eden. The latter two narratives served indeed as a worldmaking cultural technique, whereas the two former remain little more than a historical caveat and have been almost silent in the history of the image of America.

6.4. Early Voyages to New England, 1602-1614

> We [...] discovered a river, which the all-creating God, with His most liberal hand, has made above report notable with his [...] blessings, bordered with a land whose pleasant fertility [shows] itself to be the garden of nature, wherein she only intended to delight herself, having hitherto obscured it to any except to a purblind race.
>
> James Rosier, *A True Relation*

Before the Pilgrims arrived at New England's shores, several reconnaissance voyages were made to the same shores. The initially glowing image of America developed in continental European voyages and by the narratives of Barlowe or Hariot reverberate in these descriptions with ravishingly beautiful scenery and abundantly fertile soil, pleasant climate, and friendly natives.

6.4.1. John Brereton. *A Briefe and True Relation of the Discoverie of the North Part of Virginia*

Printed 1602, it is the earliest English book of discovery relating to New England. The voyage was meant to discover commodities, and the report was later circulated to inform an audience interested in New England, but also to spark financial interest in subsequent voyages to the New England coast. The ship *Concord* left Falmouth in March 1602 and returned in July the same year, with a considerable cargo of sassafras. Appended to the narrative is a "brief note of such commodities as we saw in the country notwithstanding our small time of stay".

The narrative, dedicated to Sir Walter Ralegh, was written to answer an "earnest request by a dear friend, to put down in writing, some true relation of our late performed voyage to the North parts of Virginia."[184] On May 14th, the company reached the coast of New England at Cape Neddick, Maine: "On Friday the fourteenth of May, early in the morning, we made land, being full of fair trees, the land somewhat low, certain [...] hills lying into the land, the shore full of white sand, but very stony or rocky." Only a few hours later they encountered Indians who, in their turn, had obviously had previous contact with Europeans before:

---

[184] "A Briefe and True Relation of the Discoverie of the North Part of Virginia; being a most pleasant, fruitfull and commodious soile; Made this present yeere 1602 by Captaine Bartholomew Gosnold, and Captain Bartholomew Gilbert [...] by the permission of [...] Sir Walter Ralegh. Written by John Brereton." In: George Parker Winship, ed. *Sailors' Narratives of Voyages along the New England Coast, 1524-1624*. New York: Burt Franklin, 1968: 33-50: 33.

"Six Indians, in a Bask shallop with mast and sail, an iron grapple, and a kettle of copper, came boldly aboard us, one of them apparelled with a waistcoat and breeches [...] made after our fashion, hose and shoes on his feet; all the rest (saving one that had a pair of breeches of blue cloth) were all naked." Astonishing as this may have been, they manage to make the English understand, the narrator says, "that some Basks [...] have fished and traded in this place."[185] Friendly trading relations with the natives add to a serenely peaceful picture of a small English exploring party in a land that ravishes them with its beauty and fertility.

Although the country kindles some hopes for precious metals, "the sea sides all covered with stones, many of them glistering and shining like mineral stones,"[186] the narrator leaves it at that, but notices that the Indians seem to have copper in abundance: "I was desirous to understand where they had such store of this metal, and made signs to one of them (with whom I was very familiar) who taking a piece of copper, made a hole with his finger in the ground, and withall, pointed to the mainland from whence they came." It is only logical that the narrator finds only praising words for the natives: "These people, as they are exceeding[ly] courteous, gentle of disposition, and well conditioned, excelling all others that we have seen; so for shape of body and lovely favor, I think they excell all the people of America [...], fearless of others' harms, as intending none themselves."

The area of New England which the company visited greatly impressed the European beholders: After some abundance of fowls, trees, nuts "some of them as big as hen's eggs"[187] and other natural commodities have been enumerated, the narrator's voice trails off in order "not to cloy you [i.e. Ralegh] with particular rehearsal of such things God and nature have bestowed on these places, in comparison whereof, the most fertile part of England is [...] but barren." Nevertheless, the narrator then continues his praise of the country. When coming ashore, the English "stood a while like men ravished at the beauty and delicacy of this sweet soil", mirroring the discoverer's passive gaze which takes in America's beauty and abundance and gives in to feeling "ravished". This impression is further enhanced by the fact that, in the eyes of the English, nature seems to have prepared an English garden or park for them, for "even the most woody places (I speak only of such as I saw) do grow so distinct apart, one tree from another, upon green grassy ground, [...] as if nature would show herself above her power artificial." A Garden Eden, it seems, with a built-in gardener, relieves the English of the later inclination to consider the land wild and waiting to be worked and improved by European husbandry. Instead, everything seems ready-made, including fearful

---

[185] John Brereton, "Relation": 34f.
[186] ibid.: 38.
[187] ibid.: 40.

natives who, "being emboldened by our courteous usage, and some trifles we gave them", make friendly contact with the Europeans.[188]

The narrative passages are fairly short and interspersed with lengthy digressions describing the landscape, flora and fauna. The descriptive passages are almost always couched in a rhetoric of edenic bliss, occasionally enhanced with hints at marketable commodities, yet not so strongly focused on extracting whatever is there from the earth, as was to be the case in later tracts: "There is upon this coast better fishing, and in as great plenty, as in Newfoundland; for the schools of mackerel, herrings, cod, and other fish [...] were wonderful." There are strawberries, "red and white, as sweet and much bigger than ours in England." An "incredible store of vines", combined with "excellent springs of sweet water" complete a picture of a land which truly seems to offer everything without toil, and also without danger of clashes with the natives. Instead, the natives offer the English food, spontaneously help to carry sassafras into the ship, and also keep the English company at night. All in all, it is a very optimistic picture; however, it is only optimistic in the Indians' malleability towards European civilization. Since there were no schemes of establishing colonies involved in this voyage, America is largely presented as a bountiful source of trade goods, and the native inhabitants feature alternatively as possible trade partners, guides, or extra hands in loading cargo. It is written in the same vein as Barlowe's glowing report of first sight and employs much the same narrative strategies: It enumerates commodities but has to leave off here and there because the sheer vastness of America's abundant nature exceeds European words; superlatives and claims of incredible abundance are scattered throughout the descriptive passages.

Only a few years later, both New England and Virginia would no longer evoke such ravishment in their English visitors, but become subjected to a language of pragmatism and profitability. Likewise, the edenic garden and the climate which has made the English "much fatter and in better health than when we went out of England [although] our diet and lodging was none of the best,"[189] renders this part of New England a New World paradise. Nature affords freely what the English need, and they only plant a few plants to try the quality of the soil, which is found very good. Other than that, they spend their time exploring one pleasant place after another, meet friendly yet occasionally timid Indians who make good partners in trade. Apart from sassafras and other goods listed in an appended catalogue, the narrator expects New England to yield "many other rich commodities, which we, wanting both time and means, could not possibly dis-

---

[188] John Brereton, "Relation": 41.
[189] ibid.: 47.

cover."[190] It is no surprise that this report inspired another voyage to the New England coast.

6.4.2. Martin Pring. *A Voyage set out from the Citie of Bristoll [...] for the discoverie of the North part of Virginia*

Martin Pring, in charge of this sequel to Gosnold's and Bartholomew Gilbert's 1602 voyage to New England, wrote an account of the voyage for Richard Hakluyt. It was later included in Purchas' *Pilgrimes* (1625). The ships left England on April 10, 1603, and reached the coast of Maine in June. After exploring the coast for some time, the group set up camp in the area of Plymouth harbor, gathered sassafras, and returned home with that cargo on October 2, the same year.

Pring's narrative contains many of the descriptive constituents of early North American reports; the terms "pleasant" and "goodly" appear frequently; the "same but better" technique is applied to New England fishing; Pring also uses the rhetorical device of double negation frequent in Hariot's *Briefe and True Report* ("it cannot in reason be otherwise that...") to paint future prospects of the region in a bright hue:

> We fell with a multitude of small islands on the North coast of Virginia [...] which islands we found very pleasant to behold, adorned with goodly grass and sundry sorts of trees [...] Here we found excellent fishing for cods, which are better than those of Newfoundland, and withall we saw good and rocky ground to dry them upon; also we see no reason to the contrary but that salt may be made in these parts.

In comparison to Brereton's edenic American land which "ravished" its beholders with its beauty, abundance, and friendly natives, the tone has already changed. Pring's is a trading voyage, or rather, a voyage to bring home as many marketable commodities as possible. The language of economic use and profit pervades descriptions of the land, its flora and fauna, and even the natives already figure differently in this narrative: "Going upon the main[land], we found people, with whom we had no long conversation, because here we could find no sassafras." At another place as well, "finding people, [...] not yet satisfied in our expectations, we left them and sailed over [the bay]." Places and people are left instantly, it seems, as soon as it is clear that they do not yield the commodity the English are after, sassafras. There is no description of the "people", no exchange of any kind reported. The land, however, is "pleasant"; yet the English, "upon view of the

---

[190] John Brereton, "Relation": 45.

people and sight of the place" thought it "convenient to make a small barricado to keep diligent watch and ward in."[191] This, it seems, is no longer the welcoming place that Brereton had described a year earlier, even though the financial backers of the voyage and maybe also part of the crew must have been familiar with Brereton's narrative.

The natives frequently come to the English camp, which at last gives rise to some descriptive passages: The men are "strong, swift, well proportioned, and given to treachery, as in the end we perceived."[192] Treachery is a new element in exploration accounts of the North American coast, still absent in Brereton's report, as in Barlowe's and Hariot's, but firmly in place in the later Roanoke narratives by Lane and White. Another interesting observation is that the English describe Indian cottages "abandoned by the savages", and "not far off we beheld their gardens" in which they had sown "tobacco, pompions, cucumbers, and such like" as well as wheat and maize. The natives, it can be inferred, are not as uncivilized as not to possess cottages and keep gardens. William Strachey, in his *Historie of Travell*, used this feature as a basis for describing the Virginia natives as improvident and wasters of America's natural bounty, an argument also taken up by John Smith in his *Map of Virginia*.

The narrative of Pring's voyage does not only list the natural commodities, it also reported assays concerning the quality of the soil, as required in instructions for explorers: "Although [English wheat, barley and garden seeds] were sown late, [they] came up very well, giving certain testimony of the goodness of the climate and of the soil." Plants and animals are categorized according to usefulness: Sassafras was "good against the plague and many other maladies; [...] witch-hazels, the best wood of all other to make soap-ashes withall"; animals are there "in abundance", many of "whose furs being hereafter purchased by exchange may yield no small gain to us", as was obviously the case for the French who, "as we are certainly informed brought from Canada immense value in furs." And as the land is "full of God's good blessings, so is the sea replenished with great abundance of excellent fish."[193] New England has shown to be a very commodious place, and the language of commerce and profit has largely displaced the discoverers' rhetoric of wonder and delight.

---

[191] Martin Pring. "A Voyage set out from the Citie of Bristoll at the charges of the chiefest Merchants and Inhabitants of the said Citie [...] for the discoverie of the North part of Virginia." In: George Parker Winship, *Sailors' Narratives*: 54f.
[192] ibid.: 56-58.
[193] ibid.: 59f.

6.4.3. James Rosier. *A True Relation of the Most Prosperous Voyage*

Employed by the Earl of Southampton and Thomas Arundell, Captain George Waymouth sailed to New England to explore the coast, navigable rivers, and probably also to view the area for an intended settlement. The account by James Rosier was printed in London the same year. The ship sailed with a small company of men from England on March 5, 1605 and returned on July 18 the same year. After the voyages of discovery and exploration under Gosnold and Gilbert in 1602 and under Martin Pring in 1603, this account narrates the next voyage to the New England coast under Captain George Waymouth. His concern was not so much with obtaining precious cargo like sassafras, but resembled more the first voyage in that the narrative centers largely upon viewing the coast and exploring navigable rivers, probably with some intention of finding suitable places for English settlements.

Even though the English made the natives believe that trade was their reason for coming, settlement is much more on the Englishmen's mind, for the first observations after landfall are of clay well suited for producing bricks. The next step is an assay of the soil's quality by planting some wheat and garden vegetables which do prosper beautifully "although this was but the crust of the ground, and much inferior to the mould we after found in the main[land]." Planting two crosses in the course of their voyage was part of a first step to take root in this country which is so beautiful that, right at the beginning, "many of our company wished themselves settled here, not expecting any further hopes, or better discovery to be made."[194] There are, however, better and more fruitful places to be discovered. The language of profit enters the report in the second part which almost completely leaves out the natives and treats the land as if it was empty. Fishing, "which I omit not to report" shows "how great a profit the fishing would be, they being so plentiful, so great, and so good, with such convenient drying as can be wished near at hand upon the rocks."

The river exploration which follows is the crowning event, mirrored in the rhetoric of superlatives and of unspeakable pleasure, as well as a shift from the neutral gender to feminizing the land: The river banks, "verged with a green bordure of grass, do make tender unto the beholder of *her* pleasant fertility, if by cleansing away the woods she were converted into meadow." (italics mine) The river is regarded as better and more beautiful than the Orinoco, as "some that were with Sir Walter Ralegh in his voyage to Guiana" testified. This technique of fem-

---

[194] James Rosier. "A True Relation of the most prosperous voyage made this present yeere 1605, by Captaine George Waymouth, in the Discoverie of the land of Virginia. Where he discovered 60 miles up a most excellent River, together with a most fertile land. Written by James Rosier, a Gentleman employed in the voyage." In: George P. Winship, *Sailors' Narratives*: 101-151: 110ff.

inizing the land and associating the lust for material rewards with sexual fulfilment is not new; Sir Walter Ralegh summed up his description of the "large and beautiful country of Guiana": "To conclude, Guiana is a country that has yet her maidenhead, never sacked, turned, nor wrought, the face of the earth has not been torn."[195]

The lands bordering on the St. George's River are not only better than those bordering Ralegh's Orinoco, it must be believed, but also require very little effort to convert the wilderness into usable land: It "may with small labor be made feeding ground" and may "in small time with few men be cleansed and made good arable land." This region, the narrator boasts, has everything "for our country's good, as we found [it] there (beyond our hopes) in certain, for those to whom it shall please God to grant this land for habitation." The pastoral idyll is epitomized in the narrator's impression that "surely it did all resemble a stately park,"[196] waiting to be settled, improved, and used.

The imagined New World paradise, offering abundance for a minimum of labour, surfaces here very vividly. "The excellency of this part of the river [...] did so ravish us all with variety of pleasantness, as we could not tell what to commend, but only admired;" yet it is not only the beauty of the land which is unspeakable, but it also "afforded an unspeakable profit" by its convenience for transportation. The rhetoric of exuberant pleasure in the beauty and richness of the land rises up to a mystic equation of the land with God's power to sustain His believers by faith alone. The Englishmen rowing up the river without any victuals "were so refreshed with the pleasant beholding thereof, and so loath to forsake it" that they would have continued days living on their visual pleasure alone.[197] This kind of rhetoric, though, was not exactly new; the visual pleasure of regarding a sacred object was a central aspect of medieval Christian mysticism. Now, however, it is no longer a religious object but the "virgin" land in its resplendent beauty which nourishes its beholders.

Rosier's narrative ends with this climax of unspeakable beauty and alludes to future possession and settlement by Europeans, for the natives, according to the narrator (and very much in line with the legal and moral reasoning of the time) are a "purblind generation, whose understanding it has pleased God so to darken, as

---

[195] Sir Walter Ralegh. "The Discovery of [...] Guiana." In: Giles B. Gunn, ed. *Early American Writing.* New York: Penguin, 1994: 70. Cf. also Annette Kolodny. *The Land Before Her: Fantasy and Experience of the American Frontiers, 1630-1860.* Chapel Hill: University of North Carolina Press, 1975.
[196] James Rosier, "True Relation": 131-137.
[197] ibid.: 140f.

they can neither discern, use, or rightly esteem the invaluable riches in midst whereof they live, sensually content with the bark and outward rinds."[198]

Thus, the narrative of this 1605 voyage ends where earlier narratives like Hariot's or Brereton's began: A land, full of promise and resembling an earthly paradise, equipped with friendly and cooperative natives, is there for the taking as the best place for settlement the earth seems to afford. The fact that the native inhabitants allegedly cannot claim any rights to that land because they make no use of it further enhances the glowing prospects. Rosier's narrative, along with its precursor by Brereton, established new realities by producing knowledge while at the same time perpetuating the myth of a New World Garden Eden and friendly and loving natives – with the somewhat paradoxical caveat of native treachery as a slight shadow on the glowing picture. As a result of this mixed message, the land remains enormously alluring and promising. However, the indigenous inhabitants assume a more individual shape once they are no longer stereotypically ranked as noble savages – for good and for bad: A more realistic portrayal of English-Indian relations adds a touch of reality and excitement to the narrative and probably enhanced its entertaining value; as promotion, treacherous natives in a narrative were probably less of an asset.

6.4.4. John Smith. *A Description of New England, Or, The Observations, and Discoveries, of Captain John Smith [...]*

In the *Description of New England*, John Smith presents himself for the first time as the protagonist and first-person narrator of a New World venture throughout the whole text. The narrative is composed of several elements: the description of the New England coast as Smith explored it, events during that voyage, propagandist passages praising New England's profitable fishing and agricultural potential while stirring Englishmen to action; and finally, an apology of failed subsequent voyages to New England due to technical problems and attacks by pirates.

The passages about New England praise the region for its "excellent good woods for building houses, boats, barks, or ships" and the "incredible abundance of most sorts of fish, much fowl, and sundry sorts of good fruit for man's use, [...] free stone for building, slate for tilling, [...] and iron ore sufficient." Concerning the alleged mines so ubiquitous in New World narratives of discovery and exploration, the narrator is cautious:

> Of mines of gold and silver, copper and probabilities of lead [...] I could say much if relations were good assurances: It is true indeed, I made many trials ac-

---

[198] James Rosier, "True Relation": 142.

cording to those instructions I had, which do persuade me I need not despair, but there are metals in the country: But I am no alchemist, nor will promise more than I know.

The narrator admits that much of his knowledge about North America is derived from published travel reports; he mentions Smith himself as an authority on Virginia, "within which is a country (as you may perceive by the description in a book and a map printed in my name) may well suffice 300,000 people to inhabit." South of Chesapeake Bay the authorities are "Sir Ralph Lane and that learned mathematician Thomas Hariot"; as to the regions to the North, "there is also a relation printed by Captain Bartholomew Gosnold [...] and another by Captain Waymouth [...]. From all these diligent observers, posterity may be bettered by the fruits of their labors."[199]

Instead of promising quick riches by exploiting mines, Smith praises the New England fishery as a means to gain profit, and only marginally commends agricultural investment by warning that, in some places, "it is a country rather to affright than to delight one. [...] And how to describe a more plain spectacle of desolation or more barren[ness] I know not." But this is tempered instantly by the claim that "there is no kingdom so fertile [that] has not some part barren: and New England is great enough to make many kingdoms and countries were it inhabited." In line with this claim that New England is not really inhabited is the fact that native peoples do not figure very prominently throughout the narrative. The narrator only casually mentions the names of some tribes, usually of "kind" and "well proportioned" people. Wherever conflicts arise, the English quickly gain the upper hand: "After much kindness, upon a small occasion, we fought also with forty or fifty of those; though some were hurt, and some slain, yet within an hour after they became friends." All in all, however, the natives merely pose a hindrance to settlement, for some fruitful regions are "not much inferior" to the "Paradise" of New England, the Massachusett region, "but for the multitude of people." Nevertheless, where there are natives, they may be easily subdued into providing victuals for the English and trading valuable furs and skins for "trifles". If the natives show themselves as "untoward (as is most certain they are) thirty or forty good men will be sufficient to bring them all in subjection."[200]

The picture of New England and its native inhabitants, it seems, is subjected to the narrator's purpose of making New England an attractive region for economic investment, as well as for settlements, and taking possession of the land and having natives provide for the English until they manage to grow their own

---

[199] Philip L. Barbour, ed. *Works of Captain John Smith*: 329ff.
[200] ibid.: 339f.

food sounds very easy. The narrator commends himself as a guide for future explorers, traders and settlers and accordingly paints New England in bright colors which gloss over the occasional caveats as to the existence of mines and the "barrenness" of the region. The Indians pose "no danger more than ordinary,"[201] and "the ground is so fertile that questionless it is capable of producing any grain, fruit, or seeds you will sow or plant [...] all sorts of cattle may here be bred and fed [...] securely for nothing." And if everything fails, it should be remembered, there are Indians that can be subjected into providing for the English. And even though there are numerous allusions to Indian gardens and corn fields, the narrator inserts claims here and there that the potential of the region remains as yet untapped and the land "is only as God made it when he created the world. Therefore I conclude [that] if the heart and entrails of those regions were sought, if their land were cultured, planted and manured by men of industry, judgment and experience," what doubts can there be that New England "might equalize any of those famous kingdoms [the narrator had been speaking of Persia and China] in all commodities, pleasures, and conditions?"[202]

Towards the end of the narrative, Smith once again mingles profane motifs of quick gain with more noble ones for exploring and settling the New World, seemingly trying to write something to please every kind of audience: "I am not so simple to think that ever any other motive than wealth will ever erect here a commonwealth, or draw company from their ease and humours at home."[203] For those more concerned with moral gain, he asks, "what have ever been the works of the greatest princes of the earth but planting of countries and civilizing barbarous and inhumane nations to civility and humanity, whose eternal actions fill our histories?" Accordingly, charity towards "those poor savages whose country we challenge, use, and possess" is one major reason why the narrator stirs his audience to New World ventures, to "imitate [our glorious forefathers'] virtues to be worthily their successors."[204]

With the *Description of New England*, Smith created part description, part personally involved promotion of New World riches to be gained under his guide. The narrative provides an ample stage on which he could display his personal experience, skills, and also pride in his achievements paired with offers to guide others as an expert in their first steps towards New England. Still, even the expert has to admit that not very much is known as yet of the country. This gives rise to a narrative mixture of what is there and what might one day be there. In describing

---

[201] Philip L. Barbour, ed. *Works of Captain John Smith*: 351.
[202] ibid.: 333f.
[203] ibid.: 346.
[204] ibid.: 361.

the country's "particulars", "which I intermingle thus with my projects and reasons, not being so sufficiently yet acquainted in those parts to write fully the estate of the sea, the air, the land [...] but as I gathered from the niggardly relations in a broken language to my understanding,"[205] Smith wrote part description, part fiction.

The whole mode of the narrative is prospective, describing much more what could be done with New England than its present state; what profits Europeans might be able to wring from it instead of what the country offers freely by itself. There is a crucial difference in Smith's promotional narrative in comparison to, for example, a tract like Hariot's; early Virginia is portrayed as yielding all sorts of riches by itself, for the taking with little or no labour; the paradisaic mode prevailed in the earliest English writings on Virginia over more pragmatic approaches to making use of the land by labour. Only gradually does the traditional image of a New World paradise, as if preserved for the English through the ages, recede into the background and give rise to close description, yet not so much of what is actually there, but what future potential a region might have *if* – and this little word takes center stage in many of the later English promotional tracts about North America – Englishmen are willing to invest expertise and labour. Smith is the principal advocate of the latter mode, and his *Description of New England* was realistic enough to inspire the Pilgrims' plans to emigrate to a land which was not conducive to idleness, but to honest labour and slow gain. It is somewhat ironic, however, that the considerable economic gain after the first years of hardship endangered New England's intended compact settlements and compact communities, whose settlers, in search of more profit, soon left their "ancient mother" church community.

---

[205] Philip L. Barbour, ed. *Works of Captain John Smith*: 338.

7. Narratives of Exploration and First Settlements

7.1. Jamestown

After the Lost Colony of Roanoke, the second major attempt at gaining a permanent foothold in North America began in 1607, and this time the settlement survived in the long run. However, the early hardships, especially famine, an unhealthy climate and increasing opposition of native tribes to encroachments on their lands, generated narratives that were often very contradictory in their descriptive passages on the one hand and on the narrative passages on the other. In general, a conscious effort to keep up a positive, glowing image of this New World Eden governed most of the narratives. The majority can be classed as propaganda; yet even these tracts attest to a deep and painful dichotomy between expectations and reality that was to be solved rhetorically rather than in reality.

7.1.1. George Percy. *A Discourse of the Plantation of the Southern Colonie in Virginia*

George Percy left England with the first fleet of colonists in December 1606 and arrived at Chesapeake Bay on April 26, 1607. The first sight of the coast was, according to Percy, "gay meadows and goodly tall trees, with such freshwater (creeks) running through the woods, as I was almost ravished at the first sight thereof." The first encounter with natives is violent. The group is assaulted by "the savages [who] creeping upon all four from the hills like bears charged us very desperately in the faces, hurt Captain Gabriel Archer [...] and a sailor" but finally the English chase them away. After such a violent narrative opening, the narrator takes time to describe the land, this time free of its quarrelsome native inhabitants:

> We passed through excellent ground full of flowers of diverse kinds of colours, and as goodly trees as I have seen [...] going a little further we came into a little plat of ground full of fine and beautiful strawberries, four times bigger and better than ours in England. We passed through the woods in fine paths, having most pleasant springs which issued from the mountains; we also went through the goodliest corn fields that ever were seen in any country.[206]

Exploratory trips into the land supply the English with pleasant impressions of fertility and beauty: "All the way as we went, having the most pleasant suckles,

---

[206] George Percy. "A Discourse of the Plantation..." Dec. 1606-Sept 1607. In: David B. Quinn, *New American World*, V: 266-274: 279f. It was first printed in Samuel Purchas, 1625.

the ground all flowing over with fair flowers of sundry colours and kinds as though it had been in any garden or orchard in England. [...] We kept on our way in this paradise."

In the face of natural beauty and abundance, a striking change of tone occurs when the enumeration of natural phenomena changes into an obituary. With the beginning of August 1607, the colonists (104 by that time, according to the narrator) began to die, and the frequency is further enhanced by the anaphoric construction of this passage: "The sixth of August there died John Asbie of the bloody flux. The ninth day died George Flowre of the swelling. The tenth day died William Bruster Gentleman, of a wound given by the savages..." At times, two men die in one day. Captain Gosnold, a member of the council and experienced in New World voyages, died on August 22. The the narrator simply concludes,

> our men were destroyed with cruel diseases [...] and by wars, and some departed suddenly, but for the most part they died of mere famine. There were never Englishmen left in a foreign country in such misery as we were in this new discovered Virginia. [...] Thus we lived for the space of five months in this miserable distress, not having five able men to man our bulwarks upon any occasion. If it had not pleased God to have put a terror in the savages' hearts, we had all perished by those wild and cruel pagans, being in that weak estate as we were. [...] If there were any conscience in men, it would make their hearts bleed to hear the pitiful murmurings and outcries of our sick men without relief every night and day for the space of six weeks, some departing out of the world, many times three or four in a night, in the mornings their bodies trailed out of their cabins like dogs to be buried.

The English colonists are unable to help themselves and are at the mercy of the surrounding tribes who in the end save them: "It pleased God, after a while, to send those people which were our mortal enemies to relieve us with victuals [...] which was the setting up of our feeble men, otherwise we had all perished. Also we were frequented by diverse kings in the country, bringing us store of provision to our great comfort."[207] Percy's narrative juxtaposes enthusiastic praise of American nature and catalogues of American wildlife with a sad catalogue of dying colonists – a contrast which could hardly be more striking. And yet this same juxtaposition of natural abundance with hardships and famine reappears in narratives not only of Jamestown, but also of other colonies as well.

---

[207] George Percy, "Discourse": 272f.

7.1.2. John Smith. *A True Relation of Such Occurrences and Accidents of Noate as Hath Hapned in Virginia*

The *True Relation*, originally a letter hastily finished to be sent back to London by ship, was intended to inform the Virginia Company of the first one and a half years of the Jamestown colony. However, Smith had obviously had no hand in editing or publishing it, and it remains fairly cryptic in many passages due to bad editing and printing.[208] Unlike his later texts like *A Map of Virginia* or the *General Historie*, the *True Relation* is a direct, short, and seemingly spur-of-the-moment account of the first one and a half years of the colony, from the middle of December 1606 to June 2nd, 1608, when the ship to carry the letter home left Virginia. After some less optimistic passages which might pose a hindrance to further investments in the venture had been erased, the *True Relation* was edited for publication by one I.H. on account of the Virginia Company just weeks after it had reached England. Obviously, the appetite for news from Virginia was strong, as was the Virginia Company's quest for further investors, whose purse strings the *True Relation* was supposed to help loosen.

This narrative lends itself well to investigating how a more or less first-hand account, drawn on the spot and hardly reworked by its author for publication compares to the later narratives Captain John Smith composed about his travels in North America. Smith's later writings are not included in the selection of narratives studied in this thesis because they were reworked to a degree that makes it difficult to still regard them as travel narratives. Unlike the *True Relation*, for example, his later works were *composed* in the sense that they were rearranged, abridged or expanded years after Smith's actual experiences in America to suit the author's argumentative needs. The Pocahontas episode, for example, was only a short incident in its first version, yet was later enlarged into an adventure story according to popular taste, foreshadowing what would become of this story in today's popular culture.

The *True Relation* is also a case study of early encounters between Englishmen and Indians in what was still far away from the romantic frontier often still associated with John Smith, the quintessential first American hero of popular culture. Smith's cunning dealings with the Indians and the equally cunning Powhatan show that the English were quite blind to the fact that they were taking part in a process of acculturation and were yet a far cry from cultural and technological superiority. In order to appropriately name and describe the geographical and cultural zone in which explorers like Smith and their native counterparts act, Marie-

---

[208] John Smith, "True Relation". In: Philip L. Barbour, ed. *Works of Captain John Smith*. Vol. I, 4-117: 5.

Louise Pratt uses the term "contact zone" to replace the term "frontier" because the latter retains the perspective of the invading group only and thus *per se* establishes "a European expansionist perspective" which might heavily distort power relations between the different groups. The term "contact zone" seeks to define the "social spaces where disparate cultures meet, clash, and grapple with each other" and emphasizes "how subjects are constituted in and by their relations to each other."[209]

Furthermore, the concept of a contact zone instead of frontier entails not a one-way process of cultural domination, but of acculturation. Instead of assuming a chasm that seemed insurmountable for both sides, early American travel narratives report instances of mutual acculturation. This seems clear enough for the Indians who were brought to wear European apparell to cover their nakedness or were partners in trade. Yet also the English showed instances of acculturation, often born out of sheer necessity: In order to survive, Ralph Lane had to disband his men into small groups, imitating the Indian radition of forming small hunting or fishing groups when victuals were short. This semi-nomadic life left the English unable to defend themselves sufficiently and, what is more, it made them resemble the natives who, according to travel reports of the time, lived in "herds" like the "wild beasts they hunt."

Smith's narrative establishes this contact zone between the fort in Jamestown and the surrounding Indian settlements, with John Smith as its prime, but far from sole, agent. As an active participant in contact with the natives, Smith's picture of them is derived from frequent interaction rather than close descriptions, along with some recourses to ethnographical lore, e. g. in hints at cannibalism. The English find not only abundance in nature, as some catalogue passages reveal: "More plenty of swans, cranes, geese, ducks, [...] more plain fertile planted ground, in such great proportions as there I had not seen."[210] The English also encounter "abundance" of people, and it is interesting here to note that Smith indeed observes and reports that the natives till the ground. Promotional tracts, such as Strachey's *Historie of Travell*, labored to establish English rights to the land exactly because it was allegedly untilled and the natives did not know how or care to make use of it until the English taught them the art of husbandry.[211] The natives feature quite ambiguously in Smith's description. Although he manages to establish friendly relations with Powhatan and his tribe, there are rumors of cannibals and other warlike tribes. Powhatan himself tells Smith that some days' journey

---

[209] Marie-Louise Pratt. *Imperial Eyes. Travel Writing and Transculturation*. London and New York: Routledge, 1992: 6f.
[210] John Smith, "True Relation". In: Philip L. Barbour, *Works of Captain John Smith*: 43.
[211] Compare, for example, Strachey's Praemonition to the Reader in his *Historie of Travell into Virginia Britania*.

beyond his chiefdom, there was "a fierce nation that did eat men" and beyond the "back Sea" which Smith recognizes as the South Sea, located in the interior of the continent, there lived "people with short coats and sleeves to the elbows, that passed that way in ships like ours." Rumors of a Western Ocean that might open up to the South Sea and Asia, as well as talk of cannibals in the interior and civilized people, dressed like Europeans, established a whole tableau of future enterprises to be launched in Virginia. At the same time, these rumors catered to traditional European geographical lore.

In this early instance of colonial encounter, the "contact zone" between the English and the natives is not yet characterized by the later asymmetrical power relations to the disadvantage of indigenous peoples. Here, both the English, who need to trade in order to get corn and other victuals, and the natives who highly esteem the Englishmen's iron weapons, tools, and copper products, seem to keep up a fragile balance of power. The frontier as a threshold being pushed westwards by Europeans does not yet exist as the locus of a one-sided power structure. Instead, during his travels away from the colony, Smith permanently re-invents himself and adapts his person, background or social status to the best use in every situation, which makes him the prototype of traveler after Ulysses' fashion. In the face of strong Indian clan ties, he establishes himself as "son" of Captain Newport, "whom I entitled the *Merowames* [i.e. *weroance*, tribal leader] which they call King of all the waters."[212] Not only in deeds, but also in language the narrator adapts to changing circumstances and worldviews.

Apart from uneasy relations with the natives, the infant colony has major trouble keeping people fed. While the Indians occasionally trade corn for copper or tools with the English, victuals remain scarce until a relief ship comes in. A harrowing passage in the *True Relation* is structured by a food countdown which begins depressingly enough: "Our provision being now within twenty days spent", the Indians relieve the colonists, seemingly out of the blue, with "great store both of corn and bread ready-made", and also nature steps in: "There came such abundance of fowls into the rivers, as greatly refreshed our weak estates." The passage continues parallel to declining supplies: "Our victuals being now within eighteen days spent, and the Indians' trade decreasing" and "time thus passing away, and having not above fourteen days victuals left..."[213] Smith's narrative shows the same paradoxical combination of descriptive passages praising America's abundant nature and narrative passages telling of hardship, violent encounters, hunger, and death which characterized George Percy's *Discourse*. The statement that "all our men [were] in good health and comfort" is followed by a passage narrating

---

[212] John Smith, "True Relation". In: Philip L. Barbour, *Works of Captain John Smith*: 57.
[213] ibid.: 33-37.

discontent and malice among the English, "through which disorder God (being angry with us) plagued us with such famine and sickness that the living were scarce able to bury the dead: our want of sufficient and good victuals" and constant watch day and night for fear of Indian attacks "being the chief cause."[214]

Instead of playing off English cultural and technological superiority against barbarous backwardness, the English are precariously dependent on the natives and on substantial reinforcements of people and victuals from England as well– all in the face of a seemingly abundant natural world, as others like Thomas Hariot reported home before Smith. In Smith's descriptions, however, the land appears equally and frustratingly inconstant as do the natives and their willingness to support the English. The land is sometimes described as "only a vast and wild wilderness", and the "desolateness of the country" contrasts sharply with other passages which tell of land "exceeding[ly] fertile, [featuring] good timber, mostly hills and dales, in each valley a crystal spring." Smith's desolate, vast wilderness echoes the descriptions of Puritan emigrants to New England only a few years later. Yet whereas the Puritans searched for their paradise less in the land than in the mind, Smith's Virginia is both, a paradise and a desolate wilderness, in which "more abundance of fish and fowls and a pleasanter seat cannot be imagined."[215] To add to this confusing picture, there are frequent hints at gold and other precious metals throughout the text. Despite several hints at mines Smith can, as proof, only mention rocks "interlaced with many veins of glistering spangles."[216]

The *True Relation* chronicles a very precarious period of the infant colony and encounter with American nature and indigenous inhabitants. Both seem equally kind and forbidding at once. Compared to promotional tracts, it is interesting to note that the narrator does not try to talk these paradoxes "away" but presents himself as a figure uniquely adapted to successful operations in this contact zone. It is more the story of how to successfully navigate along the crooked lines of intercultural encounter than sharing in the narrative of European success on American soil. The *True Relation* admits much futility on the side of the English, in terms of sustaining themselves and being able to wring a living from the soil which had been established as superbly fertile in so many travel reports that it could hardly have been otherwise. Hariot's *Briefe and True Report* was long in print, and so were other texts praising American abundance and promise. Furthermore, even though many early reports of the New World claimed that native populations were excessively eager to trade for glass beads and other trifles, it

---

[214] John Smith, "True Relation". In: Barbour, *Works of Captain John Smith*: 33.
[215] ibid.: 45, 53, 51.
[216] ibid.: 31.

becomes clear in the *True Relation* that they used trade for ulterior motives and could and would trade only what they could spare.

The mines that had been expected to exist in North America, waiting only to be discovered and exploited, kept mysteriously aloof throughout Smith's narrative. The *True Relation*, then, continues many themes that had become a staple in early travel reports about North America, but the longer exploring parties stayed in America, the further the hoped-for mines, gardens of ease, and friendly natives seemed to retreat into the interior, beyond the reach of the Europeans. The abrupt juxtapositions found in the *True Relation* of natural abundance and a "vast desert", and of friendly and generous natives and treachery and violence, pay tribute to the puzzling paradoxes of the new American world that differed markedly from what Englishmen must have expected it to be like based on earlier, glowing reports. Likewise, the narrator fails or refuses to take the stance of the discoverer and explorer viewing America from a superior European viewpoint. Instead, he limits descriptions to short geographical and ethnological information and curiously abstains from judgments, especially with regard to the natives. This rather neutral tone, however, somewhat diminishes the painful dichotomy between imagined and real America, by downplaying the discrepancy between the intended European actions on the American stage and the many limits America actually put on its early colonists and their aspirations.

7.1.3. John Smith. *A Map of Virginia. With a Description of the Countrey, the Commodities, People, Government and Religion*

In contrast to the *True Relation* of 1608, the *Map of Virginia* is a fairly well ordered and coherent narrative. The text accompanying Smith's map begins with the geographical location of Virginia, mentions the climate, rivers, quality of the soil, kinds of trees, and other facts about the region. The description generally favors Virginia very well, the climate agreeing "well with English constitutions being once seasoned in the country"; the summer "is hot as in Spain, the winter cold as in France or England." The first part of this quote introduces a textual strategy of letting Virginia appear in a more favorable light than may have been realistic: Structures like "once seasoned..." or "if there were" (European experts to find mines) hint at Virginia's qualities and potential as yet untapped and there for the taking *if only* skilled and hardworking Englishmen were at hand. The second part of the quote employs a familiar strategy of description, the analogy with known European phenomena. It appears frequently throughout the narrative, usually combined with some kind of superlative, and also often combined with the prospect of future rewards if properly worked: "Heaven and earth never agreed better to frame a place for man's habitation being of our constitutions, were it fully manured and inhabited by industrious people."[217]

Virginia is presented as a country yet awaiting a wake-up call to unfold its potential, and the call can only come from "industrious" men – European men, it should be added, for the natives are commonly described as idle and improvidential in this narrative. This places the *Map of Virginia* within a firmly established European colonial rhetoric originally derived from erotic concepts of the conquering male and the Virgin land waiting for its suitor, as in Ralegh's *Discoverie of ...Guiana*: "To conclude, Guiana is a country that has yet her maidenhead, never sacked, turned, nor wrought, nor the virtue and salt of the soil spent by manurance."[218] Smith leaves out the obvious eroticism but nevertheless continues a narrative thoroughly structured by the discrepancy between its present natural state and the great promises it will yield. Hints at mineral riches are part of this future program: "These waters wash from the rocks such glistering tinctures that the ground in some places seems gilded, where both the rocks and the earth are so splendent to behold, that better judgments than ours might have been persuaded [that] they contained more than probabilities."[219]

The same passage appears in the *True Relation*, but is much shorter and only casually hints at minerals: "The rocks [on one side of a river] being of a gravelly nature, [are] interlaced with many veins of glistering spangles."[220] The narrator, nevertheless, keeps away from making stronger claims: "Concerning the entrails of the earth little can be said for certainty [...] only this is certain, that many regions lying in the same latitude afford mines very rich of diverse natures." Even in this case, it is, according to the narrator, due to idle and misguided Europeans that Virginia's potential has not been tapped yet, for "there wanted good refiners, for these that took upon them to have skill this way, took up the washings from the mountains [...], flattering themselves in their own vain conceits to have been supposed what they were not. [...] Both copper and better minerals are there to be had for their labor. Other countries have it."[221] Smith connects Virginia's natural abundance and promise again and again with the exhortation that labor is necessary to turn wild nature into usable commodity. He is in line with a traditional European, and especially English distinction between nature and the garden, the

---

[217] John Smith. "A Map of Virginia". In: Barbour, *Works of Captain John Smith*. Vol. I, 131-180: 143f.
[218] Sir Walter Ralegh. "The Discoverie of [...] Guiana." In: *Early American Writing*. Ed. Giles B. Gunn. New York: Penguin, 70.
[219] John Smith, "Map of Virginia": 145.
[220] John Smith, "True Relation": 31.
[221] John Smith, "Map of Virginia": 156, 159.

latter being "used" nature, tamed, manured, and planted. Virginia is presented as a potential Garden Eden, but as yet without a gardener.

This issue has been investigated by Patricia Seed in a study about ceremonies of possession. As it was understood in the command in *Genesis*, according to Seed, man was supposed to "multiply and replenish [...] and subdue" the earth.[222] This included replenishing whatever land was there not yet occupied and cultivated. Often, interpretations combined the idea of finding vacant land with the call for improving it. Improving included drawing distinctions between wild (uncontrolled) and cultivated (controlled) flora and fauna. Since, according many early European explorers, native Americans did not cultivate land, plants, or kept domesticated animals, they themselves were not cultivated and civil either.

More than other nations, the English were, according to Seed, inclined to view and imagine the New World as a garden, hinted at, for example, in Barlowe's and Amadas' report of the first Roanoke voyage. Unrealistic expectations regarding New World fertility, abundance, and a life of ease there were bound to follow. Examples of famine in the face of wild, abundant nature must have added a very dark hue of frustration to early European experiences in America. Yet even in the face of early failures, English settlers were largely undeterred. It might have helped, though, that official instructions existed which called for explicit censoring of texts sent from the colonies to England: "Of all other things else to advertise particularly and to suffer no man to return but by passport from the President and Council nor to write any letter of anything that may discourage others."[223]

Planting as an act of taking possession meant planting whatever would grow in American soil and metaphorically included the English settlements and their inhabitants, as Alexander Whitaker would state retrospectively with regard to the Jamestown colony and its early hardships. The colony, he wrote, "has taken better root; and as a spreading herb, whose top has been often cropped off, renews its growth, and spreads itself more vigorously."[224] Garden rhetoric helped to paint prospects for the Jamestown colony in a brighter hue and also managed to convert painful setbacks into methods of strengthening the Englishmen's hold in the New World. While the *True Relation* contained lengthy descriptions of Virginia's abundant nature, hardship and famine of the English settlers at the same time, the *Map of Virginia* leaves out the harrowing experiences of how impotent the English had been in their first years as New World gardeners. What is left of the wild

---

[222] Patricia Seed. *Ceremonies of Possession in Europe's Conquest of the New World, 1492-1640.* Cambridge, MA: Cambridge University Press, 1995: 32.
[223] Quoted after Philip L. Barbour, ed. *The Jamestown Voyages under the First Charter, 1606-1609.* Cambridge: Hakluyt Society, 1969: I, 49-54.
[224] Alexander Whitaker. *Good Newes from Virginia* [1613]. Ann Arbor, MI: University Microfilms, 23.

nature-garden dichotomy is the ongoing search for a diligent and skillful gardener. Vines, for example, are never "pruned nor manured" yet will, as the narrator ensures, "prove good were they well manured."[225]

There are, however, some hints at Indian agricultural activities, for occasionally the narrator describes Indian lands as "planted and yield[ing] no less plenty and variety of fruit than the river exceeds with abundance of fish." Also, the narrator admits that the English colony is settled on Indian land. Apart from this somewhat contradictory evidence, little is said about conflicts with the Indians. The structure of the narrative follows the great rivers of the region and mentions the tribes seated at these rivers, including their present number of "able" or "fighting" men, and the numbers never rise high enough to stir anyone's concern: "On the south side [of] this river the Appamatucks have 60 fighting men." One tribe appeared to the English to consist of "giants, yea and to the neighbors, yet seemed of an honest and simple disposition, with much ado restrained from adoring the discoverers as gods."[226]

This passage appears word by word in William Strachey's *Historie of Travell*, too, very likely so because friendly giants adoring the English as gods were a pleasant and reassuring thing to report home. European superiority in other matters is mentioned in the *Map of Virginia*, too, most notably concerning religion. The English settlers try to persuade the priest of a tribe "whose devotion, apprehension, and good disposition much exceeded any in those countries" to convert to the Christian faith. The English fail, but "this he did believe that our God much exceeded theirs, as our guns did their bows and arrows and many times did send to the President at Jamestown men with presents, entreating them to pray to his God [i. e. the English] for rain, for his god would not send him any."[227]

All in all, the *Map of Virginia* can be read as a sophisticated and coherent narrative based on the *True Relation*. It has, however, lost the immediacy and much of the subversive power to be found in the earlier text and exchanged it for a clear program of promoting Virginia regardless of inept English settlers who could or would, in Smith's eyes, not exploit the potential which Virginia contained.[228] Thus, the English still did not rank much higher than the "idle" Indians who did

---

[225] John Smith, "Map of Virginia": 152.
[226] ibid.: 146, 149.
[227] ibid.: 172.
[228] For an interesting possible explanation of the desolate situation of the earliest settlers, see Karen Ordahl Kupperman. "Death and Apathy in Early Jamestown." *Journal of American History*, 66.1 (June 1979): 24-40. As a reason for the frequently observed cases of apathy and death in early Jamestown (in narratives by Strachey, Hamor, and Wood, among others) Kupperman suggests that an unsupplemented maize diet might have caused pellagra, a niacin deficiency ailment which made the sufferer anorexic and apathetic.

not make proper use of the land either, and live "from hand to mouth."[229] English settlers were obviously determined to live out New World fantasies of ease and prosperity that early reports may have bred, and thus complained bitterly of a real America falling so short of the ideal:

> They found not English cities, nor such fair houses, [...] neither such plenty of gold and silver and dissolute liberty as they expected. [They] had little or no care of anything but to pamper their bellies. [...] For the country was to them a misery, a ruin, a death, a hell, and their reports here and their own actions there according.

At the end of the narrative, the narrator switches from the predominant third-person narrator to the "I", in order to finally bring home his version of a naturally abundant, pleasant Virginia brought into disrepute by "the clamors and the ignorance of false informers" of "idle contemplatours." Smith styles himself a hero, all of his men "living near 10 months of[f] such natural means as the country naturally of itself affords, notwithstanding all this, and the worst fury of the savages, the extremity of sickness, mutinies, faction, ignorances, and want of victuall; in all that time I lost but 7 or 8 men, yet subjected the savages to our desired obedience, and received contribution from 35 of their kings."[230]

7.1.4. Robert Johnson. *Nova Britannia: Offering Most Excellent Fruites by Planting in Virginia. Exciting All such as Are Well Affected to Further the Same*

The narrative is dedicated to Sir Thomas Smith, on whose instigation it may have been produced in the first place. It is a propaganda pamphlet designed to lure investors with promises of vast profits and the taking up of vast tracts of land. Like many other early English New World reports, it claims to be

> the summe of a private speech, or discourse, touching our plantation in Virginia, uttered not long since in London, where some few adventurers [...] one among the rest stood up and began to relate (in effect) as follows. [...] There are diverse monuments already published in print to the world manifesting and showing that the coasts and parts of Virginia have been long since discovered, peopled and possessed by many English, both men, women, and children. [...] So I wish and entreat all well affected subjects, some in their persons, others in their

---
[229] John Smith, "Map of Virginia": 159.
[230] ibid.: 176f.

purses, cheerfully to adventure, and jointly take in hand this high and acceptable work.[231]

Much of Johnson's rhetoric might have been familiar by now to an English public. In the "searching" [i.e. exploring] of the James River, the colonists "were so ravished with the admirable sweetness of the stream and with the pleasant land trending along on either side, that their joy exceeded and with great admiration they praised God. [...] The country itself is large and great assuredly, though as yet, no exact discovery can be made of all. It is also commendable and hopeful in every way." In this case, the narrator cannot be bothered with specific hints at gold mines, a Northwest passage, or profits from silk works, for instance. It suffices to say that America is "hopeful in every way."

Regarding the native inhabitants, the narrator reiterates the frequent claim that they do not possess the land because they lack a sedentary lifestyle:

> It is inhabited with wild and savage people, that live and lie up and down in troupes like herds of deer in a forest; they have no law but nature, their apparell skins of beasts, but most go naked; the better sort have houses, but poor ones, [for] they have no arts nor science. [...] They are generally very loving and gentle, and do entertain and relieve our people with great kindness; they are easy to be brought to good, and would fain embrace a better condition: the land yields naturally for the sustenance of man abundance of fish [...] of land and water fowls, infinite store.

The narrator establishes a curious mixture of a promising land peopled with "savages" who do not possess the land yet are very willing to assist the English, thus posing no obstacle in any way to English possession and cultivation of the land. As for the latter, the narrator recycles the erotic terminology of a feminized, virgin land to be explored by the English, combined with hints at treasures: "There are valleys and plains streaming with sweet springs, like veins in a natural body; there are hills and mountains making a sensible proffer of hidden treasure, never yet searched; the land is full of minerals."[232]

Finally, perhaps for the sake of a bit of realism, the narrator concedes that relations with the natives might not forever be peaceful but reassures the audience: "And howsoever we hear tales and rumours of this and that, yet be not dismayed, for I tell you, if we find that any miscreants have wronged, or go about to hurt our few hundreds there, we shall be ready to right it again with many thousands."[233] It may help to remember that Richard Hakluyt had added in a marginal note that the

---
[231] Robert Johnson. "Nova Britannia". In: David B. Quinn, *New American World*, 234-248: 236.
[232] ibid.: 238f.
[233] ibid.: 247.

English were able to "deal against the savages 10 to 100"[234] when Lane and his men were not at all able to feed themselves. They were much less in danger of being wiped out by the surrounding tribes than of starving in the midst of America's stereotypically reiterated natural abundance.

7.1.5. William Strachey. *A True Reportory of the Wracke and Redemption of Sir Thomas Gates Knight*

William Strachey was shipwrecked on the Bermudas with Sir Thomas Gates, the new governor of Virginia en route to Jamestown. When the group finally arrived the next year, they found the little colony in a desolate state. Strachey's letter was sent to a lady in England but also reached the Virginia Company and showed Strachey to be a good and critical observer. On the basis of this narrative, Strachey was asked to report to the Virginia Company on the state of the colony a few years later, which he did in the *Historie of Travell*.

It is hard to assess a possible source for such pleasant olfactory sensations which Arthur Barlowe reported in 1584 and Strachey in the *True Reportory* more than two decades later, but they seem to have been a staple in early New World reports. "The twentieth [of May, 1610] about midnight, we had a marvelous sweet smell from the shore (as from the coast of Spain, short of the Straits) strong and pleasant, which did not a little glad us." Once ashore, the news about the colony's condition was more than bad "contrary to our fair hopes". After Gates had arrived at Jamestown, he summoned every one

> all such as were able to come forth of their houses" to the church "where our Minister Master Bucke made a zealous and sorrowful prayer, finding all things so contrary to our expectations, so full of misery and misgovernment. [...] Viewing the fort, we found the palisades torn down, the ports open, the gates from off the hinges, and empty houses (which owners death had taken from them) rent up and burnt, rather than the dwellers would step into the woods a stone's cast off from them to fetch other firewood; and it is true, the Indian killed as fast without, if our men stirred but beyond the bounds of their blockhouse, as famine and pestilence did within.[235]

Only shortly after Gates's arrival, however, Jamestown put on a face more in accordance with expectations of English colonial settlements:

---

[234] Ralph Lane, "Discourse". First printed in Hakluyt's 1589 *Principal Navigations*. In David B. Quinn, *Roanoke Voyages*, I: 282f.
[235] William Strachey. "A True Reportory of the Wracke and Redemption of Sir Thomas Gates Knight." In: David B. Quinn, *New American World*, V, 288-301: 289ff.

At every angle or corner [...] a bulwark or watchtower is raised and in each bulwark a piece of ordnance well mounted. To every side, a proportioned distance from the palisade, is a settled street of houses that runs along [...]. In the midst is a marketplace, a storehouse, and a corps de garde, as likewise a pretty chapel, though (at this time when we came in) as ruined and unfrequented.

The houses are as yet "in no great uniformity" concerning "the fashion or beauty of the street", but houses are decorated inside with Indian mats: "A delicate wrought fine kind of mat the Indians make with which (as they can be trucked for or snatched up) our people do dress their chambers and inward rooms, which make their houses so much the more handsome." To deal with the climate, the original roofs of houses, "plastered with bitumen or tough clay", were exchanged for the Indian way, i.e. coverings of "barks of trees"; and so the narrator concludes that "we hold ourselves well apaid, though wanting arras hangings, tapestry, and gilded Venetian cordovan, or more spruce household garniture and wanton city ornaments." Robert Johnson reported home that the Indians "have houses, but poor ones, [for] they have no arts nor science."[236] It seems that the English colonists Strachey described in the *True Reportory* were, once summoned to work, sensible enough to adapt to Indian building techniques, making early Jamestown much more a contact zone of mutual adaptation than a frontier of European superiority.

While promotional tracts emphasized Indian lack of arts and crafts, and thus ranked them with savages, Strachey's report suggests that acculturation in early Jamestown certainly was a two-way process, with the English profiting from Indian know-how. Strachey's narrative is more straightforward than quite a few others in another respect. Many texts stereotypically reiterated the healthful climate, sweet water, and wholesome air. Strachey admitted that the fort was seated "in somewhat an unwholesome and sickly air, by reason it is in a marsh ground [...] and has no fresh-water springs serving that town but what we drew from a well six or seven fathom deep, fed by the brackish river oozing into it"; the narrator admits that "many diseases and sicknesses [...] have happened to our people, who are indeed strangely afflicted with fluxes and agues, and every particular infirmity too,"[237] which the narrator blames on the poor quality of the water. Only a few years later, however, Strachey was to write that "the temperature of this country does well agree with the English constitutions."[238]

---

[236] Robert Johnson, "Nova Britannia": 238.
[237] William Strachey, "True Reportory": 294f.
[238] William Strachey. *The Historie of Travell into Virginia Britania*. Ed. Louis B. Wright and Virginia Freund. London: Hakluyt Society, 1953: 37.

Although it reached some degree of circulation, Strachey's first narrative was much rather a piece of private communication. It seems he felt free to voice criticism not only of the country and the town, but also of the English colonists there. In his second narrative, this time commissioned by the Virginia Company as internal information which also circulated widely, Strachey elaborately praised the country, the climate, and Jamestown. This time, his narrative is promotional and contains many of the stereotypical elements of "official" New World reports: The text opens with a defensive stance, authorities like Thomas Hariot are quoted to testify to the richness of the soil, mines are mentioned, and everything in Virginia seems to agree very well with Englishmen's expectations. In this sense, the *True Reportory* may be read as a reality check of the later, brightly colored picture of early Virginia composed in the *Historie of Travell*. It also shows that descriptive passages could move very far away from an eyewitness report towards a conglomerate of stereotypes in imagery and terminology. The recurrent terms "pleasant" and "goodly" are good examples; both are used to describe the American land yet are peculiarly nondescript.

7.1.6. William Strachey. *The Historie of Travell into Virginia Britania*

In July 1610, Sir Thomas Gates left Virginia and brought Strachey's Letter *A True Reportory* to England. It obviously caused much interest in officials of the Virginia company, and it ordered Strachey to write a full report on the country. The company's secretary, Martin, asked him to

> let me understand from you the nature and quality of the soil and how it is like to serve you without help from hence, the manners of the people, how the barbarians are content with your being there, but especially how our own people do brook their obedience, how they endure labor, whether willingly or upon constraint [...] and generally [...] what hope of the success." He also asked Strachey to deal "clearly with me, as I would do with you in the like case, that thereby I may be truly able to satisfy others, and to direct my counsels and endeavors for prevention of evil, if there be any.[239]

Strachey returned to England in 1611 and submitted his *Historie of Travell* to the Virginia Company the next year. He borrowed, according to a study of his life and works,[240] from earlier texts, as from "that true lover of virtue, and great learned professor [...] Mr. Hariot, who lived there in the time of the first colony, spoke

---

[239] William Strachey. *The Historie of Travell*: xxv.
[240] Doctoral Thesis by S. G. Culliford, University of London, 1950; unpublished. Quoted after: Louis B. Wright and Virginia Freund, eds. *Historie of Travell*: xviii.

the Indian language and made many proofs of the richness of the soil, and commodities thereof." Strachey also used John Smith's narratives, Richard Eden's translation of Peter Martyr, or José de Acosta's *The naturall and morall historie of the East and West Indies*. Often, the detailed observations on Indian life are not Strachey's own but quoted from others, as in the case of religious ceremonies; "the manner of [which] Captain Smith observed to be as follows..."[241] This intertextuality, often found in Strachey's narrative, is a central feature of many early American travel narratives and has to be kept in mind when judging the "truth value" of observation and interpretation contained in a narrative.

Strachey's narrative is divided into two books, the first divided into ten headings dealing with descriptions of the geography of Virginia, several chapters on the natives, their customs, religion, warfare, lifestyle, and finally, a chapter enumerating Virginia's commodities. After detailed descriptions in the first book, the second narrates the English discoveries and first colonizing ventures in America until the present (i.e. 1611, when Strachey began composing the *Historie*). In a *Praemonition to the Reader*, Strachey seeks to talk up courage in investors in a colonizing enterprise which had not earned the investors any returns by then. Also, he refutes claims by "Mouths of Ignorance, and Slander"[242] that nothing good will come of the enterprise – this defensive stance of promotional tracts had been established with Hariot's *Briefe and True Report* and would stay with American promotional narratives for decades. In order to justify an English right to North America, Strachey not only invokes the legendary Welsh prince Madoc, who is said to have reached the West Indies in the early Middle Ages, but, more convincingly, the Cabots' discoveries, and finally, the colonizing enterprises of Grenville and Ralegh in North America.

The main intention behind these undertakings, Strachey asserts, is "to communicate with these simple, and innocent people, [...] like raced and unblotted tables, apt to receive what form soever shall be first drawn thereon" with regard to civility and the Christian faith. The native inhabitants, as he terms them in the full title of his work, bear God's image like the English do and "participate with us of reason." Furthermore, he urges the English to settle in Virginia to offer the natives the benefits of religion and trade and to use the "wast[e] and vast, uninhabited grounds of their[s]." Strachey thus reiterates the common claims of English promoters of colonization, the *vacuum domicilium topos*, potential riches, and the honorable act of conversion. There is, however, a subtle hint at possible violence in the encounter: "[If] we shall find them practice violence, or treason against us

---

[241] William Strachey, *Historie of Travell*: 96.
[242] ibid.: 7.

(as they have done to our other colony at Roanoke)" they [the English colonists] will justly "draw our swords, et *vim vi repellere*."[243]

So far no close descriptions of the natives Strachey encountered during his stay in Virginia have been rendered, but only a general picture of natives eager to trade and willingly to submit to the benevolent colonizers and their faith. The quoted passage on possible violence, however, must serve as a caveat that peaceful relations are fragile at best. To assuage fears of native violence he asserts that "they never killed any man of ours, but by our men's own folly and indiscretion, suffering themselves to be beguiled", and he also counters "the common report [...] of so many men [...] to have been slain by those Indians" with the demand to know "if they can name me three men, that they ever killed of ours." This defensive stance is typical of early promotional New World reports and suggests that ample evidence existed which contradicted the rosy image of America in official narratives.

The narrator here follows the tone of early reports such as Hariot's which stressed Indian inferiority in warfare, but did without the motif of Indian treachery as the main danger to English settlers – as opposed to superior fighting techniques or morale on the part of the Indians. Those natives that seem superior (at least in numbers – "well near 600 able and mighty men") to the English appear as conveniently adoring the newcomers. When Captain Argall sets out on an exploration into the interior, he encounters a tribe of "great and well proportioned men" who "seemed like giants to the English [...] yet seemed of an honest and simple disposition with much ado restrained from adoring the discoverers as gods."[244] Yet, later in the narrative, Indian inconstancy features quite prominently to taint the first positive image of the natives with an odd juxtaposition of negative and positive features:

> They are inconstant in everything, but what fear constrains them to keep, crafty, timorous, quick of apprehension"; some are "of disposition fearful and not easily wrought herefore to trust us, [...] others again of them are so bold and audacious as they dare come into our forts, truck and trade with us and look us in the face, crying all friends, when they have but new done us a mischief [...] they are soon moved to anger, and so malicious that they seldom forget an injury; they are very thievish", and they try to steal from the English wherever possible, yet "seldom steal from one another."[245]

---

[243] William Strachey, *Historie of Travell*: 18.
[244] ibid.: 45, 48.
[245] ibid.: 75ff.

The picture these descriptions paint of the natives is ambiguous, tinged with admiration for their hardiness, physical appearance and ability to survive on what the country offers; yet, as is clear in the last descriptive passage, they appear to the narrator as treacherous and inconstant. Nevertheless, they are portrayed as non-threatening with regard to the English settlement, which may be the main point the narrator strives to make along with a general defense of Virginia against false reports and ignorance.[246]

Once English domination over the native tribes and their "lamentable ignorance"[247] would be established, the narrator claims, they "shall [be busied] by the gathering together of their several sorts of tribute somewhat else to entertain themselves withal" for, presently, they "are for the most part of the year idle, and do little else than sharpen their arrows against the English."[248] This is an interesting addition to the aim of converting the "heathens", set out in the beginning of the narrative. Forcing them to work for their tribute to the English will, it is suggested, keep them from idly passing their time plotting against the newcomers. Idleness is a central feature of natives not only in Strachey's narrative and is closely connected with the *vacuum domicilium* theory: Those who idly live on land they do not work and use have no title to it. Land is possessed not by living on it, but by living off it by clearing, planting and manuring it.[249]

Concerning some more ethnographic observations, the narrator reproduces John Smith's claim that the natives are born "from the womb indifferent white", as "Captain Smith (living sometime amongst them) affirms", and that their mothers rub a certain tawny, permanent dye into their babies' skins to protect them from heat and moskitoes. Quite a few descriptions are supported by comparisons to either "Turks", "Moors", or "Irish": The natives have wide mouths ("yet nothing so unsightly as the Moors"), sleep "stark naked on the ground from six to twelve [natives] in a house, as do the Irish", and also their dress reminds the narrator of the Irish.[250] Their "drink is (as the Turks) clear water."[251]

Obviously, Europe's own "barbarians" in Ireland, only lately subdued under English colonial rule, and on the Eastern fringe of the continent, were fairly well-known examples of uncivilized peoples and lent themselves to easy comparison

---

[246] On the *topos* of native treachery and the "inconstant savage", see Harry C. Porter. *The Inconstant Savage. England and the North American Indian, 1500-1660*. London: Duckworth, 1979.
[247] William Strachey, *Historie of Travell*: 101.
[248] ibid.: 92.
[249] Concerning different definitions of the right to possess land, see Patricia Seed. "Taking Possession and Reading Texts: Establishing the Authority of Overseas Empires." *William and Mary Quarterly*,3rd ser., 49 (1992), 183-209. See also Seed, *Ceremonies of Possession in Europe's Conquest of the New World, 1492-1640*. New York: Cambridge University Press, 1995.
[250] William Strachey, *Historie of Travell*: 70f., 79.
[251] ibid.: 81.

with the newfound "barbarians" far off Europe's shores. Thus, knowledge (or what was perceived as such) of earlier travelers like Smith was molded together with new observations, which, in order to be digestible to stay-at-home Europeans, were made more vivid and credible by drawing analogies to Europe's own "barbarians". Where own observation does not suffice for understanding, interpreters can help. The narrator gains much information, for example, on Powhatan and his tribe from "Kempes an Indian who died the last year of the scurvy at Jamestown, after he had dwelt with us almost one whole year."[252] Staying with the English has obviously extolled a high price, for it is not known that Indians died of scurvy among their own people. Even though the natives drink only clear water and are, in several chapters, accused of idleness, yet they manage to survive on what nature offers them and on what they plant, whereas the English and even Indians who choose to live with them struggle to survive. This instance is a small but subversive comment on English civilization and technological as well as spiritual "magic" which the narrator reiterates throughout the narrative.

The same reiteration is necessary, it seems, to convince readers of other commodities besides provisions. The narrator claims he need not elaborate on Virginia's riches since others have already done that: "It shall not fall here so well at large to particulate, the bounds, estate, customs, and commodities, of [Virginia], [...] as it is already set forth and expressed to public view, both in English and Latin, by Theodor de Bry, and Mr. Hariot, who was a planter there one whole year."[253] In spite of this, a long chapter is devoted to commodities. One cannot but notice that descriptions of the most precious commodities, such as gold, silver, or spices, are mentioned but carefully, the belief in their existence usually based on conjecture. Virginia's rivers

> wash from the rocks such glistering tinctures, that the ground in some places seems as gilded, where both the rocks and the earth are so splendent to behold, that very good judgments would perhaps be persuaded they contained more than probabilities, sure it is that some minerals have been found.

In the same vein, Strachey is at pains to elaborate the riches Virginia may yield yet tempers high hopes with hints that, in many cases, expectations have yet to prove true: "Besides the assurance of minerals, concerning which we do already hear the Indians talk [...] all we must submit to more clear discoveries."[254]

An entire chapter of the first book is devoted to commodities to prove "how this country is not so naked of commodity nor wretched of provision fit for the

---

[252] William Strachey, *Historie of Travell*: 61.
[253] ibid.: 37.
[254] ibid.: 34, 49.

sustenance of mankind, as some ignorantly imagine and others have falsely reported." And even though it is admitted that "albeit our ships (some will object) now returning from thence, yearly come freighted home only yet with certain precious woods," the narrator reminds critics of Virginia that it took the Spanish some time, too, "until they found out the mines, as may we (we doubt nothing) in the heart and bosom of [Virginia]." This opening statement of future riches is followed by a detailed catalogue of natural resources; some animals are only suspected to be there, but unlike in the case of mines, the author is cautious not to claim what he cannot prove: "Lions I will not positively affirm that the country has [them] since our people never saw any."[255] In terms of mines the author is much more positive: "For minerals we will promise nothing but the hope of which [...] the mountains cannot be doubted, but that in them many sorts will be found", and a silver mine is known to have been discovered by a "Helvetian". Unfortunately, "the said Helvetian died of a burning fever, and with him the knowledge of that mine, which in his lifetime he would not [...] reveal."

Mineral riches seem to be tantalizingly close in Virginia, even known to exist, as in the case of the "Helvetian"; yet the lowlands have not yet yielded anything but "glistening" rivers, and so hope and expectations turn towards the mountains, stretched into an area not yet explored and therefore suitable to keep up hopes. "Apparent proofs of natural riches"[256] have to stand in for the failure to ship any of them to England as visible proof. Virginia nevertheless remains an earthly paradise in the *Historie of Travell*, whereas in the earlier *True Reportory*, Strachey had been more straightforward concerning the colony's hardships. The tone of the *Historie of Travell* is completely in line with previous and later narratives which extolled on the natural beauty, abundance, and paradisaic state of the land. "This part [of Virginia] is not mountainous, we sometimes meet with pleasant plains, small rising hills, and fertile valleys, [...] all watered conveniently with brooks [...] other plains there are few, but only where the savages inhabit, but all overgrown with trees and woods, being a plain wilderness, as God first ordained it."[257]

Compared to the *True Reportory*, Strachey's second report from America is an extensive, yet "conservative" text in that it repeats images, terminology, and argumentative strategies out of a standardized pool of narrative items found in much official writing, yet very rarely in instances of private communication. The *Historie of Travell* describes Virginia as an earthly paradise awaiting the English; there is no longer talk of an "unwholesome, sickly air", "marish ground", moskitoes, or dying settlers. Instead, we learn that the land is "pleasant"; small rising

---

[255] William Strachey, *Historie of Travell*: 117, 124f.
[256] ibid.: 131f.
[257] ibid.: 39.

hills and pleasant brooks add up to an American *locus amoenus*, and of course the mountains "contain more than probabilities" in terms of gold and silver. Strachey also introduces the *vacuum domicilium* argument as a justification for taking up Indian land, rounding up the picture of an edenic America peopled with barbarians awaiting Europe's blessings and a "plain wilderness" waiting for a skillful gardener.

7.1.7. Robert Johnson. *The New Life of Virginea*

Robert Johnson began his second narrative about early America after *Nova Britania* in the same tone which characterizes Strachey's *Historie of Travell*. The first English settlers were admitted "a large country to inhabit" by the "barbarous King Powhatan", and the natives "brought them such relief as they had", even though the narrator makes haste to add that their own provisions, brought from England, thrived wonderfully, and consequently the settlers "wrote letters home in praise of the country, and laboured their friends to come thither."[258] To underscore such a positive development of the settlement, the author launches a catalogue of commodities linked to the settlers' activities in obtaining them: "They cut down [...] black walnut tree, spruce and cedar [...] they got rich furs, dying stuff, minerals and iron ore, [...] they planted orange trees [and] corn." The whole description of commodities is arranged to support these previous claims that everything is there and just needs "art and industry" to make use of nature, a feat the Indians obviously had not accomplished in the eyes of the English.

The joyful news "caused many willing minds to adventure their mon[ey], to furnish out a fleet of 9 good ships", whose passengers, however, seem to have been of a lesser sort: They were "bad and evil affected for the most part before they went thence; so being landed, and wanting restraint, they displayed their condition in all kind of looseness." In the end, the little colony is ruined, "our people starved" and "the poor Indians by wrongs and injuries were made our enemies."[259]

It is interesting to note this last fact, for usually Indian "treachery" was at least added to the reproach of having mistreated the Indians as an explanation why they turned against the English. The narrator claims that the "wicked impes" who proved so unable to further the colony, "writing thence, or being returned back, to cover their lewdness, [they] do fill men's ears with false reports of their miserable

---

[258] Robert Johnson. *The New Life of Virginea*. Facsimile Reprint. Amsterdam and New York: Da Capo Press, 1971 B3^v.
[259] ibid.: C1^r, C1^v.

and perilous life in Virginia."[260] Even though new supplies and new discipline arrive under Sir Thomas Gates, the narrator remains conscious of the threat of famine. He seeks to gloss it over with yet another descriptive passage enumerating the commodities of Virginia, available in "endless abundance. [...] And for the last and main objection of food, it cannot be denied by any one of reason, but with their now diligent planting and sowing of corn (whereof they have two harvests in a summer), the plentiful fishing here, the store of fowls and fruits of the earth [...] that this objection too [...] is utterly removed."[261]

Here, description serves as a rhetorical device more than anything else to refute charges that all is not well in the colony. The narrative passages, again, cannot but mention the rumors of famine and ruin in the colony that must have circulated in England. Logic and truth force authors of even the most glowing narratives to address the central issue of famine which stands in stark contrast to the standard attributes of Virginia, natural bounty and God's favor. This contradiction is often solved rhetorically rather than logically, especially in promotional pamphlets such as Ralph Hamor's or Robert Johnson's. By opposing charges of ruin with descriptive passages of Virginia's abundance in commodities, the former rumors are explained away because famine cannot persist in the face of such abundance for very long. To prove his point, the narrator also uses the rhetorically elaborate persuasive strategy of saying: "It cannot be denied by [...] reason that..." success of the infant colonies is just around the corner when in fact the colonists died daily of famine and fever in such a "healthful climate" and "endless abundance." This rhetorical model was first established for the early American exploration report by Thomas Hariot in his *Briefe and True Report* and was subsequently used whenever the colonial present was so far from promising that rhetoric, rather than facts, had to speak in America's favor.

Towards the end of the narrative, an outlook for the colony's future begins with dangers that have to be reckoned with, and here, at last, Indian "treachery" is mentioned, whereas in the look back on the colony's earliest days, it was said that the natives had been turned against the English because of mistreatment and injustice. Now, the narrator admonishes would-be leaders and settlers of the colony: "Your first conflict is from your savage enemies the natives of the country, who as you know are neither strong nor many; their strongest forces are sleights and treachery, more to be wearily prevented than much to be feared." After a long and elaborate appeal to the undertakers of colonial settlements to keep their faith in Virginia, the narrator comes once again back to his principal purpose, which is to

---

[260] Robert Johnson. *The New Life of Virginea*: C2^r.
[261] ibid.: C3^r, C3^v.

advertise Virginian settlement and its future potential while garnishing these material aspects with the gracious act of converting the natives.

> It has been already declared to the world in sundry discourses, containing sufficient encouragement to men of understanding, and therefore not needful here to lay out again, the undoubted certainty of minerals, the rich and commodious means for shipping, and other materials of great use. [...] And besides all which things, that nature has already seated there, the soil and climate is so apt and fit for industrious minds [that] no country under heaven can go beyond it.[262]

With this last quote, Johnson sums up the commonplaces reiterated in almost all "official" New Word reports – at least in those intended for publication and subjected to official censorship as well as marketability. It helped that Johnson could already quote "sundry discourses" which had said the same things about America before his narrative, thus adding further authority to *The New Life of Virginia* as well as establishing New World stereotypes even more firmly in the European imagination. What is more, the narrator feels free to leave out discussion of mineral riches, shipping goods, and healthful climate but then immediately mentions these issues again. All in all, the rhetoric Johnson applies, the careful reiteration and affirmation of New World commonplaces and strategies of persuasion are signs of a narrative anxiety to fail at glossing over early America.

7.1.8. Ralph Hamor. *A True Discourse of the Present State of Virginia*

Ralph Hamor states at the very beginning that he published his little treatise so that readers "might thereby be moved to join with others right worthily disposed, to become a hearty and devoted furtherer of an action so noble."[263] He adds that his material was first gathered during his residence in Virginia "for my own use and benefit", but since he saw that his fellow Englishmen needed to be so heavily encouraged and persuaded to support the colonizing enterprise, he decided to publish it: "Such is the perverseness of mankind, such their incredulity of every thing, save what their eyes tell them to be true", that it was necessary, even though there "should be no end of writing" [i.e. reports from Virginia], to add his voice to the proponents of Virginia. This is something rather new; it is an inversion of Robert

---

[262] Robert Johnson, *The New Life of Virginea*: G3ᵛ.
[263] Ralph Hamor. *A True Discourse of the Present State of Virginia and the successe of the affaires there till the 18 of June, 1614. Together with a relation of the severall English townes and forts, the assured hopes of that countrie and the peace concluded with the Indians. The Christening of Powhatans daughter and her mariage with an English-Man. Written by Ralphe Hamor the yonger, late Secretarie in that Colony* [London, 1615]. Facsimile reprint: New York: Da Capo Press, 1971. Dedication to Sir Thomas Smith. Not paginated.

Johnson's technique of expressedly leaving things out of his narrative because they are already widely known. Hamor adds force and authority to his narrative the opposite way, by placing it in a long line of narratives more or less saying the same thing: that America is a superbly promising place for English interests, both public and private. The results of these techniques, expressed ellipsis as well as conscious reiteration/addition, are the same.

In an epistle to the reader, the narrator once more elaborates on the modesty and credibility of his narrative, "a naked and unstudied discourse; I acknowledge, without notes reserved but in memory."[264] The religious concern for Virginia is unfolded at length:

> When these poor heathens shall be brought to entertain the honor of the name [of God], they shall break out and cry with rapture of so inexplicable mercy: Blessed be the King and Prince of England, and blessed be the English nation, and blessed for ever be the most high God, possessor of heaven and earth, that sent these English as angels to bring such glad tidings among us.

Apart from furthering the gospel in the New World, the author also promises to explain "the full unstaid repertory of every accident whereof even from his beginning, together with the causes of the backwardness in prosperity thus long." Proselytizing for the glory of God and the English nation as well as a defense of the history and success of the venture so far: Even before the narrative begins, Hamor's treatise sets forth clearly the intentions of the colonizing effort, keeps readers and would-be investors tightly gripped with the impending material rewards of the enterprise, and the narrator presents himself and his treatise as highly credible because it is an eyewitness report: The author's "filial duty" to his Father has "compelled me unwillingly thereunto, [...] merely because I have been *Oculatus testis*". His "poor relation, rich only in truth (as I shall clearly justify myself by eyewitness also)" is intended to further "the glory of God, conversion of those infidels, and the honor of our King and country." The claim of a "naked and unstudied discourse" may be seen as a *captatio benevolentiae*; it also helped to fend off charges of invention and embellishment often suspected in travel narratives. Paired with a "filial duty" to God and the eyewitness claim, these introductory phrases lend an authority to this glowingly positive narrative which it needed just as much as many others did.

The narrative begins with a flashback to the very first years of the colony, especially the "five years intestine war with the revengeful implacable Indians." Now, "a firm peace has [...] been concluded" with neighboring tribes as well as Powhatan's tribe. This is a special asset to the colony as now the English "shall be

---

[264] Ralph Hamor, *True Discourse*. To the Reader. Not paginated.

furnished with what commodities their country yields, and have all the help they may afford us." The latter aspect is especially important because Hamor hints that the majority of settlers are "for the most part no more sensible than beasts", whereas the Indians are "easily taught and may by lenity and fair usage be brought, being naturally though ingenious, yet idly given, to be no less industrious, nay to exceed our English."[265] Still, tensions remained. Powhatan had taken not only Englishmen hostage, but also stolen "many swords, pieces and other tools [...] though no use to him, he would not redeliver." It is revealing in this respect that, in the "official" narrative of this incident, they were called "hostages" of Powhatan by the English; in a letter, the governor Sir Thomas Dale wrote that these men had run away to Powhatan. The news that Powhatan was expected to redeliver these items as well as the hostages "was unwelcome to him [...] partly for the love he bore to the men his prisoners, of whom though with us they were unapt for any employment, he made great use; and those swords, and pieces of ours (which though no use to him) it delighted him to view, and look upon."[266]

The passage quoted above is revealing regarding the English hostages. We must believe that they applied themselves quite usefully to their tasks under Powhatan's rule. We also hear that they had proved quite useless workers under the colony's rule. When Captain Argall sailed up the river towards Powhatan's seat to speed up the ransoming process, "some of the men which he [i.e. Powhatan] returned (as they promised) ran to him again."[267] Winning Indians for the English side seemed to be more difficult than winning Englishmen was for the Indians. The fact that Englishmen preferred to go native testifies to an underlying fear that the American wilderness might release in civilized Europeans what they feared most: natural desires without restraint, making these men as barbarous and uncivilized as the Indians were in English eyes. The concept of barbarism, it should be added, was formed in Europe long before the European discovery of America and provided Europeans with a negative definition of that they wished not to be, or to become.[268]

This little episode hints at another deep-lying theme in early new World travel reports: The quest for an earthly paradise and the European yearning for a state of prelapsarian innocence was forever tinged with the threat of moral as well as physical degeneration. Hamor is not the only one to hint at this threat; the question of criolian degeneracy would become so important a topic that in the eight-

---

[265] Ralph Hamor, *True Discourse*: 2.
[266] ibid.: 5f.
[267] ibid.: 7.
[268] On this topic, cf. James Axtell. "The White Indians of Colonial America." *William and Mary Quarterly*, 3rd ser., 32 (1975): 55-88.

eenth century an essay contest was staged in France whether the discovery of America had been beneficial for mankind or not. Possible moral and physical degeneracy caused by "going native" was at the heart of the negative assessments voiced in the contributions. The debate has remained with American literature ever since. The Lost Colony of Roanoke owes much of its fascination to this issue but the possibility that the colonists had simply blended into surrounding Indian tribes excluded the Roanoke colony from American beginnings.[269]

Hamor makes adequate use of the marriage of John Rolfe to Pocahontas within his narrative strategy:

> The greatest, and many enemies and disturbers of our proceedings, and that which has hitherto deterred our people to address themselves into those parts have been only two: enmity with the naturals, and the bruit of famine: One of these two [...] I have already removed [by citing this marriage as an example of future racial harmony], and shall as easily take away the other.

It is admitted that there has been famine among the colonists, yet it was "occasioned merely by misgovernment, idleness, and faction." Now, the narrator claims, "there is plenty of food", the main reason for this betterment being that communal labor and keeping a communal store had been abandoned for the higher incentives of independent labor. It is a nice little comment on the efforts of a communal enterprise, which had to be abandoned almost right after the beginning in Virginia and was to prove equally unsuitable in New England as well, but for different reasons.

What is more, this textual strategy aims at "writing away" what endangers the colony rhetorically: "One of these two [dangers, namely enmity with the natives and famine] I have already removed" – thus summing up the sense behind narrating the Powhatan and Pocahontas affair – "and shall just as easily take away the other" by describing how a man might make his living in Virginia. This passage remains utterly prospective. The narrator discourages idle men from removing to Virginia, for "they have been the occasions of the manifold imputations and disgraces which Virginia has innocently undergone through their defaults." Far from saying that the country is too barren and life there too harsh to sustain idle men, the narrator seeks to deter such "ill livers from addressing themselves thither" because Virginia "is a country too worthy for them, and altogether disconsonant to

---

[269] On the degeneracy thesis, see e.g. Roy H. Pearce. *Savagism and Civilization*. London: University of California Press, 1988; Bernard W. Sheehan. *Savagism and Civility: Indians and Englishmen in Colonial Virginia*. Cambridge: Cambridge University Press, 1980. On Beginnings and suitable and less suitable ones for social origins and mythmaking, see Edward Said. *Beginnings: Intention and Method*. London: Granta, 1997.

their natures."[270] Here, the text obviously grapples with the problem of presenting the Virginia colony as an evolving success while paying tribute to rumors that life there is not as easy as could have been expected from previous and glowing reports.

At the beginning of the narrative, in the address to the reader, Virginia is asked to yield "out of those great plenties and havings which God has lent thee to spare a little-little portion to the full settling and finishing up"[271] of the English settlement: great plenties of which only a "little-little portion" would be necessary to sustain the English. Once again American nature is personified, though in this image it is not the virgin land awaiting the romantic and heroic male explorer. Instead, Virginia resembles Ceres, the Roman goddess of agriculture and is a benign, nurturing caregiver to the still male, but much less heroic European colonists in the New World. The picture of Virginia and the colony in Hamor's *True Discourse* is a very ambiguous one, and the narrative consequently labors under the pressure of coherently telling a promising story while remaining credible. The shift from personifying America as a virgin [land] to be conquered by powerful Englishmen to a caregiver asked to spare a "little-little portion" of her riches to sustain the explorers is part of the picture.

Glowing propaganda of a difficult cause is not easy, witnessed in such contradictions or necessary shifts in imagery as mentioned above. In order to find a way out of this dilemma, the narrator invites only those English to come to Virginia who "either through crosses in this world, or wrecked rents, or else great charge of children and family live here [i.e. in England] [in] extreme poverty: For those this country [Virginia] has present remedy: Every such person, so well disposed to adventure thither shall soon find the difference between their own and that country." Those will live happily, "as many do there, who I am sure will never return."[272] The effect of such a limited invitation has to be, of course, positive, for those who have lost everything in England can hardly encounter more hardships in Virginia than they could if they remained in England. After so much talk of food, which in essence centered around corn and corn bread, the narrator begins a description of commodities to be found in Virginia.

> Now, least any man should yet rest discouraged because as yet no mention is made of any other provision of victuals save only of bread-corn, which grant[ed ...] will afford but a bare and miserable living, I think there is no man so ignorant to conceive that such a main continent as is Virginia, boundless, for ought we have discovered, and so goodly rivers, nowhere else to be paralleled, should

---

[270] Ralph Hamor, *True Discourse*: 16-19.
[271] Ralph Hamor, *True Discourse*. To the reader: Not paginated.
[272] Ralph Hamor, *True Discourse*: 19f.

be more barren of cattle, fish, and fowl, than other lands, assuredly they are not.[273]

A pure catalogue of wild animals follows. Allusions to plenty are interspersed with comparatives: "Wild turkeys much bigger than our English" or "wild pigeons, in winter beyond number or imagination, [as I] myself have seen three or four hours together flock in the air, so thick that even they have shadowed the sky from us." Consequently, after such enumerations interspersed with allusions to enormous quantity and superior quality, the narrator asks: "Why should any man that has his limbs [...] so much as dream of starving?" To help render this a rhetorical question, the superlative form of Virginian attributes is a grammatical strategy employed for this end: "I myself know no one country yielding without art or industry so many fruits [or] berries" and other naturally growing food.[274]

A narrative passage, inserted after the long description of Virginia's commodities, deals with the time since the arrival of Governor Sir Thomas Dale. He went to Jamestown "where the most company were, and their daily and usual works bowling in the streets, [...] the houses ready to fall upon their heads."[275] Strong laws are introduced, the narrator goes on, "so as if the law should have not restrained by execution, I see not how the utter subversion and ruin of the colony should have been prevented", and deserters to the Indians and even to the Spanish arch-enemy are mentioned, too. The latter were rediscovered by Indians, "hired by us to hunt them down to receive their deserts [i.e. punishment]."[276] The immediate juxtaposition of descriptive passages about America's riches, clothed in a rhetoric of exuberant praise, with narrative passages dealing with human failure and even desertion to the Spanish shows the painful dichotomy characterizing many early American experience. While descriptive passages were devoted to establishing and perpetuating an image of a land of ease, abundance, and pleasure, narrative passages were the *locus* for American colonial reality often marked by a deep chasm between expectations and experience.

---

[273] Ralph Hamor, *True Discourse*: 20.
[274] ibid.: 21.
[275] In *A Map of Virginia*, John Smith reported much the same impression of Jamestown's early settlers. For an interesting possible explanation of the desolate situation of the earliest settlers, see Karen Ordahl Kupperman. "Death and Apathy in Early Jamestown." *Journal of American History*, 66.1 (June 1979): 24-40. As a reason for the frequently observed cases of apathy and death in early Jamestown (in narratives by Strachey, Hamor, and Wood, among others) Kupperman suggests that an unsupplemented maize diet might have caused pellagra, a niacin deficiency ailment which made the sufferer anorexic and apathetic.
[276] Ralph Hamor, *True Discourse*: 26f. Again, Englishmen who had gone "native" were mentioned in quite a few early English narratives. Cf. James Axtell. "The White Indians of Colonial America." *William and Mary Quarterly*, 3rd ser., 32 (1975): 55-88.

It is especially interesting to see how the usual allusions to precious metals are handled in this respect:

> I have purposely omitted the relation of the country commodities, which every former treatise has abundantly, the hope of the better mines, [...] perfectly discovered, and made trial of, and surely of these things I cannot make so ample relation, as others, who in the discovery of those affaires have been [...] more conversant.

This may be understood as the narrator's elaborate evasion of decisive information on precious metals, for the failure of having "discovered" them. Obviously, however, talk about these commodities was expected in narratives of Virginia, and the narrator simply refers the reader to other texts which have "perfectly discovered" these things – or just discovered the hope of finding such mines?[277]

In a letter which is appended to the main narrative, Sir Thomas Dale writes to a minister in England about Virginia that "no country of the world affords more assured hopes of infinite riches, which both by my people's discovery and the relation of such savages, whose fidelity we have often found assured me." Virginia's riches are a promise rather than a fact; the whole honorable, glorious and fruitful character of the enterprise is only projected, not proved. In order to support hopes and expectations, the natives, who at other times were usually described as treacherous, function as witnesses to support what the English alone may not credibly maintain.

There is an obvious rift in the logic of the "official" narrative by Hamor and also in the letter. Hamor's Virginia is abundantly rich in natural resources but will satisfy only those who have lost everything in England anyway and can expect no worse. There is abundance of every kind, but not for the taking; only those willing to work hard will gain access to it. On another sheet, however, the narrator claims that husbandmen in Virginia will have to work considerably less for the same yield than in England. Balancing the widespread expectations among Englishmen of American abundance with the early experiences of hardship and starvation results in this split character of the *True Discourse*. Whenever Indians are necessary to assuage English fears of attacks or lack of material rewards, they make good and credible witnesses. But the threat of mistrust, rebellion and violence in general pervades several passages of the narrative. The generally rosy outlook which the *True Discourse* is at pains to keep up is counterbalanced by the fragile peace and prosperity of the young colony, which forces its Governor Dale to stay on in

---

[277] Ralph Hamor, *True Discourse*: 34f.

Virginia after his time is over "rather than see [...] these poor people I have the charge of ruined."[278]

In the *True Discourse*, as in narratives like Ralph Lane's or Thomas Hariot's, the narrative passages relate what happened, albeit from the English point of view, and risk painting a less than glowing picture of the colony's situation. The descriptive passages, however, remain strikingly stereotypical throughout much of the early texts about Virginia: Material riches are promised, mines might still be there, the animals breed more fertilely than in Europe, and the soil promises abundant yields of corn, wheat, or silk grass. Indian women are "comely"[279] and, in the case of Pocahontas, can be Europeanized sufficiently to provide a (however utopian) model of interracial harmony. Description, accordingly, is the part in early American travel narratives which maintains images of abundance and harmony, overshadowed by hints at violence and unrest in the narrative passages against which descriptions of "classic" features of America are inserted to keep the balance tipped to the positive side.

7.1.9. Edward Waterhouse. *A Declaration of the State of the Colony in Virginia*

Waterhouse's narrative was written in the style of a sermon under the impression of the so-called Virginia massacre of 1622. In the foreword to the Virginia Company, the narrator claims to

> present you with these my poor labours, the collection of the truth thereof, drawn from the relation of some of those that were beholders of that tragedy [...] also from the letters sent you by the governor and other gentlemen of quality [...] that so the world may see that it was not the strength of a professed enemy that brought this slaughter on them, but contrived by the perfidious treachery of a false-hearted people. [...] The discovery of their falsehood will prove (as shall appear by this treatise following) many ways advantageable to us.

The *Declaration* begins by mentioning the "many and sundry treatises written of Virginia, and the commodities thereof." Despite of this, the narrator intends to "sum up the benefits of that country" again, "partly because they daily increase by new discoveries made" and because readers usually do not gather all that has been

---

[278] Ralph Hamor, *True Discourse*: 58f.
[279] ibid.: 39.

written about a subject and thus "gain but a lame and parcel-knowledge."[280] Like Hamor, Waterhouse consciously adds his voice and view to an already considerable body of writing, as if by mere addition the success of the colony could be furthered. Reiterating terminology and qualifications already familiar to an English audience was part of that strategy. The terms fruitful, spacious, rich, temperate, healthful, abounding, replenished, or goodly are used liberally in almost every promotional English report from early America. The following passage from Waterhouse's narrative contains all of these in one sentence: "This spacious and fruitful country of Virginia is (as is generally known to all) naturally rich, and exceedingly well watered, very temperate, and healthful to the inhabitants, abounding with as many natural blessings, and replenished with as many goodly woods [...] as any country in the world is known to afford." The geographical situation promises, according to the belief of the day, "the richest commodities of most parts of the earth."

Concerning food supplies, there "is no place better [than Virginia]", and the narrator launches into a lengthy catalogue of different kinds of timber, fish, fowl, game, fruit, and nuts. Further signs of Virginia's astounding fertility are the increase in height, weight, and fertility of cattle and horses. Virginia "out of certain advertisements so often reiterated from thence, as well as by the relations of hundreds now yearly coming and going [is a] country which nothing but ignorance can think ill of." It promises "richer mines of the best and most desired metals [...] when the colony shall be of sufficient strength to open and defend them."[281]

The years of 1619-1621 saw, according to the narrator, "forty-two sail of ships with 3570 men and women for plantation", and the governor and treasurer of the colony wrote to England that salt works, iron works, and glass works were established, plenty of corn sowed, the quantity of tobacco "restrained" yet the quality "increased", vines and mulberry trees planted and a whole range of other crops planted. An inn "for the better entertainment of newcomers" was planned in Jamestown.[282] One description of how things prosper in Virginia and how nature seems to help is followed by another. The place where iron works have been set up is so "fitting for that purpose as if nature had applied herself to the wish and direction of the workman"; vines grow and prosper, as do the silk worms – a project that would soon be discontinued for lack of profit.[283]

---

[280] Edward Waterhouse. *A Declaration of the State of the Colony in Virginia [...] With a Relation of the Barbarous Massacre in the Time of Peace and League, Treacherously Executed by the Native Infidels.* Facsimile Reprint. Amsterdam and New York: Da Capo Press, 1970: 2.
[281] Edward Waterhouse, *Declaration*: 4f.
[282] ibid.: 7.
[283] ibid.: 10.

Unlike previous narratives, however, Waterhouse's seizes on the 1622 massacre as an incentive to rout out the Indians. The Indians launched their attack early one morning and, in the end, killed 347 men, women and children, according to the narrator. Further details of how corpses were cut and torn apart, some parts carried away, and even those English slain brutally with which the Indians had established personal relations added to the terror: They did "so many barbarous despights and foul scorns after [to some dead bodies of the English] as are unbefitting to be heard by any civil ear." It is interesting to note that the narrator expresses his wonder over the fact that the natives could plot and execute this massacre "at one instant of time, though our several plantations were a hundred and forty miles up one river on both sides." Yet the passage immediately following claims that the natives lack any recognizable political or social organization on a larger scale, for "these wild naked natives live not in great numbers together but dispersed [...] and many miles distant from one another"[284], making the scale of the attack even more shocking. A Jamestown resident's report in the winter of 1622 put these 347 deaths in another perspective:

> There having been, as it is thought, not fewer than ten thousand souls transported thither, there are not, through the aforenamed abuses and neglects [of the colony's administration and settlers], above two thousand of them at the present to be found alive. [...] Instead of a plantation, it will shortly get the name of a slaughterhouse.[285]

Another source suggests that, unlike Waterhouse's narrative puts it, the attack was not exactly a surprise. The father of Governor Wyatt wrote to his son in Virginia about the massacre, and the letter testifies to the fact that, unlike public opinion had it, the so-called massacre was not an inexplicable, irrational and unprovoked act.[286]

The narrator mentions the "instigation of the devil" as a reason for the attack, and "the daily fear possessed them that in time we by our growing continually upon them, would dispossess them of this country as they had been formerly of the West Indies by the Spaniard produced this bloody act." As a consequence of the attack, the narrator uses a medical analogy saying that in the end

---

[284] Edward Waterhouse, *Declaration*: 17-19.
[285] Quoted after: Francis Jennings. *The Invasion of America: Indians, Colonialism, and the Cant of Conquest*. Chapel Hill, North Carolina: University of North Carolina Press, 1975: 79. Cf. also Karen Ordahl Kupperman. "Death and Apathy in Early Jamestown." *Journal of American History*, 66.1 (June 1979): 24-40: 35. "In 1622, the massacre killed 347 colonists, but roughly 3000 colonists had died of other causes in the preceding three years, presumably from malnutrition above all."
[286] J. Frederick Fausz and John Kukla. "A Letter of Advice to the Governor of Virginia, 1624." *William and Mary Quarterly*, 3rd ser., 34 (1977): 104-129.

this must needs be for the good of the plantation" through the "loss of this blood to make the body more healthful. [...] Our hands which before were tied with gentleness and fair usage are now set at liberty by the treacherous violence of the savages, not untying the knot, but cutting it so that we [...] may now by right of war and law of nations invade the country, and destroy them who sought to destroy us; whereby we shall enjoy their cultivated places [which is a considerable advantage because now] their cleared grounds in all their villages [...] shall be inhabited by us.[287]

Another "positive" side effect of the massacre is the fact that "the way of conquering them [with the sword] is easier than of civilizing them by fair means, for they are a rude, barbarous, and naked people, scattered in small companies, which are helps to victory, but hindrances to civility." To conclude, the narrator suggests an infinite number of ways to destroy the natives, such as driving them to their enemies and making use of the factions and enmities between and within tribes; destruction of fishing weirs, burning of villages and corn fields, putting bloodhounds on their tracks - all to show that, as the narrator quotes the French proverb, "ill luck is good for something."[288] Waterhouse's narrative does away with "fair usage" and suggests subjecting the Indians once and for all. The "glorious" attempts at bringing the gospel to the New World came to an end with the massacre of 1622 and Waterhouse's narrative. Colonial policy would soon concentrate increasingly on driving the natives farther into the interior as English settlements and land usage extended inland from the Eastern seaboard. Still, instead of closing with a catalogue of Virginia's commodities, the narrator adds a list of those colonists killed in the attack on various English plantations to the end of the *Declaration*.

7.1.10. Richard Frethorne. *Letter from Virginia*

Frethorne's letter is a rare account of a simple man's situation in early Virginia and a rare extant piece of private communication. He lived in Martin's Hundred, about 10 miles away from Jamestown. This letter, dated 1623, of a poor laborer may be read to complement (or rather, contradict) the tone of the official tracts which were sent to London from Virginia and were usually written as promotion. While someof those admit that the climate is not very healthy during the summer but hurry up to make up for this disadvantage, Frethorne writes to his parents that

---

[287] Edward Waterhouse, *Declaration*: 22f.
[288] ibid.: 24-26.

the country "causes much sickness, as the scurvy and the bloody flux and diverse other diseases, which make the body very poor and weak. And when we are sick, there is nothing to comfort us."[289]

The shortage of food, obviously still a central problem in the colony sixteen years after its foundation, is at the center of the letter. Frethorne contradicts tales of natural abundance, claiming that "since I came out of the ship I never ate anything but peas and loblollie (that is, water gruel). As for deer or venison, I never saw any since I came into this land. There is indeed some fowl, but we are not allowed to go and get it, but must work hard both early and late for a mess of water gruel and a mouthful of bread and beef." The vicinity of hostile tribes does not help the overall picture either: "We live in fear of the enemy every hour [...] for our plantation is very weak, by reasons of the death and sickness of our company." As a consequence, the rest of the narrative is a pitiful obituary and a plea for his parents' compassion and help. Of the twenty labourers who arrived with Frethorne, half of them are dead by the time of this letter; and "we look every hour when two more should go. Yet there came some four other men yet to live with us, of which there is but one alive, and our Lieutenant is dead, and his father, and his brother [...] and yet we are just 32 to fight against 3,000 [i.e. Indians] if they should come."

Frethorne's account mirrored the strong impact the "Virginia Massacre" of the previous year must have had on the settlers; yet there is reason to doubt the number of 3,000 fighting Indians among the neighbouring tribes after sicknesses and frequent attacks in retaliation for the "Massacre". Still, the memory of the sudden and concerted attack, together with frequent deaths, sickness, and famine, combined to form a sad report of early Virginia: "There is nothing to be gotten here but sickness and death." The frequent claim that the climate "agreed well with English constitutions"[290] and made the colonists strong and healthy is countered here: "I am not a quarter so strong as I was in England." Frethorne's letter must have been an example of the "slanderous reports" of dissatisfied colonists that the "official" narratives sought to silence. As early as 1612, John Smith mentioned that reports like Frethorne's existed, and also explained the reasons for such dissatisfaction with Virginia:

> They [i.e. the colonists] found not English cities, nor such fair houses, [...] neither such plenty of gold and silver and dissolute liberty as they expected. [They] had little or no care of anything but to pamper their bellies. [...] For the country

---

[289] Richard Frethorne. "Letter from Virginia." In: Myra Jehlen, ed. *The English Literatures of America*. London: Routledge, 1997: 123-125.
[290] John Smith. "A Map of Virginia": 143.

was to them a misery, a ruin, a death, a hell, and their reports here and their own actions there according.[291]

Frethorne's letter shows that English discourse about North America was a contested field of narrative dominance. This feature seems to have been central to European contact with North America, as we have already seen in the narratives of Hariot or the Frobisher voyages, for example. Hariot claimed that "there have been diverse and variable reports with some slanderous and shameful speeches bruited abroad by many that returned from thence [i.e. Virginia]. [...] Which reports have not done a little wrong to many that otherwise would have also favoured and adventured [i.e. invested] in the action."[292] As a consequence, Hariot claims to have written his narrative, which has remained the single most influential and esteemed narrative of the Roanoke voyages and a classic of early American literature. Nothing is known about Frethorne's fate, but his narrative, though much less influential that Hariot's, tells a very different story than the dominant promotional narratives of its time.

7.1.11. Jamestown: Epilogue

Some decades later, visitors from England reported home what the colony looked like, and what success had come out of the often reiterated task to convert the "heathens". John Clayton wrote in a letter to "A Doctor of Physik" about Virginia:

> I would now give you a further account of the country but that then my thoughts might be as wild as the place, that is all one continued wood, but take this in short: It is a place where plenty makes poverty, ignorance ingenuity, and covetousness causes hospitality that is thus: Every one covets so much and there is such vast extent of land that they spread so far they cannot manage well a hundredth part of what they have. Every one can live at ease and therefore they scorn and hate to work to advantage themselves, so are poor with abundance.[293]

The Anglican minister and university-trained naturalist John Banister reported about the Indians in the vicinity of English settlements that "amongst all this variety of food, nature has taught them to use of no other drink but water, so that to be drunk and swear is the only piece of civility these barbarous people have learned

---

[291] John Smith. "A Map of Virginia": 176.
[292] Thomas Hariot, *Briefe and True Report*: 9.
[293] John Clayton, "Letter". In: Richard Beale Davis, C. Hugh Holman and Louis D. Rubin, Jr., eds. *Southern Writing, 1585-1920*. New York: The Odyssey Press, 1970: 81.

from us Europeans." Lasting peace, too, would still be elusive were it not for trade and making the Indians covet what they neither knew nor needed before:

> The Indian trade [...] is, if rightly weighed and considered, our *vinculum pacis*, and the only means we have to live in quiet with them, for since there has been any way laid open for trade, and many things now are become absolutely necessary to the preservation of their lives which they wanted not before, because they never had them; if obstruction be made, so that they cannot supply their wants by barter, no marvel if they do it by force.[294]

Clayton's and Banister's reports serve as a sobering antidote for the early pious claims that voyages to and settlements in Virginia were noble ventures with the aim of saving Indian souls on the one hand, and promises of individual gain and social betterment through hard labor on the other hand.

7.2. Newfoundland, Four Decades after the Frobisher Voyages

7.2.1. Richard Whitbourne. *A Discourse and Discovery of New-Found-Land*

Like other authors of travel narratives before him, Whitbourne promises that "the following discourse will satisfy [those interested in the topic] if they will forgive the unhandsomeness of the form it is put into and look into the matter itself only." The "island of New-Found-Land" is "large, temperate and fruitful, the fruitfulness of it consisting not only in things of sustenance for those that shall inhabit it, but in many sorts of commodities likewise of good value and use to be transported. The natives in it are ingenuous and apt by discreet and moderate governments to be brought to obedience."[295]

The arguments in favor of a proposed settlement in Newfoundland are first, to find an outlet for England's surplus population; second, catching up with the Dutch in Atlantic fishing; enlarging the dominion of the English crown and third, "that which will crown the work", the advancement of God's glory by converting the natives. Interestingly, the narrator proposes settlements in the part of the "island" where no natives live, and they figure only marginally in this narrative that is as much a description of Newfoundland as a promotional pamphlet, promoting the first person narrator as a competent leading figure in Atlantic sailing and ex-

---
[294] *John Banister and His Natural History of Virginia, 1678-1692*. Ed. Joseph and Nesta Ewan. Urbana, Chicago, London: University of Illinois Press, 1970: 377, 385.
[295] Richard Whitbourne. *A Discourse and Discovery of New-Found-Land* [London, 1620]. Facsimile Reprint New York: Da Capo Press, 1971: B^v.

perience in Newfoundland. During the narrative, however, more motives appear: Newfoundland might serve as a privateering base to attack the Spanish fleet returning from the West Indies and South America; the region might also serve as a good basis for the discovery of a Northwest passage. Civilizing and converting the natives is only mentioned in passing after the initial emphasis on that motivation.

The narrative itself is entitled *A Relation of the New-Found-Land* and describes Newfoundland as "an island almost as spacious as Ireland" and most apt for Englishmen due to its geographic situation. "I shall not much need to commend the wholesome temperature of that country." The narrator also tells of the large number of fishing vessels from various European ports which rendezvous yearly at Newfoundland's shores. Thus, it may be assumed that, judging the number of Europeans ("many thousands of English, French, Portuguese and others") yearly visiting these shores, there already existed a considerable deal of familiarity with the coastal region and its climate, albeit only during the summer season. Newfoundland mainly served as a fishing region, and inland explorations were so scarce that neither much was known of the natives nor of the country itself. [296]

To further promote Newfoundland, the narrator dedicates long passages to the fertility of the soil and the abundance of flora and fauna; many commodities are to be had "without the labor of man's hand", yet if the land "were manured and husbanded" it would be even more profitable. The major part of the narrative is accordingly devoted to the benefits which might arise from this region once peopled with and worked by Englishmen. Whitbourne's narrative abounds with stereotypes of description which, perhaps surprisingly, appear in earlier narratives from Virginia and New England and would later reappear in descriptions of colonies as far from each other gegraphically as New York and the Carolinas. All of these regions are described with the ubiquitous passages on fertility, healthful climate, abundant nature, and prospects of mines. What is more, Newfoundlad, just like John Smith's New England in *A Description*, is a future paradise "if only" manured and brought to yield its riches by skilled Europeans. This way, present shortcomings in terms of material rewards, especially in precious metals and rich agricultural returns, are amended in advance by pointing to an assuredly glorious future.

7.2.2. George Calvert. *Letter to King Charles I*

George Calvert, Lord Baltimore, corrected such fatal misconceptions like Whitbourne's concerning the climate in Newfoundland. In the 1570s, we may recall,

---

[296] Richard Whitbourne, *Discourse*: D^r.

one of the Frobisher voyages was financed and equipped to establish a permanent English settlement in Newfoundland. The plan failed because the late summer brought forebodings of a severe winter, and the designated colonists lost heart and returned to England with the fleet. Nine years after Whitbourne's narrative, in 1629, George Calvert wrote to the King of England,

> I have found by too dearly bought experience which other men for their private interests always concealed from me, that from the midst of October to the midst of May there is a sad face of winter upon all this land, both sea and land so frozen for the greatest part of the time as they are not penetrable, no plant or vegetable thing appearing out of the earth until it be about the beginning of May, nor fish in the sea. Besides, the air [is] so intolerably cold [that] it is hardly to be endured. [...] My house has been a hospital all this winter, of 100 persons 50 sick at a time, myself being one, and nine or ten of them died.[297]

Like Frethorne's letter from Virginia, George Calvert's short account is one of the few examples of narratives without a promotional tinge, and both texts shed a very different light on the general image of America which narratives like Hariot's, Johnson's, or Strachey's had developed. Instead of catalogues of natural abundance, superlatives or allusions to paradise, these narratives tell of terrible hardships, a very unparadisaical climate, and hunger and sickness as the typical constituents of everyday life in the early English colonies in North America.

7.3. New England, 1620-1674

After the first series of voyages to the New England coast between 1602 and 1614, Puritan emigrants from England were the next travelers to these shores. Even though many of them came seeking a spiritual asylum rather than an earthly Eden or quick material gains, their narratives nevertheless feature many of the commonplaces found in most other English New World narratives as well: The propagandistic passages which lured ever more people to New England set the new settlers up for disappointments, as Thomas Dudley's letter (cf. chapter 7.3.2.) shows.

---

[297] George Calvert. "A Letter from Newfoundland." In Myra Jehlen, ed. *The English Literatures of America*. London: Routledge, 1997: 127.

7.3.1 Edward Winslow. *Good Newes from New England. A True Relation of Things very Remarkable at the Plantation of Plimoth in New England*

In the dedication, the narrator mentions the usual truth claims and other men's "vile and clamorous reports" and comes back to them and the reasons for writing his narrative at the end:

> When I first penned this discourse, I intended it chiefly for the satisfaction of my private friends; but since that time have been persuaded to publish the same. And the rather, because [people who came over to New England and who] were a strain to Old England that bred them [...] so, it is to be feared, will be no less to New England, in their vile and clamorous reports, because she would not foster them in their desired idle courses. [...] Thus I have made a true and full narration of the state of our plantation, and such things as were most remarkable therein since December, 1621.[298]

Winslow's attempt to counter "vile and clamorous reports" echoes Thomas Hariot's reports from "mouths of ignorance and slander" and shows that early American narratives were composed on a contested field of public discourse. Hostile native tribes in the vicinity of the New England settlements as well as recurring food shortages are serious problems which the narrator mentions. He often balances them with lengthy descriptive passages of natural beauty and abundance. Between the lines, however, the reader can learn that the settlements were still strongly dependent on reinforcements of people as well as goods and provisions from Old England. Nevertheless, the chances for successful Indian attacks were now significantly lower than at the beginning of the colony, Winslow claims: "Our number of men is increased, our town better fortified, and our store better victualled."

Winslow's text is characterized, like many other English New World travel narratives, by a peculiar shift back and forth between passages dealing with good progress of the settlements and passages dealing with native hostility, European ineptitude and famine: In this "so healthful and hopeful country", the English had "to mew up ourselves in our new-enclosed town; partly because our store was almost empty, and therefore [we] must seek out for our daily food, without which we could not long subsist; but especially for that thereby they would see us dismayed, and be encouraged to prosecute their malicious purposes."[299] We may

---

[298] Edward Winslow. *Good Newes from New England. A True Relation of Things Very Remarkable at the Plantation of Plimoth in New England.* [1624] Bedford, MA: Applewood Books, no date: 6, 57.
[299] ibid.: 12.

wish to remember that instructions to hide sick Englishmen from Indians and put on a face of military power were central to most early colonial ventures, as the example of the 1606 instructions for Virginia show: "Above all things do not advertise the killing of any of your men. [...] You shall do well also not to let them see or know of your sick men if you have any which may also encourage them to many enterprises."[300]

Contrary to the general assumption that the New England Puritan settlements were much more successful from the beginning than the ones in Virginia, Winslow's narrative reports the same difficulties of continually facing starvation and being wiped out by native tribes. And as in Virginia, early reports of natural abundance, a life of ease and promising material rewards were one reason for these difficulties:

> About the end of May, 1622 [...] our store of victuals was wholly spent, having lived long before with a bare and short allowance", one reason for this being that "certain amongst ourselves [had been] too prodigal in their writing and reporting of that plenty we enjoyed. [...] It may be said, if the country abound with fish and fowl in such measure as is reported, how could men undergo such measure of hardness, except through their own negligence? I answer, every thing must be expected in its proper season.[301]

In fact, the Indians were still the principal supplier of corn, which may be gathered out of several passages: "The savages, upon our motion, had planted much corn for us."[302] If the English in Plymouth had to "mew up" themselves and hide their weak state from Indians as best as they could, another English New England settlement fared even worse. In Plymouth, many Indians complained about the new settlement at Wessagusset, under the command of Thomas Weston, and the colonists' behaviour, as the narrator reported:

> We heard many complaints, both by the Indians, and some others of best desert amongst Master Weston's colony, how exceedingly their company abased themselves by indirect means, to get victuals from the Indians, who dwelt not far from them, fetching them wood and water and all for a meal's meat; whereas, in the meantime, they might with diligence have gotten enough to have served them three or four times. Others by night broke the earth and robbed the Indians' store; for which they had been publicly stocked and whipped, and yet there was small amendment.

---

[300] Quoted after Barbour, ed. *The Jamestown Voyages* I, 49-54.
[301] Edward Winslow, *Good Newes*: 16f.
[302] ibid.: 23.

The Plymouth colony, it seems, fared little better: "For our own parts, our case was almost the same with theirs, having but a small quantity of corn left, and were enforced to live on ground nuts, clams [...], and such other things as naturally the country afforded, and which did and would maintain strength."[303] But unlike the Plymouth settlement which managed to maintain its colonists, the Wessagusset men were doomed.

> They hanged one of them that stole their corn, and yet they regarded it not; that another of their company was turned savage; that their people had most forsaken the town, and made their rendezvous where they got their victuals, because they would not take pains to bring it home; that they had sold their clothes for corn, and were ready to starve both with cold and hunger also because they could not endure to get victuals by reason of their nakedness.[304]

At Wessagusset, Englishmen's worst fears became true when men turned "native". The New World paradise proved less than welcoming to civilized man, and the fate of Thomas Weston's men must have been a strong reminder that going native was considered a horrible thing to do, making men and beasts alike. The 1589 *Principal Navigations* included a narrative of discovery to the New England coast which made men turn into cannibals in order to avoid starvation.[305]

Due to this peculiar mixture of exuberant praise in its descriptive passages and narrative parts often centering around violent encounters with natives and hardships, Winslow's narrative shares many features with earlier reports from Virginia, including a final scheme of success:

> Though at some times in some seasons at noon I have seen men stagger by reason of faintness for want of food, yet before night, by the good providence and blessing of God, we have enjoyed such plenty as though the windows of heaven had been opened unto us. How few, weak, and raw were we at our first beginning, and there settling, and in the midst of barbarous enemies! [...] So that when I seriously consider of things, I cannot but think that God has a purpose to give that land as an inheritance to our nation, and great pity it were that it should long lie in so desolate a state, considering it agrees so well with the constitution of our bodies, being both fertile, and so temperate for heat and cold, as in that respect one can scarce distinguish New England from Old.[306]

---

[303] Edward Winslow. *Good Newes from New England*: 40f.
[304] ibid.: 44.
[305] "A Voyage of Master Hore and divers other Gentlemen to Newfound Land, and Cape Breton" in 1536, recorded in Richard Hakluyt's 1589 edition of the *Principal Navigations*.
[306] Edward Winslow, *Good Newes*: 58.

Winslow's narrative is as much a little chronicle as it is a promotional pamphlet of New England. Now that future success is made to seem only a few steps away, Winslow adds to his narrative a long description of natives who are portrayed quite positively. Even though they are heathens in Winslow's eyes, he admits that they observe some kind of religion which he compares to that of the ancient Greeks: "And as in former ages Apollo had his temple at Delphos, and Diana at Ephesus, so have I heard them call upon some [spirits] as if they had their residence in some certain places." Once it seems opportune to show natives in a positive light, they are no longer described by analogy to Europe's own "barbarians" of the time (Turks, Lapplanders, Irish), but to ancient Greeks. Furthermore, Winslow claims that the Indians are of a very hardy nature, including women and infants; he also buys into the assumption that Indians do sacrifice children, possibly alluding to the Huskenaw initiation ritual. About their chief men, the *pnieses*, Winslow says, "they are commonly men of the greatest stature and strength, and such as will endure most hardness, and yet are more discreet, courteous and humane in their carriages than any amongst them, scorning theft, lying, and the like base dealings, and stand as much upon their reputation as any men."[307]

While the first appendix established a favourable image of the New England tribes surrounding the English settlements, a second appendix is dedicated to the geographical situation, climate, and agricultural potential of New England. In all descriptions, be it the quality of the soil, the climatic likeness of New England to Old England, or else, a favourable picture is created, including "our Indians" as witnesses to the soil's fertility or partners in the fur trade. There is no longer talk of incessant threats of native treachery, which dominated many narrative passages before. Instead, Winslow focuses on economic gain. The fur trade may yearly bring "many thousand pounds profit by trade only from that island on which we are seated." Fishing is another profitable industry and "may be had in as great abundance as in any other part of the world; witness the west-country merchants of England, who return incredible gains yearly from there." In this passage, the stereotypical terms which were applied in the earliest reports to describe America's paradisaic state of natural abundance are here introduced into a language of use and economic profit.

> Not that we altogether, or principally, propound profit to be the main end of what we have undertaken, but the glory of God, and the honour of our country [...] hoping that where religion and profit jump together (which is rare) in so honorable an action, it will encourage every honest man, either in person or

---

[307] Edward Winslow. *Good Newes from New England*: 59-61.

purse, to set forward the same." Passages like this appear almost verbatim in promotional narratives of all English colonies.[308]

After many harrowing passages of famine, sickness, threats of native violence, and the Wessagusset incident of men going native, Winslow achieves a narrative turnaround towards the end of *Good Newes* by once again resorting to a strong focus on future economic gain. Terms like "abundance", "yearly returns", and "profitable" establish positive associations with New England once again; and in Winslow's narrative, the future of (Yankee) Northeast America seems foreshadowed in the statement that "religion and profit will jump together" to create a glorious future for New England.

7.3.2. Francis Higginson to His Friends in England

Several letters from New England during the first decades of English settlement open with hints at the great interest Englishmen back home took in the voyages to New England and the colony there: Francis Higginson, for example, introduced his relation of the crossing, dated July 24, 1629, as a letter of events "faithfully recorded according to the very truth for the satisfaction of very many my loving friends who have earnestly requested to be truly certified in these things."[309] After long weeks at sea, the company on the boats bound for Naumkeag approach the shore of America, and first impressions change the narrative flow from daily recordings during the sea voyage to a description of the first impressions of America's shore, echoing what may have become by then the standard rhetoric of first sight accounts:

> Now we saw an abundance of mackerel, a great store of great whales [...], infinite multitudes of mackerel [...] and we saw every hill and dale and every island full of gay woods and high trees. The nearer we came to the shore the more flowers [were] in abundance, sometimes scattered abroad, sometime joined in sheets nine or ten yards long. [It] made us all desirous to see our new paradise of New England, whence we saw such fore-running signals of fertility afar off.[310]

Descriptions of natural beauty, the term "abundance", and the enumeration of flora and fauna were by now long established constituents of such descriptions.

---

[308] Edward Winslow, *Good Newes*: 69-70.
[309] "Francis Higginson to His Friends in England. July 24, 1629." In: Everett Emerson, ed. *Letters from New England. The Massachusetts Bay Colony, 1629-1638.* Amherst, MA: University of Massachusetts Press, 1976: 12.
[310] ibid.: 21.

Heterogeneous opinions about the country's fertility may have prompted Higginson to look for "fore-running signals of fertility".

After having entered the harbor, some men fetch "ripe strawberries and gooseberries and sweet single roses. Thus God was merciful to us in giving us a taste and smell of the sweet fruit as an earnest of his bountiful goodness to welcome us at our first arrival."[311] And even though Higginson was conscious of the enormous effort that building a plantation would require, nature seemed to lend a helping hand once in a while. At the end of another letter instructing would-be settlers, later enlarged into *New-Englands Plantation*, he adds: "Whilst I was writing my wife brought me word that the fishers had caught sixteen hundred brass at one draught, which if they were in England were worth many a pound."[312] References to truth abound in Higginson's text like in many other narratives:

> I will endeavor [...] to report nothing but the naked truth [in telling you] of the discommodities as well as the commodities, though as the idle proverb is, 'travelers may lie by authority'. [...] I have been careful to report nothing of New England but what I have partly seen with my own eyes and partly heard and inquired from the mouths of very honest and religious persons, who by living in the country a good space of time have had experience and knowledge.[313]

This elaborate truth claim is followed by a description of the soil in New England: "The fertility of the soil is to be admired at. [...] Of minerals there has yet been but little trial made, yet we are not without great hope of being furnished in that soil. This country abounds naturally" in corn, wheat, roots and garden vegetables, and the narrator assures prospective planters that the yield of corn will be many times beyond what can ordinarily be expected. Also, "for wood there is no better in the world." The narrator also supports claims early Virginia settlers had made about the fertility of wild animals, a claim to be found in Ralph Hamor's narrative and many others as well: The deer "bring three or four young ones at once, which is not ordinary in England." What is true for the land is true for the sea as well. "The abundance of sea fish are almost beyond believing, and sure I would scarce have believed it except I had seen it with mine own eyes." To sum it up, "thus we see both land and sea abound with store of blessings for the comfortable sustenance of man's life in New England."[314]

Higginson's letter, intended for circulation among friends, features the same narrative strategies found in promotional texts like Hamor's or Strachey's. Typi-

---

[311] "Francis Higginson to His Friends in England. July 24, 1629": 22.
[312] ibid.: 27.
[313] ibid.: 39.
[314] ibid.: 31-34.

cal claims of abundance, amazing fertility, superlatives, and even double negations ("we are not without great hope" concerning minerals) when talking about expected commodities America has not yielded so far appear in the descriptive passages and show a surprising stability of stereotypes. Given the fact that Higginson did not write for a colonizing company or financial backers, it is especially interesting to see how much he, too, seems to have been indebted to narrative models of New World reports that we find little in his narrative that we have not read before. But then again, Higginson may have been anxious to present America in just the same positive light in which previous reports had put it in order to lure more settlers to New England. Thomas Dudley wrote about the "ill effects" of such glowing propaganda for those that followed promises of New World abundance and ease of living in a letter from New England.[315] Dudley's letter is very detailed and straightforward in its description of the first two years of settlement in New England and is a strong antidote to Higginson's description:

> The same year [1628] we sent Mr. John Endicott and some with him to begin a plantation and to strengthen such as he should find there, which we sent hither [...], from whom the same year receiving hopeful news, the next year, 1629, we sent divers ships over [...] These [settlers] by their too large commendations of the country and the commodities thereof invited us so strongly to go on that [...] in April 1630 we set sail from old England.[316]

They, however, find the colony in a sad condition, "above eighty of them being dead" after the first winter. "Many died weekly, yea almost daily," and a sad catalogue of the deceased follows.

> In a word, we yet enjoy little to be envied but endure much to be pitied in the sickness and mortality of our people. And I do the more willingly use this open and plain dealing, lest other men should fall short of their expectations when they come hither, as we to our great prejudice did, by means of letters sent us from hence into England, wherein honest men out of a desire to draw over others to them wrote somewhat hyperbolically of many things here.[317]

Dudley's letter alternates narrative passages, almost all of them dealing with the death of some worthy persons or other fateful enterprises, and descriptive passages or rather catalogues. Unlike the more common sort of catalogue, of commodities or description of the Indians, Dudley's letter catalogues the opposite:

---

[315] Thomas Dudley to the Lady Bridget, Countess of Lincoln. March 12 and 28, 1631. In: Everett Emerson, *Letters*: 67-83.
[316] "Francis Higginson to His Friends in England. July 24, 1629": 70.
[317] ibid.: 75.

newly arrived settlers who die during the first year and a half. Description here does not function as an antidote to depressing news from America, balancing present disappointment with future potential; rather, it is used here to underscore sad narratives of the early colony, the effect only lessened by frequent recourses to God's trial and eventual mercy.

Higginson's *Letter to His Friends* says nothing of that kind. After mentioning some "discommodities", namely moskitoes in hot summers and the cold New England winters, as well as rattlesnakes, the narrator moves on to the native inhabitants. The *sagamores* ("kings") cannot rise up more than three hundred men because

> their subjects about twelve years since were swept away by a great and grievous plague [...] so that there are very few left to inhabit the country. The Indians are not able to make use of the land, neither have they any settled places, as towns to dwell in, nor any ground as they challenge for their own possession but change their habitation from place to place.

The semi-yearly nomadic lifestyle of many New England tribes was conveniently used as an argument for settling in an "empty land" in almost all regions, from Newfoundland to Georgia. Thus the Indians allegedly lacked a central feature of civility, which further impeded proselytizing and establishing congregations of praying Indians. Concerning the general situation of Indian-European encounter, the narrator says that "they do generally profess to like well of our coming and planting here, partly because there is abundance of ground that they cannot possess nor make use of, and partly because our being here will be a means both of relief to them when they want and also a defense from their enemies." It is an ironic turn that the narrator mentions the Indians are happy with their neighbors because they might help out with supplies in times of want – it used to be quite the other way round during the first years of European settlement in the New World. The narrator says, "we neither fear them nor trust them. [...] We purpose to learn the language as soon as we can, which will be a means to do them good."[318]

A letter from John Winthrop to his wife Margaret[319], still in England, sheds some more light on Higginson's positive picture of New England. Instead of enumerating and praising what the country offers, Winthrop recounts the early hardships of settling there:

---

[318] "Francis Higginson to His Friends in England. July 24, 1629": 37f.
[319] John Winthrop to Margaret Winthrop. November 29, 1630. In: Everett Emerson, *Letters*: 60.

You shall understand by this [letter] how it is with us since I wrote last. [...] That thou mayest see the goodness of the Lord towards me, that when so many have died and many yet languish, myself and my children are yet living and in health. Yet I have lost twelve of my family, viz., Walters and his wife and two of his children, Mr Gager and his man, Smith of Buxall and his wife and two children", and the sad catalogue goes on. Winthrop himself, however, adds, "My dear wife, we are here in a paradise. Though we have not beef and mutton, etc. yet [...] we want them not; our Indian corn answers for all.[320]

The letters by Thomas Dudley and John Winthrop show a peculiar inversion of the most common technique of New World description, the catalogue. The same happened before, for example in George Percy's *Discourse* about the Jamestown plantation. Instead of enumerating natural commodities, Percy's catalogue turns into an obituary of colonists dying every day. In the face of such stark contrasts of an idealized America with real experiences, Higginson's narrative testifies, like many others, to a deep-rooted narrative anxiety that America might fall short of the high expectations which the earliest narratives like Hariot's or Brereton's had created. Therefore, even narratives intended at least in part for circulation among friends catered to these expectations and were to a considerable extent composed out of narrative commonplaces which appeared in narratives of all future English colonies on the Eastern seaboard throughout roughly the first century of contact. The rare departures from this narrative model can be found in letters like Frethorne's from Jamestown or Dudley's and Winthrop's from New England.

7.3.3. William Wood. *New England's Prospect*

Before Wood's tract was published, there was very little information available for Englishmen interested in New England's geography, indigenous inhabitants and English settlements apart from the letters studied above, which may or may not have reached wide circulation. Among the few reports publicly accessible were John Brereton's *Briefe and True Relation* (1602), James Rosier's *True Relation of the Voyage of Captaine George Waymouth* (1605), John Smith's *Description of New England* (1616), and Francis Higginson's *New Englands Plantation* (1630), of which Higginson's *Letter to His Friends* was the basis. Wood had lived in New England for four years before he returned to London to see his book published in 1634. His narrative was cited repeatedly by Thomas Morton in his *New English Canaan*.

---

[320] "Francis Higginson to His Friends in England. July 24, 1629": 60f.

Like many writers of promotional tracts before him, Wood claimed he wrote his narrative because "there have some relations heretofore passed the press which have been very imperfect, as also because there have been many scandalous and false reports passed upon the country, even from the sulphurious breath of every base ballad-monger."[321] Even before he mentions this, the narrator assures the reader that he "dare presume to present thee with the true and faithful relation of some few years' travels and experience" to avoid the common charge that travelers "may lie by authority because none can control them. [...] What I speak is the very truth."[322] Wood's elaborate truth claims echo Thomas Hariot's claim to authority based on empiricism and also his intention to counter "shameful and slanderous speeches" discrediting the New World.

Wood's narrative is divided into chapters dealing respectively with the geographical situation and features of New England, the climate, flora and fauna, some English plantations, and chapters on "evils and such things as are hurtful in the plantation." The native inhabitants feature in the second part of the narrative, and Wood presented a fairly respectful and thorough portrait of them.

Even though there were few narratives Wood could draw upon for information, he quoted John Smith and referred the reader to the *Description of New England* for a detailed geographical description.[323] Wood repeated the common misconception that New England was an island or a peninsula "as the Indians do certainly inform us" and "those who have best skill in discovery." When describing the climate, the narrator reiterates the standard description that "that part of the country wherein most of the English have their habitation [...] is for certain the best ground and sweetest climate in all those parts bearing the name of New England, agreeing well with the temper of our English bodies."[324] This, again, is a standard element in descriptions of early America and appeared for example in Ralph Lane's narrative of the Roanoke colony: "The territory [of the Chesapeake] is for temperature of climate [...] not to be excelled."[325]

In order to make his description sound impartial, Wood adds, "not to smother anything, lest you judge me too partial in reciting good of the country and not bad, true it is that some venturing too nakedly in extremity of cold, being more foolhardy than wise, have for a time lost the use of their feet [...] but time and surgery afterwards recovered them."[326] This strategy of abundant praise with the little and

---

[321] William Wood. *New England's Prospect*. Ed. Alden T. Vaughan. Amherst, MA: University of Massachusetts Press, 1977: 20.
[322] ibid.: 19f.
[323] ibid.: 25.
[324] ibid.: 25ff.
[325] Ralph Lane, "Discourse": 257.
[326] William Wood, *New England's Prospect*: 29.

seemingly constructed caveats regarding less-than-perfect aspects of New England structures the narrative. Wood did intend to write a promotional tract, it seems, yet also tried to counterbalance charges that he was being too indulgent of his topic. After such "balanced" descriptions of New England's climate and the rumours that the winters there were severe, Wood compares New England to Virginia where

> extremely hot summers have dried up much English blood and by pestiferous diseases swept away many lusty bodies, changing their complexion not into swarthiness ["swarthy" being a standard adjective to describe Indian complexions] but into paleness, so that when they come for trading into our parts we can know many of them by their faces.[327]

New England also compares favourably in terms of fertility of soil, availability of pasture land and increase in farm animals. The usual comparatives and superlatives appear frequently in Wood's narrative, following a long-standing tradition of describing New World nature with exuberant praise: "I dare not think England can show fairer cattle either in winter or summer than is in those parts both winter and summer, being generally larger and better of milk." And even where New England falls short of the ideal for the time being, prospective rhetoric steps in, describing what may be "if only" there were more experienced English husbandmen, the fields better manured, etc. "It is neither impossible nor much improbable that upon improvements the soil may be as good in time as [in] England."[328]

This narrative strategy of prospective praise, couched grammatically in double negations, already featured prominently in New World descriptions as early as Thomas Hariot's *Briefe and True Report*, or John Smith's *Description of New England*. Apart from these strategies, the regular allusions to natural abundance feature prominently in Wood's report, too. "Whatsoever grows well in England grows as well there, many things better and larger. [There are] strawberries in abundance, very large ones, some being two inches about." Mines have at least to be mentioned, too, in order to satisfy the usual expectations, even though Wood himself cannot come up with any tangible proof: "For such commodities as lie underground, I cannot out of my own experience or knowledge say much." The standard references to hearsay (taken from the Indians and even the Spanish) follow instantly in order not to disappoint the expectations of a European audience: "It is certainly reported that there is ironstone; and the Indians inform us that they can lead us to the mountains of black lead [...] and though nobody dare confi-

---

[327] William Wood. *New England's Prospect*: 32.
[328] ibid.: 34f.

dently conclude, yet dare they not utterly deny, but that the Spaniard's bliss [i.e. gold] may lie hidden in the barren mountains."[329]

Other literary props of a paradisaical *locus amoenus* are found throughout the descriptive passages as well: "Every two families hav[e] a spring of sweet waters bewtixt them", and though summers are hotter than in England, "they are tolerable, being often cooled with fresh blowing winds."[330] And yet even Wood has to admit that there is a fine line between fact and fantasy:

> I have myself heard some say that they heard it was a rich land, a brave country, but when they came there they could see nothing but a few canvas booths and old houses, supposing at the first to have found walled towns, fortifications, and corn fields, as if towns could have built themselves or corn fields have grown of themselves without the husbandry of man. These men, missing of their expectations, returned home and railed upon the country.

Likewise, Wood suggests such unrealistic expectations and rumors of New World riches and abundance were the reasons for the early years of famine: "The root of their [i.e. the early colonists'] want sprung up in England, for many hundreds hearing of the plenty of the country were so much their own foes and country's hindrance as to come without provision."[331]

The bottom line of these passages, then, is that whatever hardships the New World poses, they are man-made and can thus easily be alleviated. Also, Wood points out that some New World reports established an unrealistic image of early America which accounted for much disappointment among early colonists. Nevertheless, Wood's narrative is part of such New World propaganda centering not so much on what is there; instead, much of this narrative is made up of standard images and rhetorical devices.

The second part of Wood's narrative deals with the native inhabitants and is both more realistic and original in its content. Wood does not fail to narrate some gruesome stories of acts of torture which were conveniently committed by tribes living far away from the English settlement. Cannibalism is part of the picture of these "savage" tribes, but there are also some signs of degeneration which have been induced by contact with Europeans. Some Indian tribes have been provided with guns and/or ammunition by the French, so that whenever they have guns but no ammunition, they visit the English settlements. When boats arrive at a harbour, these Indians

---

[329] William Wood. *New England's Prospect*: 36f.
[330] ibid.: 30f.
[331] ibid.: 67.

present them with a volley of shot, asking for sack and strong liquors which they so much love, since the English used to trade it with them, that they will scarce trade for anything else, lashing out into excessive abuse, first taught by the example of our English who, to unclothe them of their beaver coat, clad them with the infection of swearing and drinking, which was never in fashion with them before [according to] our bestial example [...] from which I am sure have sprung many evil consequences.[332]

Some decades later, John Lawson would report from the Carolinas that "rum [is] a liquor now so much in use with them that they will part with the dearest thing they have to purchase it." His glossary, appended to his *New Voyage to Carolina*, contains the sentence "all the Indians are drunk" translated into several Indian languages.[333] This is a new aspect in English New World narratives but one which became more prominent as contacts between Europeans and native tribes became more frequent. In many passages, Wood's New England still appears like a pristine paradise, but its exotic appeal is waning quickly as the native tribes become contaminated not only with European diseases, but also with Europeans' vices, most of all the abuse of alcohol.

7.3.4. John Josselyn. *An Account of Two Voyages to New-England*

Forty years after William Wood's *New England's Prospect*, John Josselyn wrote *An Account of Two Voyages to New England*, a long and detailed narrative of two voyages to New England from 1638 to 1639 and from 1663 to 1671. The first edition of the narratives appeared in London in 1674, a second edition the next year. Josselyn had already published *New Englands Rarities Discovered* (1672), to which he refers throughout the text.

In many ways, Josselyn's narrative repeats the stock components of early New World descriptions. Even though he was a very well-educated man, he seems nevertheless to have been attracted to the various myths and fables surrounding the New World. He tells tales of lions, sea serpents, mermaids and mermen, "the credit whereof I will neither impeach nor enforce."[334] Josselyn's America is thus peopled with fabled creatures and certainly appealed to the taste of readers long

---

[332] William Wood, *New England's Prospect*: 79.
[333] John Lawson. *A New Voyage to Carolina. Containing the Exact Description and Natural History of that Country; together with the present state thereof. And a Journal of a Thousand Miles, Travel'd thro' several Nations of Indians*. Ed. Hugh Talmage Lefler. Chapel Hill: University of North Carolina Press, 1967: 238.
[334] John Josselyn: *An Account of two Voyages to New England*. Ed. Paul J. Lindholdt. Hanover: University Press of New England, 1988: 20f.

used to stories of pygmies, Patagonian giants, or mermaids. Like many before him, Josselyn naturally referred to authorities like Pliny.

Descriptive passages of the countryside echo almost verbally many previous narratives:

> Between the mountains are many ample rich and pregnant valleys as ever eye beheld, beset on each side with variety of goodly trees, the grass man-high unmowed, uneaten and uselessly withering; within these valleys are spacious lakes or ponds well stored with fish and beavers [and surrounded by trees] under the shades whereof you may freely walk two or three miles together; being goodly large trees, and convenient for masts and sail yards. The whole country produces springs in abundance replenished with excellent waters, having all the properties ascribed to the best in the world. The mountains are richly furnished with mines of lead, silver, copper, tin, and diverse sorts of minerals.[335]

Abundance, natural beauty, sweet springs and ample valleys echo earlier descriptions of a New World paradise; little seems to have changed, at least in narrative strategies and stereotypes, after almost 100 years of English exploration and settlement on the Eastern seaboard. In fact, Josselyn even uses the same terms which occur frequently in early American narratives of discovery: "Abundance", "replenished", "excellent", "richly furnished", enhanced finally with "the best in the world."

Apart from these general descriptions of the land and its indigenous inhabitants, by Josselyn's time there also was something to be said about the transplanted English population on New England soil. Boston anno 1638 is described as "rather a village than a town, there being not above twenty or thirty houses", and "the country all along as I sailed, being no more than a mere wilderness, here and there by the seaside a few scattered plantations, with as few houses."[336] Nevertheless, social life in Boston already takes shape before the eyes of English readers, complete with virtues and vices. Due to his royalist leanings, however, Josselyn might have decided to leave out most of the virtues and instead focused on the vices:

> For being drunk, they [i.e. the administration in Boston] either whip or impose a fine of five shillings; so for swearing and cursing, or boring though the tongue with a hot iron. [...] An English woman suffering an Indian to have carnal knowledge of her, had an Indian cut out exactly in red cloth sewn upon her right

---

[335] John Josselyn, *Account of Two Voyages*: 33f.
[336] ibid.: 18.

arm, and enjoined to wear it twelve months. Scolds they gag and set them at their doors for certain hours, for all comers and goers-by to gaze at.[337]

Some passages, including the sentences just quoted, reappear verbatim in an autobiographical collection of letters which the sometime printer and bookseller John Dunton published in 1686, after a long visit to Boston.[338] Josselyn warns against "trading for a stranger with them but with a Grecian faith, which is not to part with your ware without ready money, for they are generally in their payments recusant and slow, great syndics, or censors, or controllers of other men's manners, and savagely factious amongst themselves."[339] Dunton goes one step further in his unfavourable portrait of the Bostonians: In trade

> they are generally very backward in their payments, great censors of other men's manners, but extremely careless of their own, yet they have a ready correction for every vice. [...] The Quakers here have been a suffering generation, [...] for the Bostonians, though their forefathers fled thither to enjoy liberty of conscience, are very unwilling any should enjoy it but themselves: But now they are grown more moderate.[340]

In fact, these passages on Boston and community life in early New England are the parts in which Josselyn's individual look on America and his wit shine through. Like in many other English New World reports, the narrative passages are dedicated to a real America, individual experience, and often paint a less-than-perfect picture of its object. In contrast to this, the descriptive passages display an amazing stability over decades and across regions. The pool of images, terminology and rhetorical strategies most narratives drew upon remained uniform, modeled on such narratives of first contact like Laudonnière's *Florida* or Hariot's *Briefe and True Report* even even after many decades of English experience.

---

[337] John Josselyn, *Account of Two Voyages:* 124.
[338] John Dunton. *Letters Written from New England. AD 1686, in which are described his voyages by sea, his travels on land and the characters of his friends and acquaintances.* With notes and an appendix, ed. W.H. Whitmore. New York: Burt Franklin, n.d.
[339] John Josselyn, *Account of Two Voyages*: 126.
[340] John Dunton, *Letters*: 69.

7.4. Maryland

7.4.1. George Alsop. *A Character of the Province of Maryland*

George Alsop came to Maryland as an indentured servant at a very young age. Although he praised Maryland lavishly in his narrative, he returned to England after only a few years in the colony. *A Character of the Province of Maryland*, which was published in England shortly after his return, is yet another early report and promotional pamphlet about North America. This time, Maryland is the best place to be, and Alsop clothes his description in the familiar narrative strategies of favourable comparison with Old England. Many passages enumerate natural bounty and the paradisaic setting of the colony, and an underlying eroticization of the feminized land further supports Maryland's allure:

> Maryland is a province situated upon the large extending bowels of America [...] dwelling pleasantly upon the Bay of Chesapeake. [...] Pleasant, in respect of the multitude of navigable rivers and creeks that conveniently and most profitably lodge within the arms of her green, spreading, and delightful woods; whose natural womb (by her plenty) maintains and preserves several diversities of animals that rangingly inhabit her woods.[341]

Nature, it seems, is now a nurturing mother, always at the inhabitants' command to "offer her benefits daily to supply the want of the inhabitant." America is no longer the virgin land awaiting the European (male) conquering hero as in Ralegh's *Guiana* or in the quintessential engraving entitled "Vespucci discovering America" by Theodor Galle after Jan van der Straet.[342] Now, the feminization of the land focuses on presenting America as a benign and nurturing mother earth providing freely for the European settlers. In Ralph Hamor's *True Discourse*, Virginia is asked "out of those great plenties and havings which God has lent thee to spare a little-little portion to the full settling and finishing up"[343] of the colonists in Virginia. In Alsop's narrative, Maryland presents herself to the eye of the observer

---

[341] George Alsop. "A Character of the Province of Maryland."[1666] In: Richard Beale Davis, C. Hugh Holman and Louis D. Rubin, Jr., eds. *Southern Writing, 1585-1920*. New York: The Odyssey Press, 1970: 41.
[342] In Hugh Honour. *The New Golden Land*. London: Lane, 1975, p.88f. See especially Chapter 4, "A Land of Allegory". On European conquest and iconography, especially with regard to the Roanoke Voyages and John White, cf. Bernadette Bucher. *Icon and Conquest: A Structural Analysis of the Illustrations of de Bry's Great Voyages*. Chicago: University of Chicago Press, 1981.
[343] Ralph Hamor, *True Discourse*. To the reader: Not paginated.

dressed in her green and fragrant mantle of the spring. Neither do I think there is any place under the heavenly altitude [...] that can parallel this fertile and pleasant piece of ground in its multiplicity, or rather nature's extravagancy of a super-abounding plenty. For so much does this country increase in a swelling spring-tide of rich variety and diversities of all things, not only common provisions that supply the reaching stomach of man with a satisfactory plenty, but also extends with its liberality and free convenient benefits to each sensitive faculty, according to their several desiring appetites.

Nature could not have told man "in more convenient terms [...] dwell here, live plentifully and be rich."[344] Thus, Alsop very early sums up America's promise to the newcomers of a life of ease and rich material rewards. Like in many other English reports from North America in the seventeenth century, a standard set of images and terms is used in Alsop's narrative to compose a stereotypical picture of America as a terrestrial paradise: Nature is no longer just abundant but offers "super-abounding plenty"; the country is "pleasant" and "fertile", and America not only satisfies man's material interests but ravishes its European beholders with pleasant sensual impressions, too: The land is "fragrant" and emits "odoriferous" scents – the same term was used repeatedly when Europeans described their first approach to the American shore, like for example Arthur Barlowe in his narrative.

The latter aspect especially establishes Maryland as *the* American paradise: The fruitful flora of Maryland, the narrator claims, is "the only emblem or hieroglyphic of our Adamitical or primitive situation, as well as for [the] odoriferous smells", and plants "still bear the effigy of innocence according to their original grafts, which by their dumb vegetable oratory, each hour speaks to the inhabitant in silent acts, that they need not look for any other terrestrial paradise."[345] Eight decades after Arthur Barlowe's exuberant praise of America's paradisaic state, riches to nurture man without much toil, and a benevolent feminine nature bound on pleasing the English newcomers, Alsop's narrative utilizes the same *topoi*, rhetoric, and narrative strategies. These include mentioning *over-abundant* nature, the promise of becoming rich without much toil, and a prelapsarian state of innocence, but in fact the report says very little about Maryland that has not been said before about any given region on the eastern seaboard.

---

[344] George Alsop, "A Character": 41.
[345] ibid.: 41f.

7.5. New York, 1670-1695

7.5.1. John Miller. *A Description of the Province and City of New York*

Miller's narrative reports the current state of the colony of New York and begins very much like a travel guide: "The province of New York is a country very pleasant and delightful, and well improved for the time it has been settled and the number of its inhabitants. It lies in the latitude of 40 and 41."[346] The narrative contains all aspects a reader might have grown to expect from a New World travel narrative, including the fairly nondescript terms "pleasant" and "delightful" and the claim that the climate is "very agreeable" to Englishmen's constitutions. Miller discusses possible mineral riches, a healthy climate, natural fertility and abundance, inserts prospective rhetoric of rich gains, and stresses the promising development of the English settlements.

> I dare boldly affirm it to be [...] the best province his Majesty has in all America, and very agreeable to the constitution of his subjects. [...] It is true, many rocks and mountains [reduce the quality of the land], but I believe the goodness of their inside as to metals and minerals will, when searched, make amends for the barrenness of the outside.

The natural resources which the author mentions are grouped neatly together into categories of use. The province offers "walnut, cedar, oak of several kinds and many other sorts of wood proper for building ships or houses; [...] turpentine for physical uses, and pitch and tar for the seaman's service, [...] and much wild fowl, as swans, geese, ducks [...] and no less store of good venison." Furthermore, the region abounds in

> many herbs such and as good as we have growing in our gardens [...] and some other fruits in great abundance, especially grapes which, I am persuaded, if well improved, would yield good wine. [...] The soil black and rich, brings forth corn in abundance. [...] Fish there is in great store, both in the sea and rivers. [...] This, joined to the healthfulness, pleasantness and fruitfulness thereof, are great encouragements to people rather to seek the bettering of their fortunes here than elsewhere.[347]

---

[346] John Miller. *A Description of the Province and City of New York; with plans of the city* [1695]. In: *A Two Years Journal*, ed. Cornell Jaray. Historic Chronicles of New Amsterdam, Colonial New York and Early Long Island. Port Washington, NY: Friedman, 1968: 27.

[347] John Miller, *Description*: 32ff.

In this passage Miller sums up stereotypes of New World descriptions like Hariot's "merchantable commodities" for shipbuilding, the ubiquitous grapes and the subsequent claim that they, "if only improved", will yield wine of good quality. Furthermore, "abundance", "healthfulness" and the promise that people will be "bettering their fortunes" in America complete the by now quite standardized description of America, enhanced by the promise of personal future success.

As soon as the narrator turns to describing the (European) inhabitants of the province, the picture is less glossy. "The number of the inhabitants in this province are about 3000 families whereof almost one half are naturally Dutch, a great part English, and the rest French. [...] As to their religion, they are very much divided; few of them intelligent and sincere, but the most part ignorant and conceited, fickle and regardless."[348] Next, the narrator discusses the "evils and inconveniences" in New York. He names six "evils", among them the "wickedness and irreligion of the inhabitants [i.e. Europeans]", the "want of ministers", the "difference of opinion in religion", the "heathenism of the Indians" and also the nearness of Canada and the threat of the French "papists". As for the first evil, wickedness combines, according to the narrator, with drunkenness. "Cursing" and "swearing" are some other vices of the European-born people so that, "joined with their profane, atheistical and scoffing method of discourse [...] their company [is] extremely uneasy to sober and religious men."[349]

This "evil" of badly-mannered backwoodsmen in the province of New York is as much man-made as another "evil", the "heathenism" of the Indians. This is another interesting point of criticism. The French to the North have, one may infer, been very successful in converting their neighboring tribes like the Oneidas, and have also influenced "our Mohawks", as the narrator says. The English, in contrast, must have been either singularly incompetent or disinterested in winning over native tribes to their faith. Charged with infidelity to the English when he converted to French Catholicism, a Mohawk Indian claimed that "he had lived long among the English, but they had never all that while had so much love for him as to instruct him in the concerns of his soul, and show him the way to salvation, which the French had done upon their first acquaintance with him."[350]

In Miller's narrative, description of the land is, like in so many other narratives, composed of stereotypes found in most promotional, and quite a few non-promotional reports from early North America. Miller's attitude towards and portrayal of New York's crude and irreligious inhabitants of European descent, however, marks the beginning of something new in reports from and about America:

---

[348] John Miller, *Description*: 31.
[349] ibid.: 38-40.
[350] ibid.: 53.

The stance of a disengaged, sometimes condescending narrator allows for criticism of the European inhabitants' shortcomings in Miller's *Description*. Soon this stance would become the source for satire and humor. Sarah Kemble Knight's *Journal* is one of the best early examples. It confirms Miller's observation that the European inhabitants of the colonies take little action to "civilize" the Indians. Knight reports that "the natives of the country [are] the most savage of all the savages of that kind, [...] little or no care taken (as I heard upon inquiry) to make them otherwise." Knight also supports observations like William Wood's that contact with Europeans has done native tribes more bad than good, especially with regard to alcohol: The Indians "trade most for rum, for which they hazard their lives; and the English fit them generally as well by seasoning it plentifully with water."[351] The counterpart to Knight's drunk Indians are the ubiquitous country bumpkins of European descent, heavily criticized by Miller, who make for funny entertainment in Knight's *Journal* and are forerunners of stock characters in American satirical literature.

7.5.2. Daniel Denton. *A Brief Description of New-York: Formerly Called New-Netherlands*

Daniel Denton opens his narrative with the standard claim to present a "brief but true" eyewitness report from North America, assuming right at the beginning an authority which many authors obviously felt their narratives badly needed:

> I have here through the instigation of diverse persons in England and elsewhere presented you with a brief but true relation of a known unknown part of America. The known part which is either inhabited, or lies near the sea, I have described to you, and have written nothing but what I have been an eyewitness to all or the greatest part of it. [...] For the unknown part, which is either some places lying to the Northward yet undiscovered by any English, or the bowels of the earth not yet opened, though the natives tell us of glittering stones, diamonds, and pearl in the one, and the Dutch have boasted of gold and silver in the other; yet I shall not feed your expectation with anything of that nature, but leave it until a better discovery shall make way for such a relation.[352]

---

[351] Sarah Kemble Knight. "The Journal of Madam Knight", ed. Sargent Bush, Jr. In: *Journeys in New Worlds. Early American Women's Narratives*. Ed. William L. Andrews. Madison, WI: University of Wisconsin Press, 1990, 69-116: 105f.

[352] Daniel Denton. *A Brief Description of New-York: Formerly Called New-Netherlands. Together with the Manner of its Situation, Fertility of the Soil, Healthfulness of the Climate, and the Commodities thence Produced. Also Some Directions and Advice for Such as shall go thither* [London, 1670]. Ann Arbor, MI: University Microfilms, 1971: A3^v.

This technique of inserting little teasers into a narrative and then refraining from "feeding" an audience's "expectations" is a very common narrative strategy in early reports from North America. It was most often used when mines were mentioned and obviously had to bridge a gap between empirical evidence (no mines) and stereotypically reiterated claims that North America would offer England rich rewards in precious metals, just like Spain's colonies had done. John Smith's various reports from North America show just how strong expectations were and how intent authors were on catering to them wihout sacrificing the truth.

Like Smith, Denton cannot come up with tangible evidence but only with promises of future success. The overall picture he paints of the province of New York is glowingly positive. Towards the end of the narrative, Denton claims that if his narrative is found lacking in any way,

> it is principally in not giving it [the land] its due recommendation, for besides those earthly blessings where it is stored, heaven has not been wanting to open its treasure, in sending down seasonable showers upon the earth, blessing it with a sweet and pleasant air, and a continuation of such influences as tend to the health both of man and beast; [...] I may say truly, that if there be any terrestrial happiness to be had by people of all ranks, especially of an inferior rank, it must certainly be here. [...] And how prodigal, if I may so say, has nature been to furnish the country with all sorts of wild beasts and fowl, which everyone has interest in and may hunt at his pleasure. [...] But that which adds happiness to all the rest, is the healthfulness of the place [...] where besides the sweetness of the air, the country itself sends forth such a fragrant smell that it may be perceived at sea before they can make the land. [...] If there be any terrestrial Canaan, 'tis surely here, where the land flows with milk and honey. The inhabitants are blessed with peace and plenty.[353]

Denton's America, "flowing with milk and honey", is yet another New World Canaan, benevolently prepared to welcome and nurture Europeans. European language is not fit to give the land "due recommendation"; Denton utilizes the complete palette of narrative commonplaces for promotional New World travel narratives. Their early models seemed to have had a lasting influence on European visitors to the New World. Alsop's Maryland, Higginson's New England, or Denton's New York are naturally and respectively the best place to be, to "dwell here, live plentifully and be rich", for the land "flows with milk and honey". In fact, these narratives, like the ones discussed before, reveal very little individual observation, but instead a strong indebtedness to established literary models. Only in some letters does the New World take on an individual, and occasionally less than

---

[353] Daniel Denton, *A Brief Description*: 17ff.

pleasant face. Given the sheer amount of promotional narratives, however, we may assume that the New World was "made" for an English, and European, audience by narratives like Denton's.

7.6. The Carolinas

7.6.1. Letters by Edward Bland and Francis Yeardley

From the 1650s onward, exploring parties set out from Virginia towards the South in search of good land for settlements, trade with the Indians, the South Sea (Yeardley's "great salt sea", see below), or mineral riches. Like Virginia at the end of the sixteenth century, the Carolinas generated narratives of first encounter which were as enthusiastic and full of the ubiquitous catalogues, superlatives, claims of superior fertility and natural beauty as were the narratives of Barlowe or Hariot. Even the search for silver and gold was simply continued towards the South, and like in the case of the Northern colonies and settlements, when these metals remained elusive, hearsay or native sources were quoted to uphold hopes. Edward Bland, a merchant who embarked on an exploring voyage South of Virginia in 1650, combined the praise of a healthful climate with promises of mineral riches: "The climate according to our opinions was far more temperate than ours in Virginia, and the inhabitants full of children; we saw among them copper and were informed that they tip their pipes with silver [...] and 'tis very probable that there may be gold and other metals among the hills."[354]

Francis Yeardley, son of Virginia governor Sir George Yeardley, wrote home similar observations in a letter. Yeardley reports the discovery of "South Virginia or Carolina, the which we find a most fertile, gallant, rich soil, flourishing in all the abundance of nature [...] and experimentally rich in precious metals." Yeardley's terminology is straight out of the pool of descriptive commonplaces applied somewhat indiscriminately to any North American region of first contact. Despite all praise, there are already monuments testifying to futile attempts at settlement by Europeans. The ruins at Roanoke have become some kind of historical sight shown to foreign visitors by the Indians of that region. When a group of English explorers met an Indian hunting party, the Indians "received them civilly, and showed them the ruins of Sir Walter Ralegh's fort."[355] In this narrative, the recent past of English colonizing efforts, embodied in the ruins of "Sir Walter Ralegh's fort", and the undeterred optimism of European explorers meet, the latter sparked

---
[354] Edward Bland. "The Discoverie of New Brittanie." In: Alexander S. Salley, ed. *Narratives of Early Carolina*. New York: Barnes and Noble, 1911, rpt. 1967: 17.
[355] Francis Yeardley. "Letter to John Ferrar Esq." In: Alexander S. Salley, ed. *Narratives*: 25-27.

by expectations of a "rich" and "flourishing soil" enhanced by a land "empirically rich in precious metals."

7.6.2. Thomas Ashe. *Carolina, Or a Description of the Present State of that Country*

Thomas Ashe wrote an early promotional narrative of Carolina after a brief stay in Charlestown in 1680. His glowing description of Carolina yet increased the reputation of the proprietary colony which had already taken on the hue of an earthly Eden in the previous narratives by Bland and Yeardley. Here again, Carolina is presented as the place to be, complete with a healthy climate and the beauty of the land "ravishing" its beholder. Obviously, there were already enough voices to testify to the country's numerous blessings:

> The discourses of many ingenuous travelers (who have lately seen this part of the West Indies) have for salubrity of air, for the luxuriant and indulgent blessings of nature, justly rendered Carolina famous. [...] Since my arrival at London, I have observed many with pleasing ideas, and contemplations, as if ravished with admiration, discourse of its pleasures.[356]

The land close to the sea, echoing Arthur Barlowe's perceptions one hundred years earlier, "is clothed with odoriferous and fragrant woods, flourishing in perpetual and constant verdures." And yet the woods are not there to please the spectator, but to make "goodly boxes, chests, tables, and cabinets." Ashe combines Carolina's beauty with prospective economic success by exploiting its resources. In this narrative, like in many others, the natives feature more like decoration of an exotic destination than neighbors of English settlements: "The natives of the country are from time immemorial, *ab origine* Indians, of a deep chestnut color, their hair black and straight, tied various ways", and the narrator adds that they are all well-featured, excellent hunters, and many of them also experts at medicine. And even though "their drink is water", they are "lovers of the spirits of wine and sugar. [...] They have hitherto lived in good correspondence and amity with the English, who by their just and equitable carriage have extremely won and obliged them, justice being exactly and impartially administered."[357] We may assume that Ashe chose to leave out the detrimental effects of alcohol abuse among native inhabitants which some other authors like Daniel Denton or William Wood chose to report.

---

[356] Thomas Ashe. "Carolina, Or a Description of the Present State of that Country." [1682] In: Alexander S. Salley, *Narratives*: 139.
[357] Thomas Ashe. "Carolina, Or a Description of the Present State of that Country.": 142, 157.

7.6.3. John Lawson. A New Voyage to Carolina

The *New Voyage* is a collection of several texts, beginning with the journal of a surveying voyage 1700/1701 and enlarged with *A Description of North Carolina*, *The Present State of North Carolina*, and chapters on natural history, flora, and fauna. The text ends with *An Account of the Indians of North Carolina*, complete with a little dictionary of some terms in English and two Indian tongues. At the beginning of his voyage, Lawson opens his *Journal* with a description of Charleston, which he praises for its pleasant seat, "large, beautiful buildings", "good and pleasant roads", prospering trade, and "wise and industrious inhabitants" who have risen to "great estates" in a very short time. The latter fact has made the colony, according to Lawson, "of more advantage to the Crown of Great Britain than any other of the more Northerly Plantations (Virginia and Maryland excepted)." All Christian faiths are freely professed, and the government is described as just and based on equality rather than rank; the colony's militiamen are "absolute masters over the Indians and carry so strict a hand over [them] that none do the least injury to any of the English. [The Indians] are very warlike people, ever faithful to the English, and have proved themselves brave and true on all occasions, and are a great help and strength to this colony."[358]

This is, compared with earlier reports of exploration, quite a step away from the reiterated charges of Indian treachery and idleness, which made the native inhabitants appear to be mere obstacles to English settlement and proper use of the land. Lawson's report describes a colony no longer in its infant years, but already in first bloom and offering considerable comforts, one of the chiefest being peaceful relations with the colony's Indian tribes. It is a historic irony, then, that Lawson would become one of the first victims of the Tuscarora Indians' uprising.

Lawson's picture of the colony is very much in tune with his first impressions of Charleston. The country is described as generally fruitful and beautiful, except for a few swampy, sandy or rocky areas towards the coast. All in all, the soil is fruitful and affords whatever is necessary to build settlements, from lime, clay, stone, and marble for building materials to iron ore, fertile land fit for agricultural use, plenty of water, and a healthy climate. Occasionally, the narrator is ravished by beautiful scenery and echoes the rhetoric of superlatives so prevalent in early reports of North America. Still, it is already tinged with the explorers's prospective gaze, submitting the land to European husbandry and civilized settlement before his eye:

---

[358] John Lawson. *A New Voyage to Carolina: Containing the Exact Description and Natural History of that Country*. Ed. Hugh Talmage Lefler. Chapel Hill, NC: University of North Carolina Press, 1967: 8-10.

We passed through a delicious country (none that I ever saw exceeds it). We saw fine bladed grass [...] along the banks of pleasant rivulets. [...] That day, we reached the fertile and pleasant banks of Sapona River [i.e. Yadkin River], whereon stands the Indian town and fort. Nor could all Europe afford a pleasanter stream, were it inhabited by Christians, and cultivated by ingenious hands. [...] There is a most pleasant and convenient neck of land [between two rivers] where many thousand acres may be fenced in, without much cost or labour. [Another area is] parceled out into most convenient necks [...] easy to be fenced in [...] whereby, with a small trouble of fencing, almost every man may enjoy, to himself, an entire plantation or rather park.[359]

This long quote abounds with terminology and images derived from a standard set of New World descriptions: The term "pleasant" is used so often that it becomes almost devoid of meaning. Comparatives help define America which surpasses Europe with its "pleasanter streams"; land may be put to good use without much labor involved, and Lawson envisions the wild land converted into a park.

His is no longer the stance of the passive discovering beholder, taking in pristine sights and letting himself be ravished by their beauty. During George Waymouth's voyage along the New England coast one hundred years earlier, James Rosier experienced the beauty of the country as such, and not yet with a discriminating eye for economic profit: "The excellency of this part of the river [...] did so ravish us all with variety of pleasantness, as we could not tell what to commend, but only admired."[360] Now, the European explorer takes his perspective and his narrative into a human time frame subjected to utility; yet it is not the present but rather the future of the land and its (European) inhabitants which guide the narrator's observations. Accordingly, the natural riches fit for future use are enhanced by the expectation to find mines. Now they are, at least those containing lead, already present, and it is only gold and silver that seems to be still elusive, yet surely located somewhere in the mountains. The Indians, the narrator says, "make use of lead-ore to paint their faces" but "as for the refining of minerals, the Indians are wholly ignorant of it." However, "were a good mine of lead [...] worked by an ingenious hand, it might be of no small advantage to the undertaker [...], and the working of these mines might discover some that are much richer."[361] Like most other authors of New World reports, Lawson has to resort to double negation and prospective rhetoric when talking about precious metals. What is more, he finds another reason why there have not yet been discoveries of gold and silver mines:

---

[359] John Lawson, *A New Voyage*: 52, 55, 87.
[360] James Rosier. "A True Relation of the most prosperous voyage made this present yeere 1605, by Captaine George Waymouth." In: George P. Winship, ed. *Sailors' Narratives*: 101-151: 140f.
[361] John Lawson, *New Voyage*: 56f.

"As [these minerals] are subterraneous products, so in all new countries, they are the species that are last discovered; and especially in Carolina, where the Indians never look for anything lower than the [surface] of the earth [...] As good if not better mines than those the Spaniards possess in America lie full West from us."

The westward quest for gold has been with European settlement in North America right from the start, beginning with De Soto's fateful voyage in the sixteenth century and continued in many of the narratives studied here. Lawson's narrative is no exception. Later, in *An Account of the Indians of North Carolina*, the narrator muses about other reasons why so far no mines have been discovered and exploited: While the Indians know of some mines, "they say, it is this metal that the English covet. [...] If we should discover these minerals to the English, they would settle at or near these mountains and bereave us of the best hunting quarters we have, as they have already done wherever they have inhabited."[362]

As a result, the true potential of the Carolinas remains, the narrator admits, untapped for the reasons mentioned, and the best places still in Indian hands: "The savages do indeed possess the flower of Carolina, the English enjoying only the fag-end of that fine country." And while the narrator admonishes his English audience to not wrong the natives by depriving them of their land and judging them by European standards, he cannot but note that the detrimental effect of European encroachment on Indian tribes is already strongly visible:

> The Sewees have been formerly a large nation, though now very much decreased, since the English have seated [themselves on] their land, and all other nations of Indians are observed to partake of the same fate where the Europeans come, the Indians being a people very apt to catch any distemper they are afflicted withal [...].[363]

Apart from the disastrous effect of European diseases, alcohol is another plague brought into the land by the Europeans. Instances of alcohol abuse by Indians and all sorts of accidents resulting from this appear frequently throughout Lawson's journey. "Rum [is] a liquor now so much in use with them that they will part with the dearest thing they have to purchase it." Consequently, he includes the sentence "All the Indians are drunk" in his glossary at the end of the book, translated into two Indian tongues right after several translated expressions testifying to the great hospitality Indians showed towards the English. Indeed, the narrator recounts frequently the friendly reception of the traveling party at Indian camps and villages wherever they went, being supplied with food and drink to the best abilities of the respective tribes. Early maltreatment of Indians by Carolina's first settlers had

---

[362] John Lawson, *New Voyage*: 166, 215.
[363] ibid.: 62, 17.

been violently avenged, and "were it not for such ill practices, [North Carolina] might, in all probability, have been, at this day, the best settlement."[364]

This is quite a departure from the recurrent claims that America is the land "flowing with milk and honey" and the best place to be. Due to such observations, the narrator exhorts his countrymen to set the Indians a good example by morally impeccable behaviour and mildness towards the natives.

> They are really better to us than we are to them; they always give us victuals at their quarters. [...] We look upon them with scorn and disdain, and think them little better than beasts in human shape, though if well examined, we shall find that, for all our religion and education, we possess more moral deformities and evils than these savages do.

Concerning previous narratives of the New World and the way they describe the natives, Lawson says that "these savages are described in their proper colours but by a very few; for those that generally write histories of this new world are such as interest, preferment, and merchandize drew thither, and know no more of that people than I do of the Laplanders, which is only by hearsay."[365]

Lawson's *Journal* and the appended descriptions and accounts are surprisingly honest and straightforward about the difficult relationship between the native inhabitants of the Carolinas and the European newcomers. Yet while the *Journal* gives ample evidence of Indian hospitality, bravery, and natural wisdom in their present state, the *Account of the Indians* paints a much more pessimistic future of these peoples in the face of an increasing influx of Europeans to the Carolinas. Still, the description of the natives is far from being ethnologically sound or without prejudices based on eurocentrism; the easy living which the fertile country affords its inhabitants is apt to make Europeans "degenerate" into natives, which the narrator suspects was the case with the Lost Colony of Roanoke: "We may reasonably suppose that the English were forced to cohabit with [the surrounding tribes] for relief and conversation; and that in process of time they conformed themselves to the manners of their Indian relations. And thus we see how apt human nature is to degenerate."[366] It is clear from this quote that, notwithstanding frequent praise of Indians and their superior adaptation to American nature, their way of life is a sign of human degeneration and can only be amended by setting them examples of civilized living.

The *Journal* was composed to be read, it is clear, not just for its informative content, but also as an entertaining report for the armchair traveler. The more sci-

---

[364] John Lawson, *New Voyage*: 238, 80.
[365] ibid.: 242f.
[366] ibid.: 69.

entifically interested readers are satisfied by the very detailed *Descriptions* and the *Account of the Indians*; the latter is probably the most interesting text in this book with its sympathetic, often surprisingly enlightened portrayals of Indian life, manners, and customs. Nevertheless, a dominating eurocentric voice of a paternalistic onlooker watching the native tribes perish slowly before the ongoing conquest – a term Lawson uses at the end of the *Account* – of the European settlers characterizes many passages of the narrative. It is telling in this context that the "incredible abundance" featuring so prominently in early narratives of discovery and exploration is here, roughly a century after the first permanent English settlement in North America, applied to typically European phenomena: "This place is more plentiful in money than most, or indeed, any of the plantations on the continent; [...] their stocks of cattle are incredible." Natural abundance of timber is not mentioned for itself anymore, to delight the reader's imagination, but to fire a prospective settler's interest, as timber is now converted into abundance of "vessels of cedar" or "pitch and tar", of which "none of the plantations are comparable for affording the vast quantities of naval stores."[367] The America of Lawson's *Carolina* has already been Europeanized to a degree that time cannot be turned back anymore to the innocent natural paradise which English discoverers like Barlowe, Hariot, Rosier, or even John Smith had described in their narratives. The ruins of the Roanoke colony "are to be seen at this day, as well as some old English coins which have been lately found", and the Indians living near the area, descendants, it must be believed, of intermarriage with the Lost Colonists, "value themselves extremely for their affinity to the English."[368]

The passages describing Lawson's America, like Daniel Denton's or John Josselyn's, still echo the first discoverers' fascination with a beautiful and abundantly fertile land. However, narrative strategies had to be developed to cope with increasingly numerous instances of futility. An elaborate defensive or prospective rhetoric was used to gloss over the fact that America neither yielded the expected gold and silver, nor did it turn out to be a lubberland of ease offering every man rich returns on little labor.

---

[367] John Lawson, *New Voyage*: 11.
[368] ibid.: 69.

8. Conclusion

The study of travel narratives about English experiences in early North America reveals, especially when texts are read in chronological succession, a surprising stability of narrative strategies and stock elements which unify texts as diverse as descriptions of Higginson's New England and Lawson's Carolina. American historiography has often privileged Plymouth over Jamestown as the first "true" permanent settlement. The Puritan "errand into the wilderness" seemingly offered a more rewarding substance for a narrative of grand success, of civilizing an American wilderness without the moral and economic turmoil of early Jamestown or even Roanoke. A settlement which remained on the brink of extinction by famine, incompetent leadership, and native hostility for decades after its founding did not lend itself well to such a beginning; neither did the narratives it produced function well for a mythification of origins. Only John Smith occasionally styled himself as a suitable "first American". He has been "used" accordingly as a central reference point, as for example in Sharon Rogers Brown's study of American travel narratives as a literary genre: "American literature begins with John Smith's summons to a new frontier of romantic adventure."[369]

Close readings of his early narratives dealing with this frontier, however, have shown that his early America was less a frontier and more a contact zone which offered little space for heroism in reality. Narratives, though, were a different story. In retrospect, Smith was indeed an extremely suitable hero due to his worldmaking narratives. The numerous reworkings around the Pocahontas episode in his writings offer an exciting, yet distorted moment of cultural harmony which has gladly been taken up by popular culture as a positive myth of origin. Nevertheless, the very fact that the "final" Pocahontas episode is a result of intense textual reworking – we might also say fictionalization - shows that this popular myth has much to do with narrative strategy and little with historical facts, as Mary Fuller points out in an analysis of Smith's writings: "The plethora of writing *about* Jamestown evidence a massive investment in fashioning a representation of metaphorical success which would palliate or compensate for material lacks and defailments."[370]

News of every kind is susceptible to manipulation and distortion. News about early America, transmitted to Europe in travel reports, was no exception, and it has been the central aim of this study to expose the narrative strategies by which a

---

[369] Sharon Rogers Brown. *American Travel Narratives as a Literary Genre from 1542 to 1832.* Lewiston, NY: Mellen, 1993.
[370] Mary Fuller. *Voyages in Print: English Travel to America, 1576-1624.* Cambridge: Cambridge University Press, 1995: 91.

report could be fashioned and composed in order to uphold an image in writing that often had little resemblance with reality. In focusing on the major "worldmaking" narratives as historical sources, for example John Smith's accounts of Jamestown or Hariot's of Roanoke, today's canon of early American literature reflects this lasting dominance of narratives over history.

The early attempt at establishing a colony at Roanoke had its own peculiar status in history as well as literature. Perhaps this historical and literary episode exemplifies best the dichotomy between fact and fiction which characterizes so much early English travel writing about North America. Even though the experiment was costly in lives and eventually failed, the colony secured its own niche in history with a "durable, well-defined, mythologized role in popular history as the site of the Lost Colony."[371]

Roanoke and Jamestown had their precursors in the Frobisher and Gilbert voyages to Newfoundland in the 1570s and early 1580s. The narratives which chronicled these voyages set the stage for rhetorical, instead of actual, rehabilitation of failed English ventures in early North America. Narratives about early New England fall into two categories: The first is made up of reports of reconnaissance and trading voyages to the New England coast between 1602 and 1614. While the first two narratives studied here continue to describe the edenic, "superabundant", ravishingly beautiful New World of Barlowe and Hariot, the later ones, especially John Smith's *Description of New England*, resort to a prospective rhetoric of success in the face of contemporary hardships and failure. The second group is made up of narratives originating from the Puritan settlements along the New England coast. The narratives by Edward Winslow and William Wood were structured according to established characteristics of the New World travel report and abundantly praised the "paradise", as John Winthrop termed New England in a letter to his wife. As in the case of Roanoke and Jamestown, however, some narratives also reveal that much of the praise of New England was only rhetoric, or rather propaganda. Thomas Dudley's letter sums up the ill effects of New World propaganda which New England brought forth in the same vein as Jamestown or Roanoke had done before.

The reports from New England are surprisingly similar to reports written about the Southern regions of English settlement on the Eastern seaboard. Reports of New England as well as of Virginia or the Carolinas employed much the same rhetorical strategies when dealing with futility and failure: Whenever mines were mentioned, narrators had to resort to elaborate rhetorical strategies to uphold probabilities even though no mines were found. Examples of such efforts can be found in almost every narrative: "The mountains make show of mineral sub-

---

[371] Mary Fuller, *Voyages in Print*: 39.

stance", and "more than hope may be conceived thereof" (Edward Hayes, *A Report of the Voyage ... by Sir Humphrey Gilbert*); "it cannot in reason be otherwise", or "there cannot be shown any reason to the contrary" (Hariot, *Briefe and True Report*). A river allegedly contains "more than probabilities" (Smith, *Map of Virginia*; Strachey, *Historie of Travell*); "there are hills and mountains making a sensible proffer of hidden treasure" (Robert Johnson, *Nova Britannia*).

Another instance of failure was the paradoxical threat of famine and sickness in midst of a country usually described as incredibly fertile and naturally abundant, as well as "agreeing well" with English constitutions: Edward Hayes reported about Newfoundland that "God [had] superabundantly replenished the earth with creatures serving for the use of man"; Barlowe wrote about Roanoke that "there is such plenty [...] that I think in all the world the like abundance is not to be found"; Hariot was even more precise by saying that "one man may prepare and husband so much ground [...] with less than four and twenty hours labor, as shall yield him victual in a large proportion for a twelve month." Ralph Lane commended the Chesapeake region for its "temperature of climate [and] for fertility of soil" yet his men faced starvation repeatedly when native tribes failed to supply the English with food; George Percy could hardly put his fascination with Virginia's abundant and beautiful nature in words and termed it "this paradise." Yet in the same narrative, he reported that the English died of diseases and famine, sometimes several men a day.

While some narratives like Percy's or letters like Frethorne's or Thomas Dudley's hint at a less-than-perfect early America, the majority of narratives from Newfoundland to South Carolina perpetuated *topoi* of natural abundance, healthful climate, fertile soil, and prospective success. Some features of the New World were repeated almost verbatim again and again. The terms "abundance", "fruitful", and "pleasant" appear in most texts, ranging from Arthur Barlowe to Martin Pring, John Smith's narratives, and from private letters from New England and the Carolinas to promotional tracts like William Wood's or John Josselyn's. Sometimes Old World terminology seemed insufficient; Robert Johnson's *New Life of Virginea* mentioned "endless abundance"; Edward Hayes' narrative of Sir Humphrey Gilbert's Newfoundland voyage describes the land as "superabundantly replenished."

In the face of such extreme praise, the descriptive passages often had to be supported by truth claims and an emphasis of the eyewitness report, as in Francis Higginson's *Letter* to friends in England: "The abundance of sea fish are [sic] almost beyond believing, and sure I would scarce have believed it except I had seen it with mine own eyes."[372] A few decades later, however, reports warned that

---

[372] Francis Higginson, "Letter to H." In: Everett Emerson, *Letters*: 21.

such a life of ease might have negative effects on European settlers in America. John Clayton wrote from Virginia that "every one can live at ease and therefore they scorn and hate to work to advantage themselves, so are poor with abundance."[373] John Archdale wrote a *Description Of that Fertile and Pleasant Province of Carolina* and greatly praised that region; still, he had to mention that natural abundance did not bring out the best in the European settlers there: "In short, its natural fertility and easy manurement is apt to make the people incline to sloth; for should they be as industrious as the Northern colonies, riches would flow in upon them."[374]

Most narratives, however, perpetuated positive descriptions and images of North America, regardless of the region of origin, and possibly contrary evidence. They followed a literary model established decades before the first English voyages to North America by continental European travelers, published in England in early collections like Richard Hakluyt's *Divers Voyages* or Richard Eden's *Decades*. Richard Whitbourne commended Newfoundland as "temperate and fruitful"[375] whereas a letter by George Calvert, Lord Baltimore, reveals the disastrous effect of such propaganda: "I have found by too dearly bought experience which other men for their private interests always concealed from me" that Newfoundland was less than apt for man's easy sustenance.[376] The same is largely true for the other regions which generated narratives of discovery and exploration. Descriptive passages were the common *loci* for standardized praise, whereas narrative passages often reported hardships, death by famine, or violent clashes with natives. Arthur Barlowe and Thomas Hariot established a New World Eden in which man could live in prelapsarian innocence and ease; George Alsop reported that Maryland offered "superabounding plenty." Early reports from New England claimed that regions were "above report notable with His [...] blessings" so much that the Englishmen were "ravished" by the "beauty and delicacy of this sweet soil."[377] George Alsop compared Maryland to a Garden Eden: European settlers "need not look for any other terrestrial paradise to suspend or tire their curiosity upon while she [i.e. Maryland] is extant."[378] John Archdale believed that the settlers' lot in Virginia "is fallen, by the divine hand of providence, into the Ameri-

---

[373] John Clayton. "Letter to a Doctor of Physik." In: Richard Beale Davis, C. Hugh Holman and Louis D. Rubin, Jr., eds. *Southern Writing, 1585-1920*. New York: The Odyssey Press, 1970: 81.
[374] John Archdale. "A New Description of that fertile and Pleasant Province of Carolina." [1707] In Alexander S. Salley, *Narratives*: 290.
[375] Richard Whitbourne. *A Discourse and Discovery of New-Found-Land*. [London, 1620] Facsimile Reprint. Amsterdam, New York: Da Capo Press, 1971: B^v.
[376] George Calvert. "A Letter from Newfoundland." In Myra Jehlen, ed. *The English Literatures of America*. London: Routledge, 1997: 127.
[377] George Alsop. *A Character of Maryland*: 3; John Brereton, "Briefe and True Relation": 41.
[378] George Alsop, *A Character of Maryland*: 4.

can Canaan, a land that flows with milk and honey."[379] It seems that "this earthly paradise"[380] could be found in every region which the English explored, according to the narratives studied here.

Narrative passages were the parts of early English reports from North America where an often grim reality could find expression. In Ralph Lane's report, for example, his America at the end differs markedly from the New World Eden he had described at the beginning. His men were close to starvation, and an upriver voyage of exploration was no longer structured chronologically by days, but by a countdown to zero days of victuals left and imminent starvation. A letter by John Winthrop to his wife in England is characterized by the same dichotomy between a New World paradise and human tragedy when Winthrop enumerates recently deceased settlers but then adds that America to them is a paradise.

Another feature which most New World reports share is a discussion of the reasons for exploring and settling the North American seaboard. These centered primarily on the *vacuum domicilium* thesis and on the glorious project of civilizing and converting the indigenous inhabitants. Questions of natural versus civil rights, the legal status of "barbarians", and questions of land use are closely related to the intense reasoning in many narratives. At the beginning of the seventeenth century, the Eastern seaboard was neither a uniformly aboriginal wilderness nor a virgin land. Even though estimates of Indian population figures along the Eastern seaboard at the time of the first English voyages to America vary, the first Europeans arrived at a populated coastal region, as T. Brasser lays out in a study of coastal Algonkian tribes. "These lowlands as well as the broad river valleys were, in Indian times as in the present, the most densely populated portions of the entire area."[381] Also, the slash-and-burn technique had already changed the face of the land in many places, prompting newly arrived Englishmen to marvel at the "parks" that seemed to have been prepared and maintained by a gardener when other parts of the coast looked like a "howling wilderness."

The issue of settling an allegedly *vacuum domicilium* is at the heart of many early North American travel narratives, and it has been continued into modern times, prompting Perry Miller to root America's origins in the "vacant wilderness" of New England.[382] The strategies devised to support this theory of an "empty wilderness" were, firstly, references to the English discoveries of the Cabots, and

---

[379] John Archdale, "A New Description". In: Salley, *Narratives*: 308.
[380] Robert Johnson, "Nova Britannia": 235-237.
[381] T.J.C. Brasser. "The Coastal Algonkians: People of the First Frontiers." In Eleanor Burke Leacock and Nancy Oestreich Lurie, eds. *North American Indians in Historical Perspective*. New York: Random House, 1971: 64-91: 65.
[382] Perry Miller. *Errand Into the Wilderness*. Cambridge, MA: Belknap Press, 12th printing, 1996: vii.

sometimes even legendary figures like the Welsh prince Madoc[383] were invoked; secondly, in order to strengthen English claims a rhetoric of adequate use of the New World garden was developed to support English expansion on American soil. Indian villages and gardens were disregarded as acceptable permanent settlements and appropriate use of the land: The natives, according to James Rosier in his *True Relation* of 1605 (and very much in line with the legal and moral reasoning of the time) were a "purblind generation, whose understanding it has pleased God so to darken, as they can neither discern, use, or rightly esteem the invaluable riches in midst whereof they live, sensually content with the bark and outward rinds."[384] Even though many narratives mention Indian corn fields and list several garden vegetables the Indians planted, the same narratives reiterated claims that the Indians did not make use of the land and let it lay waste. A special emphasis was placed on adequate manuring, a technique the Indians were usually reported to be ignorant of. Consequently, many early narratives elaborately pictured a future America peopled with able (English) husbandmen, reaping ever greater yields than the narratives already promised with regard to the ubiquitous claims concerning the soil's fertility.

Apart from such a bright future, however, the contemporary English agricultural yields were often so negligible that whole colonies were in danger of starvation and often only kept alive by trading with the Indians for corn. While the quest for gold, silver, or pearls remained on the general agenda, early English colonies were much more desperate to procure food. The task of settling a world and the "if only..." rhetoric designing a future America peopled with skilled and hardworking Englishmen suggests that the Indians, in the eyes of the early colonists, neither settled nor used the land satisfactorily. The English settlers continued to depend on reinforcements from England and trade for corn with the Indians well into the second decade of settlement, attesting to a peculiar gap between rhetoric and reality that is the central characteristic of almost all narratives studied in this thesis. Francis Jennings describes the paradoxical situation of early colonists: "The European 'settlers', who knew nothing of tillage methods in America and were often revolted at the labour of farming, depended on Indian gardens for subsistence between the deliveries of cargoes from overseas."[385]

---

[383] Hakluyt's 1589 edition of the *Principal Voyages* contains "The Voyage of Madoc [...] to the West Indies in the Yeere 1170"; Madoc is said to have declared the countries "pleasant and fruitful" and "without inhabitants". *Principal Navigations*, 506-507.
[384] James Rosier. "A True Relation of the Most Prosperous Voyage." In: George P. Winship, *Sailors' Narratives*: 142.
[385] Francis Jennings. *The Invasion of America: Indians, Colonialism, and the Cant of Conquest.* Chapel Hill, NC: University of North Carolina Press, 1975: 33.

Edward Winslow expressed precisely this dichotomy between imagined and real America in his narrative of 1624: In this "so healthful and hopeful country", the English had "to mew up ourselves in our new-enclosed town; partly because our store was almost empty, and therefore [we] must seek out for our daily food, without which we could not long subsist; but especially for that thereby they [i.e. the Indians] would see us dismayed, and be encouraged to prosecute their malicious purposes."[386] Nevertheless, questions of a just appropriation of Indian land almost always used the *vacuum domicilium* rhetoric, often in connection with the claim of bringing civilization and Christianity to the New World.

The first seal of Massachusetts[387] adequately gave pictorial expression to this rhetoric. The question of converting the Indians featured prominently in official propaganda, but the early narratives from America report little tangible evidence of such efforts, let alone of successfully converted natives. The anonymously published compilation *New England's First Fruits* opens with a chapter "in respect of the Indians", and the "first fruits [...] He has begun to gather in amongst" them.[388] However, the number of these first fruits – converted Indians – pales before the number of "white Indians", of Englishmen who chose to live with Indian tribes.[389] *New England's First Fruits* offers yet another interesting turn on the "come and help us" topic: The motto is not only implicitly applied to the Indians, but also expressly to English plantations in Virginia and the West Indies, they "crying out unto us [...] come and help us" to keep these plantations from starvation. Now, it is no longer the Indians who cry out "come and help us", but European plantations in the New World which are portrayed as relying on victuals from prospering New England.[390]

This rhetoric aimed at Englishmen morally concerned with bringing civilization and the gospel to the "heathens" of the world and their "waste lands" has been a central feature in the rhetoric of imperial powers and echoed throughout history decades before the colony of Massachusetts and long after. Whereas the first Englishmen claimed to have come to America's "heathens" and their "vast wilder-

---

[386] Edward Winslow, *Good Newes:* 12.
[387] Available for example at: http://www.sec.state.ma.us/pre/presea/sealhis.htm. Dec., 2005. "In 1629, King Charles I granted a charter to the Massachusetts Bay Colony, which included the authority to use a seal. It featured an Indian holding an arrow pointed down in a gesture of peace, with the words 'Come over and help us,' emphasizing the missionary and commercial intentions of the original colonists. This seal was used until 1686, shortly after the charter was annulled, and again from 1689-1692."
[388] [Anon.] "New England's First Fruits" [1642]. In: Samuel Eliot Morison. *The Founding of Harvard College.* Cambridge, MA, and London: Harvard University Press, 1995: 421.
[389] cf. James Axtell, "The White Indians of Colonial America". *William and Mary Quarterly,* 3rd ser., 32 (1975): 55-88.
[390] "New Englands First Fruits": 428ff.

ness", in later centuries this rhetoric remained with America (among other nations) and was adapted by politicians who promised to come to the world's "heathens", a topic Eric Cheyfitz discusses in his essay *Tarzan of the Apes*:

> The "object lesson of expansion", as Teddy Roosevelt said, [is] that "peace must be brought about the world's *waste spaces*. [...] Peace cannot be had until the civilized nations have expanded in some shape over the barbarous nations." [...] "It is our duty toward the people living in barbarism to see that they are freed from their chains, and we can free them only by destroying barbarism itself."[391] (italics mine)

Even before English settlements were established on American soil, the younger Richard Hakluyt had claimed that the indigenous peoples of North America "cry out unto us [...] to come and help them."[392]

Another central feature which most of the narratives share has to do with the failure of gaining rich economic rewards in America and also with the failure of converting and civilizing the natives: Many narratives are characterized by a strongly defensive stance; this concerned the question whether it was righteous or not to take away land from Indians, whether the whole effort of outfitting and financing voyages of exploration to America was worthwhile, and whether glowing reports were lying or at least exaggerating. Thomas Hariot set the stage when he admitted that "there have been diverse and variable reports with some slanderous and shameful speeches bruited abroad by many that returned from thence."[393]

John Smith claimed that he had written the description of Virginia in *A Map of Virginia* "to satisfy my friends of the true worth and quality of Virginia. Yet some bad natures will not stick to slander the country [...]." Previous narratives of New World discovery and exploration had established expectations which could hardly be met by infant colonies, and disappointment followed, as John Smith had to concede: "They found not English cities, nor such fair houses, [...] neither such plenty of gold and silver and dissolute liberty as they expected. [...] For the country was to them a misery [...] and their reports here and their own actions there according."[394] These issues were also mentioned by Robert Johnson in *Nova Britannia*: "There are diverse monuments already published in print to the world"; William Strachey wrote of "mouths of ignorance, and slander."[395]

---

[391] Eric Cheyfitz. "Tarzan of the Apes: US Foreign Policy in the Twentieth Century." *American Literary History*, 1/2 (1989): 339-60: 340.
[392] Quoted after: Alden T. Vaughan. "'Expulsion of the Savages'." *William and Mary Quarterly*, 3rd ser., 35 (1978): 60.
[393] Thomas Hariot, *Briefe and True Report*. Reprint of the second edition. London, 1893: 9.
[394] John Smith, "A Map of Virginia." In Philip L. Barbour, *Works of Captain John Smith*: 175f.
[395] Robert Johnson, *Nova Britannia*: 236. William Strachey, *Historie of Travell*: 7.

Edward Winslow spoke of "vile and clamorous reports", and William Wood claimed he had written *New England's Prospect* because "there have some relations heretofore passed the press which have been very imperfect, [being] scandalous and false reports."[396]

Along with such a defensive stance testifying to negative reports about North America, most narrators maintained that their narratives were true because they had been eyewitnesses, and thus authorities on North America. Still, the previous passages point to a contested field of discourse about North America with increasing numbers of participants. Some few narratives were written to counterbalance the propaganda perpetuated in travel narratives of North America and a newfound paradise, incredible fertility, friendly natives, and marvelous chances of economic profit. Christopher Levett, "one of the Council of New England", as the title page states, wrote *A Voyage Into New England*. The narrative was meant to inform his patron, George Duke of Buckingham, of

> the country and the people, commodities and discommodities. [...] To say something of the country: I will not do therein as some have done, to my knowledge speak more than is true: I will not tell you that you may smell the corn fields before you see the land, neither must men think that corn grows naturally (or on trees) nor will the deer come when they are called, or stand still and look at a man, until he shoots him [...] nor the fish leap into the kettle, nor on the dry land, nor are they so plentiful that you may dip them up in baskets [...] which is not truer than that the fowls will present themselves to you with spits through them.[397]

The central rhetorical strategy which made it possible to maintain a positive image of the New World and keep funds flowing for colonizing ventures was developed very early on, in Thomas Hariot's *Briefe and True Report* and later applied in many other narratives. A prospective rhetoric of economic gain enabled the narratives to balance high expectations with present futility. Hariot's narrative is to a considerable extent an enumeration of what America might be or what it might yield.

Ralph Lane devoted much space in his narrative to what he could have accomplished had his colonists not been threatened with starvation and native hostility: He "would have raised a sconce with a small trench" along the way to this said tribe; at some place he "would have raised a main fort. "[398] Robert Johnson

---
[396] Edward Winslow, *Good Newes from New England*: 6; William Wood, *New England's Prospect*: 20.
[397] Christopher Levett. *A Voyage Into New England Begun in 1623*. Ann Arbor, MI: University Microfilms: 22.
[398] Ralph Lane, "Discourse." In: David B. Quinn. *Roanoke Voyages*: 263ff.

applied the same kind of prospective rhetoric because he did not know enough empirically about the country but obviously did not want to let down his audience: "The country [...] is commendable and hopeful in every way." George Alsop suggested that nature's motto for Maryland was "dwell here, live plentifully and be rich."[399] This strategy of transferring America's rewards into the future when the present proved frustratingly unrewarding made it possible for many narratives to establish English colonial activities in a grander narrative frame of eventual success. In a *Geographical Description of the Kingdoms of England, Scotland and Ireland and the Western colonies*, first published in 1673, Richard Blome summed up this unifying effect when he wrote with regard to Virginia that

> much time was spent in the discovery of this country, with vast expenses in the setting forth of ships and not without the great loss of many a poor wretches' life before it could be brought to perfection; but at length, through the industry of Captain John Smith, and other worthy persons, who took great pains for the advancement of these discoveries, fortune began to smile on her.[400]

Some decades later, such prospective rhetoric, together with the feminization of American nature as a benign, nurturing mother, had become a constituent in America's own early literature. Crèvecœur's Farmer James, in *Letters from an American Farmer*, found a worthy American topic of conversation with a Cambridge-educated Englishman in America's abundantly fruitful nature and the future promise to all mankind: "Here [in America]", an acquaintance of Farmer James points out to him, "nature opens her broad lap to receive the perpetual accession of new comers, and to supply them with food. [...] The spectacle afforded by these pleasing scenes must be more entertaining" than many ancient cultural spectacles Europe had to offer. In America, the "anticipated fields of future cultivation and improvement, to the future extent of those generations which are to replenish and embellish this boundless continent" were the peculiar promise and treasure of the New World when compared with the Old.[401]

Mark Twain obviously found in the elaborately exaggerated descriptions of American nature and its sheer vastness, established in many early English reports of the New World, a ready fund for satire. In *The Innocents Abroad*, the sights of the Holy Land pale before every comparison with America. Now, to the innocent American tourist, the writers elaborately describing and praising the Holy Land

---

[399] George Alsop, *A Character*: 4; Robert Johnson, *Nova Britannia*: 238f.
[400] Richard Blome, *Britannia, or a Geographical Description* [1673]. Ann Arbor, MI: University Microfilms: 140.
[401] Hector St John de Crèvecoeur. *Letters from an American Farmer*. London: Dent, 1962: 11f.

are the ones who have to go to considerable lengths in trying to make that destination sound marvelous:

> Every rivulet that gurgles out of the rocks and sands of this part of the world is dubbed with the title of 'fountain', and people familiar with the Hudson, the Great Lakes, and the Mississippi fall into transports of admiration over them and exhaust their powers of composition in writing their praises. If all the poetry and nonsense that have been discharged upon the fountains and the bland scenery of this region were collected in a book, it would make a most valuable volume to burn.[402]

For Twain's American traveler of the nineteenth century, the stereotypical abundance, beauty, and vastness of the American landscape first described by European visitors who quite "exhausted their powers of composition" in finding Old World words to describe the New, has been so deeply ingrained that no words will do anymore to help the American tourist appreciate the Holy Land. The "descriptive benchmarking" begun in sixteenth- and seventeenth-century English reports about North America is firmly in place in later American literature, be it Crèvecoeur's *Letters From an American farmer* or Twain's satirical *Innocents Abroad*.

In the course of this thesis, it has been my aim to unearth the reasons for, and the strategies of, such a "descriptive benchmarking" of early North America for an English, and often also European audience. Many constituent parts of the travel reports analyzed here were derived much less from observation than from classical and medieval legends of faraway lands, images of an earthly Eden, and the first glowing reports of European travelers to the American shores. Reports by Verazzano or Ribaut, published in Richard Eden's and Richard Hakluyt's early compilations of European travel to America, set the stage for a whole tableau of abundant nature, marvelous fertility, exotic flora and fauna, noble or ignoble savages, quick material gain, and rumors of immense riches in precious metals. As a consequence, most of the English reports about North America were composed with, and out of, such a background. Close observation only gradually made its way into these narratives which were often further influenced by promotional interests of a company funding the voyages and settlements. Censorship is another issue which influenced the body of sources as we find them today: Official instructions for voyages of discovery and exploration explicitly asked that no negative reports reach Europe. Therefore, what we find in early American reports are not the "harbingers of [America's] first literature" but a peculiar composition, to repeat Mark Twain's assessment, of fact and fiction, located respectively in narra-

---

[402] Mark Twain. *The Innocents Abroad, Or, the New Pilgrims Progress.* New York: Penguin, 1966: 366f.

tive and descriptive passages. Truth, in these narratives, was indeed a "docile and obedient servant."[403]

The latter, which are usually responsible for creating a certain *effet de réel* in fictional literature, are used to achieve quite the opposite in early English travel reports of North America: They maintain utopian images of paradise, a life of ease, and superabundant natural beauty almost regardless of what the traveler actually experienced. Narrative passages, in contrast, are the locus of a more realistic view on early North America in travel accounts whereas, in fiction, they are the quintessential playground of invention. This stunning inversion of the narrative principle of fiction characterizes much of early English American travel writing and is the central technique by which such narratives could uphold the image of an ideal America, whose very fictionality begins to shine through in reports as early as Thomas Hariot's or Ralph Lane's.

Even though most narratives claimed to be eyewitness accounts and to tell nothing but the truth, their value as reports establishing and transmitting knowledge of early North America is best accessed through the literary techniques employed in narrating events and describing the New World. Only when the narratives are read as a body can the stereotypes applied to various North American regions in descriptions and the rhetorical strategies of "talking away" failure be made visible, as Mary Fuller points out in a study of early English travel narratives and their role in the genesis of an English national consciousness: "If the history of those early decades is about one thing, it is about the ways in which the failure of voyages and colonies were recuperated by rhetoric."[404] In other words, the early history of English contact with North America was largely "made" less by deeds than by words.

Read as a body of sources, these narratives reveal the formation of an ideology which concentrated strongly on a glorious future, on what could be expected instead of what was there in reality. Only in the narratives and their prospective rhetoric does America's promise as a newfound paradise continue to exist, resulting in an America of the future perfect. The present, it seems, was frequently ignored if it was found not to suit prior expectations. Material rewards were then largely projected either temporally into the future, expressed in terms of "if only", or geographically into the as yet unexplored interior of the continent. Either way, eventual fulfilment remained possible. Narratives of English New World exploration and the early stages of settlement were more often than not narratives of futility. However, by taking part in a larger, teleological narrative enterprise, the original, optimistic concept of North America as a land of opportunity and prom-

---

[403] Nelson Goodman, *Ways of Worldmaking*: 18.
[404] Mary Fuller, *Voyages in Print*: 12.

ise remained intact, even if removed into the realm of future possibilities. Description served as the tool by which the image could continue to dominate the facts. Read as a body of worldmaking texts, these narratives establish a coherence and teleology of the English colonial venture that allowed for the accommodation of hardship and failure because they could be couched in this larger context of future progress towards success and cultural sophistication which often remained elusive in individual experience.

Appendix

Chronology

1492	Columbus' first voyage to America
1497	John Cabot sails from Bristol to America and arrives at Newfoundland; the next year, he sets out again but disappears at sea
1507	Francanzano da Montalboddo, *Paesi Nuovamente Retrovati*. Early Account in Italian of Spanish and Portuguese Voyages
1524	Verazzano explores North American coast
1544	Sebastian Münster, *Cosmographia Universalis*. Early German account containing New World voyages
1550	Giovanni Battista Ramusio, *Navigationi et Viaggi*, first major collection of narratives of early modern travel
1554	Richard Eden, *The Decades of the Newe Worlde or West India*
1558	Accession of Elizabeth I
1576	First voyage of Martin Frobisher to Newfoundland; Christopher Hall's narrative *The First Voyage of Master Martin Frobisher to the Northwest*
	Sir Humphrey Gilbert, *A Discourse of a Discoverie for a new passage to Cataia*
1577	Second Frobisher voyage to Newfoundland; Dionyse Settle, *The last voyage into the west and northwest regions [...] by Captaine Frobisher* is published
	Francis Drake begins circumnavigation (returns 1580)
1578	Letters Patent granted to Humphrey Gilbert
	Third voyage of Martin Frobisher to Newfoundland
	George Best, *A True Discourse of the late voyages of discoverie*
	Thomas Ellis, *A true report of the third and last voyage into Meta Incognita*
1582	Richard Hakluyt the younger's *Divers Voyages Touching the Discoverie of America*
1583	George Peckham's *A True Reporte, of the Late Discoveries of Humphrey Gilbert* contained news of America based on Gilbert's fatal voyage

1584	Reconnaisance voyage under the command of Arthur Barlowe to the Carolina banks at Roanoke (Wingandacoa). Natives Manteo and Wanchese are brought to England. Barlowe' narrative is first published in the 1589 *Principal Navigations*
1585	A fleet sails to Carolina (Wococon Inlet) under Sir Richard Grenville
1586	Grenville's relief ships arrive at Roanoke only shortly after the colonists have left with Sir Francis Drake for England. Grenville leaves a few men to hold the fort who are later ambushed by Indians and are never seen again
1587	A new group of colonists arrives at the Carolina Banks under John White who soon returns to England to procure supplies, an effort which failed and only allowed him to return to America in 1590, when the colony had already disappeared
1588	Thomas Hariot, *A Briefe and True Report of the New-Found Land of Virginia*
	Defeat of the Spanish Armada
1589	First edition of Hakluyt's *Principal Navigations*
1590	Theodor de Bry begins publication of the multi-volume *America*
1596	Sir Walter Ralegh, *The Discoverie of the large, rich and bewtiful Empyre of Guiana*
1598-1600	Second, enlarged edition of Hakluyt's *Principal Navigations*
1602	Exploration voyage along the coast of Maine under Cpts. Bartholomew Gosnold and Bartholomew Gilbert. John Brereton wrote a report, *A Briefe and True Relation*, published the same year
1603	Accession of James I
	Martin Pring explores the area around Cape Cod on a trading voyage backed by Richard Hakluyt. A report, *A Voyage Set Out [...] for the Discoverie* was published the same year
1605	George Waymouth explores the area around Monhegan Island. James Rosier wrote an account of the voyage, published the same year, as *A True Relation of the Most Prosperous Voyage*
1606	Two charters for regions in North America are granted to two English groups, the London (chartered for Virginia) and Westcountry (New England) group
1607	Jamestown is founded by the London Company. The first year sees clashes with Indians and explorations inland during which John

	Smith is captured by Powahatan and meets Pocahontas
	George Percy, *Observations gathered out of a discourse of [...] Virginia*
1608	Smith writes the *True Report*; he is elected President of the Virginia Council
	Champlain's third voyage to Canada; Quebec founded
1609	John Smith leaves Jamestown for good
	Lord De La Warr is named Lord Governor and Captain General for Virginia; appoints William Strachey secretary of the colony the next year
	Robert Johnson's *Nova Britannia* is entered for publication
1612	Smith writes *A Map of Virginia*
	Robert Johnson's *The New Life of Virginea* is published as promotion of the colony
	William Strachey. *The Historie of Travell into Virginia Britannia*
1613	Samuel Purchas' *Purchas His Pilgrimage* published
1614	Pocahontas marries John Rolfe
	John Smith sails for New England and returns in late August with only little profit in furs and fish
	Smith's *A Description of New England*
1615	Smith sets out for New England again, and his ship brings back considerable merchandize
	Ralph Hamor publishes an account of the Jamestown colony until June 1614: *A True Discourse of the Present State of Virginia*
1616	Printing of Smith's *The Description of New England* is finished
1617	Ralegh sets sail for Guiana
	Pocahontas dies in England
1618	Ralegh returns to England and is executed
1619	The Pilgrims are granted a patent to settle in Virginia
1620	The Pilgrims arrive at Cape Cod, much farther North than planned
	The Mayflower Compact is signed
	John Smith's *New Englands Trials* is entered for publication

1622	William Bradford succeeds John Carver as governor of the Plymouth colony
	On Good Friday, Indians attack the settlements surrounding Jamestown and kill 347 colonists ("Virginia Massacre")
	Edward Waterhouse. *A Declaration of the State of the Colonie [...] in Virginia. With a relation of the barbarous massacre [...]*
	Mourt's Relation is published anonymously and reports the first years of the Plymouth settlement
1623	Richard Frethorne. *Letter* to his parents.
1624	Smith's *General Historie* is published
1625	James I dies and is succeeded by Charles I
1628	Thomas Morton of Merry Mount upsets the Plymouth colony's leaders and is sent back to England after a punitive expedition led by Miles Standish
1629	Francis Higginson's *Letter to His Friends in England* (later enlarged into *New-Englands Plantation*)
1630	Puritan settlement at Massachusetts Bay
	William Bradford begins writing *Of Plymouth Plantation*
1634	Maryland founded by Lord Baltimore
	William Wood, *New England's Prospect*
1635	Connecticut founded by Thomas Hooker
1636	Rhode Island founded by Roger Williams; Harvard College founded
	-1637 Pequot War
1637	Thomas Morton publishes *New English Canaan*
1642	*New England's First Fruits*
1643	Roger Williams, *A Key into the Language of America*
1653	North Carolina founded
1661	- 1664 British conquest of New Netherland (New York)
1663	South Carolina founded as a proprietary colony
1664	New Jersey founded by Lord Berkeley and Sir George Carteret
	New York founded by the Duke of York after surrender of the Dutch governor

APPENDIX

1666	George Alsop, *A Character of the Province of Maryland*
1670	Daniel Denton, *A Brief Description of New York*
1673	John Josselyn, *An Account of two voyages to New England*
1675	-1678 King Philip's War
1686	John Dunton travels to New England and writes *Letters Written from New England*
1682	Pennsylvania founded by William Penn
1695	John Miller, chaplain to the troops in New York, writes his *Description of the Province and City of New York*
1700-1	John Lawson sets out on a surveying voyage through North and South Carolina; he publishes an account of it, *A New Voyage to Carolina*

9. List of Works Cited

9.1. Primary Sources

Alsop, George. "A Character of the Province of Maryland." In: Richard Beale Davis, C. Hugh Holman and Louis D. Rubin, Jr., eds. *Southern Writing, 1585-1920*. New York: The Odyssey Press, 1970.

[Anon.] "New England's First Fruits". In: Samuel Eliot Morison. *The Founding of Harvard College*. Cambridge, MA, and London: Harvard University Press, 1995: 421-447.

[Anon.] "The Relation of David Ingram." In: *The Principal Navigations, Voiages and Discoveries of the English Nation*. First edition, 1589. Facsimile Reprint ed. David B. Quinn and Raleigh A. Skelton. Cambridge: Hakluyt Society, 1965: 557-559.

Archdale, John. "A New Description of that fertile and Pleasant Province of Carolina". In: Alexander S. Salley Jr, ed. *Narratives of Early Carolina*. New York: Barnes and Noble, 1911, rpt. 1967: 282-311.

Ashe, Thomas. "Carolina, or a Description of the Present State of that Country." In: Alexander S. Salley Jr, ed. *Narratives of Early Carolina*. New York: Barnes and Noble, 1911, rpt. 1967: 138-159.

Banister, John. *John Banister and His Natural History of Virginia, 1678-1692*. Joseph and Nesta Ewan, eds. Urbana, Chicago, London: University of Illinois Press, 1970.

Barlowe, Arthur. "The First Voyage made to the Coastes of America..." In: David B. Quinn. *The Roanoke Voyages. Documents to Illustrate the English Voyages to North America Under the Patent Granted to Walter Raleigh in 1584*. London: Hakluyt Society, 1955, Vol. 1: 91-115.

Bland, Edward. "The Discoverie of New Brittanie". In: Alexander S. Salley Jr, ed. *Narratives of Early Carolina*. New York: Barnes and Noble, 1911, rpt. 1967: 1-19.

Blome, Richard. *Britannia, or a Geographical Description....* [London, 1673]. Ann Arbor, MI: University Microfilms, n.d.

Bradford, William. *Of Plymouth Plantation, 1620-1647*. Ed. Samuel Eliot Morison. New York: The Modern Library, 1967.

Brereton, John. "A Briefe and True Relation of the Discoverie of the North Part of Virginia; being a most pleasant, fruitfull and commodious soile; Made this present yeere 1602 by Captaine Bartholomew Gosnold, and Captain Bartholomew Gilbert by the permission of Sir Walter Ralegh. Written by John Brereton." In: George Parker Winship, ed. *Sailors' Narratives of Voyages along the New England Coast, 1524-1624*. New York: Burt Franklin, 1968: 33-50.

Calvert, George. "A Letter from Newfoundland." In: Myra Jehlen, ed. *The English Literatures of America*. London, New York: Routledge, 1997: 127.

Clayton, John. "Letter to a Doctor of Physik." In: Richard Beale Davis, C. Hugh Holman and Louis D. Rubin, Jr., eds. *Southern Writing, 1585-1920*. New York: The Odyssey Press, 1970: 81.

Crèvecoeur, Hector St. John de. *Letters from an American Farmer*. London: Dent, 1962.

Denton, Daniel. *A Brief Description of New-York: Formerly Called New-Netherlands. Together with the Manner of its Situation, Fertility of the Soil, Healthfulness of the Climate, and the Commodities thence Produced. Also Some Directions and Advice for Such as shall go thither.* [London, 1670]. Ann Arbor, MI: University Microfilms, 1971.

Dudley, Thomas. "Letter to the Lady Bridget." March 12 and 28, 1630/31. In: Everett Emerson, ed. *Letters from New England. The Massachusetts Bay Colony, 1629-1638*. Amherst, MA: University of Massachusetts Press, 1976: 67-83.

Dunton, John. *Letters Written from New England. AD 1686, in which are described his voyages by sea, his travels on land and the characters of his friends and acquaintances*. Ed. W.H. Whitmore. New York: Burt Franklin, no date.

Frethorne, Richard. "Letter to His Parents, March 20, April 2 and 3, 1623." In: Myra Jehlen, ed. *The English Literatures of America*. London: Routledge, 1997: 123-125.

Eden, Richard. *The Decades of the Newe Worlde*. [Ed. Edward Arber. *The First Three English Books on America. Being Chiefly Translations, Compilations, &c., by Richard Eden.*] Rptd. New York: Kraus Reprint Co., 1971.

Ellis, Thomas. "The Third and Last Voyage into Meta Incognita, Made by M. Martin Frobisher in the Yeere 1578, Written by Thomas Ellis." In: *The Principal Navigations, Voiages and Discoveries of the English Nation*. First edition, 1589. Facsimile Reprint ed. David B. Quinn and Raleigh A. Skelton. Cambridge: Hakluyt Society, 1965: 630-635.

Hakluyt, Richard. *Divers Voyages touching the discoverie of America, and the Islands adiacent unto the same, made first of all by our Englishmen, and afterward by the Frenchmen and Britons.* London, 1582. Facsimile Reprint. Amsterdam: Theatrum Orbis Terrarum, 1967.

--- *The Principal Navigations, Voiages and Discoveries of the English Nation.* First edition, 1589. Facsimile Reprint ed. David B. Quinn and Raleigh A. Skelton. Cambridge: Hakluyt Society, 1965.

Hall, Christopher. "The First Voyage of Master Martin Frobisher to the Northwest for the Search of the Straight or Passage to China, Written by Christopher Hall." In: *The Principal Navigations, Voiages and Discoveries of the English Nation.* First edition, 1589. Facsimile Reprint ed. David B. Quinn and Raleigh A. Skelton. Cambridge: Hakluyt Society, 1965: 615-622.

Hamor, Ralph. *A True Discourse of the Present State of Virginia, and the successe of the affaires there till the 18 of June, 1614. Together with a relation of the severall English townes and forts, the assured hopes of that countrie and the peace concluded with the Indians. The Christening of Powhatans daughter and her mariage with an English-Man. Written by Ralphe Hamor the yonger, late Secretarie in that Colony.* [London, 1615]. Facsimile Reprint, New York: Da Capo Press, 1971.

Hariot, Thomas. *A Briefe and True Report of the Newfound Land of Virginia.* Reprint of the Second Edition. London, 1893.

Hayes, Edward. "A Report of the Voyage and the Success Thereof, Attempted in the Year of Our Lord 1583 by Sir Humphrey Gilbert Knight, Intended to Discover and to Plant Christian Inhabitants in Places Convenient [...] Written by Edward Hayes." In: *The Principal Navigations,* ed. David B. Quinn and Raleigh A. Skelton. Cambridge: Hakluyt Society, 1965: 679-697.

Higginson, Francis. "Letter to His Friends in England". In: Everett Emerson, ed. *Letters from New England. The Massachusetts bay Colony, 1629-1638.* Amherst, MA: University of Massachusetts Press, 1976.

Johnson, Robert. "Nova Britannia: Offering most excellent fruites by planting in Virginia. Exciting all such as are well affected to further the same." [London, 1609] In: David B. Quinn, ed. *New American World. A Documentary History of North America to 1612*, 5 vols. New York: Arno Press and Hector Bye, 1979: 234-248.

--- *The New Life of Virginea.* London 1612. New York: Da Capo Press, 1971. Facsimile Reprint.

Josselyn, John. *An Account of two Voyages to New England.* Ed. Paul J. Lindholdt. Hanover: University Press of New England, 1988.

Knight, Sarah Kemble. "The Journal of Madam Knight". Ed. Sargent Bush, Jr. In: *Journeys in New Worlds. Early American Women's Narratives*. Ed. William L. Andrews. Madison, WI: University of Wisconsin Press, 1990: 69-116.

Lane, Ralph. "An Account of the Particularities of the Employments of the English Men left in Virginia by Sir Richard Grenville Under the Charge of Master Ralph Lane." In: David B. Quinn. *The Roanoke Voyages. Documents to Illustrate the English Voyages to North America Under the Patent Granted to Walter Raleigh in 1584*. London: Hakluyt Society, 1955. Vol. I: 255-294.

--- Letters sent from Roanoke. In: David B. Quinn. *The Roanoke Voyages. Documents to Illustrate the English Voyages to North America Under the Patent Granted to Walter Raleigh in 1584*. London: Hakluyt Society, 1955. Vol. I: 199-214.

Lawson, John. *A New Voyage to Carolina. Containing the Exact Description and Natural History of that Country; together with the present state thereof.* Ed. Hugh Talmage Lefler. Chapel Hill, NC: University of North Carolina Press, 1967.

Levett, Christopher. *A Voyage Into New England Begun in 1623*. Ann Arbor, MI: University Microfilms, n. d.

Miller, John. "A Description of the Province and City of New York; With Plans of the City and several Forts as they Existed in the Year 1695." Ed. Cornell Jaray. *Historic Chronicles of New Amsterdam, Colonial New York and Early Long Island*. Port Washington, New York: 1968.

Percy, George. "A Discourse of the Plantation of the Southern Colonie in Virginia." In: David B. Quinn, ed. *New American World. A Documentary History of North America to 1612*, 5 vols. New York: Arno Press and Hector Bye, 1979. Vol. V: 266-274.

Pond, John. "Letter to William Pond. March 15, 1631." In: Everett Emerson, ed. *Letters from New England. The Massachusetts Bay Colony, 1629-1638*. Amherst, MA: University of Massachusetts Press, 1976: 64-67.

Pring, Martin. "A Voyage set out from the Citie of Bristoll at the charges of the chiefest Merchants and Inhabitants of the said Citie [...] for the discoverie of the North part of Virginia [1603]." In: George Parker Winship, ed. *Sailors' Narratives of Voyages along the New England Coast, 1524-1624*. New York: Burt Franklin, 1968: 53-63.

Purchas, Samuel. *Hakluytus Postumus* [London, 1625]. Rpt. Glasgow: MacLehose, 1905.

Ralegh, Sir Walter. "The Discoverie of [...] Guiana." In: Giles B. Gunn, ed. *Early American Writing*. New York: Penguin, 70.

Rosier, James. "A True Relation of the Most Prosperous Voyage Made this Present Year 1605 by Captain George Waymouth in the Discovery of the Land of Virginia." In: George Parker Winship, ed. *Sailors' Narratives of Voyages along the New England Coast, 1524-1624*. New York: Burt Franklin, 1968: 101-151.

Settle, Dionyse. "The Second Voyage of Master Martin Frobisher, Made to the West and Northwest Regions, in the Yeere 1577 [...]." In: *The Principal Navigations, Voiages and Discoveries of the English Nation*. First edition, 1589. Facsimile Reprint ed. David B. Quinn and Raleigh A. Skelton. Cambridge: Hakluyt Society, 1965: 622-630.

Smith, John. "A True Relation of Such Occurrences and Accidents of Noate as Hath Happened in Virginia." In: Philip L. Barbour, ed. *The Complete Works of Captain John Smith*. Chapel Hill, NC and London: University of North Carolina Press, 1986. Vol. I: 4-117.

---"A Map of Virginia. With a Description of the Countrey, the Commodities, People, Government and Religion." In: Philip L. Barbour, ed. *The Complete Works of Captain John Smith*. Chapel Hill, NC and London: University of North Carolina Press, 1986. Vol. I: 131-180.

--- "A Description of New England, Or, The Observations, and Discoveries, of Captain John Smith (Admirall of that Country) in the North of America, in the year of our Lord 1614. With the proofe of the present benefit this Countrey affoords." In: Philip L. Barbour, ed. *The Complete Works of Captain John Smith*. Chapel Hill, NC and London: University of North Carolina Press, 1986. Vol. I: 305-363.

--- "The General History of Virginia, New England, And the Summer Isles." In: Philip L. Barbour, ed. *The Complete Works of Captain John Smith*. Chapel Hill, NC and London: University of North Carolina Press, 1986.

Strachey, William. "A True Reportory of the Wracke, and Redemption, of Sir Thomas Gates Knight." In: David B. Quinn, ed. *New American World. A Documentary History of North America to 1612*, 5 vols. New York: Arno Press and Hector Bye, 1979. Vol. V: 288-301.

--- *The Historie of Travell into Virginia Britania*. Ed. Louis B. Wright and Virginia Freund. London: Hakluyt Society, 1953.

Twain, Mark. *The Innocents Abroad, Or, the New Pilgrims Progress*. New York: Penguin, 1966.

Underhill, John. *Newes from America. Or, a New and Experimentall Discoverie of New England* [London, 1638]. New York: Da Capo Press, 1971.

Waterhouse, Edward. *A Declaration of the State of the Colony of Virginia [...] With a Relation of the Barbarous Massacre in the Time of Peace and League.* [London, 1622]. Amsterdam, New York: Da Capo Press, 1970.

Whitaker, Alexander. *Good Newes from Virginia* [1613]: Ann Arbor, MI: University Microfilms, n.d.

Whitbourne, Richard. *A Discourse and Discovery of New-Found-Land* [London, 1620]. Facsimile Reprint. New York: Da Capo Press, 1971.

White, John. "The Fourth Voyage Made to Virginia, With Three Shippes, in the Yeere 1587." In: David B. Quinn, ed. *The Roanoke Voyages. Documents to Illustrate the English Voyages to North America Under the Patent Granted to Walter Raleigh in 1584.* London: Hakluyt Society, 1955: Vol. II: 515-539.

--- "The Fifth Voyage of Master John White Into the West Indies and Parts of America Called Virginia, in the Yeere 1590." In: David B. Quinn, ed. *The Roanoke Voyages. Documents to Illustrate the English Voyages to North America Under the Patent Granted to Walter Raleigh in 1584.* London: Hakluyt Society, 1955. Vol. II: 598-622.

Winslow, Edward. *Good Newes from New England* [1624]. Bedford, MA: Applewood Books, no date.

Winthrop, John. "Letter to Margaret Winthrop." In: Everett Emerson, ed. *Letters from New England. The Massachusetts Bay Colony, 1629-1638.* Amherst, MA: University of Massachusetts Press, 1976: 60-61.

Wood, William. *New England's Prospect.* Ed. Alden T. Vaughan. Amherst, MA: University of Massachusetts Press, 1977.

Yeardley, Francis. "Letter to John Ferrar Esq." In: Alexander S. Salley Jr, ed. *Narratives of Early Carolina.* New York: Barnes and Noble, 1911, rpt. 1967: 25-27.

9.2. Secondary Sources

Adams, Percy G. *Travellers and Travel Liars, 1600-1800*. Berkeley: University of California Press, 1962.

--- *Travel Literature and the Evolution of the Novel*. Lexington, KY: University of Kentucky Press, 1983.

---*Travel Literature through the Ages*. New York: Garland, 1988.

Allen, John. "Lands of Myth, Waters of Wonder: The Place of the Imagination in the History of Geographical Exploration." In: David Lowenthal and Martyn J. Bowden, eds. *Geographies of the Mind. Essays in Historical Geography*. New York: Oxford University Press, 1976: 41-61.

Allen, John Logan. *North American Exploration*. Lincoln, NE: University of Nebraska Press, 1997.

Alpers, Svetlana. "Describe or Narrate? A Problem in Realistic Representation." In: *New Literary History*, Vol. VIII (1976): 16-41.

Anderson, Benedict. *Imagined Communities*. London: Verso, 1983.

Andrews, William L., and Arthur G. Bradley, eds. *Travels and Works of Captain John Smith*. Rpt. New York: Franklin, 1965.

--- , ed. *Journeys in New Worlds: Early American Women's Narratives*. Madison: University of Wisconsin Press, 1990.

Axtell, James. "The White Indians of Colonial America." *William and Mary Quarterly*, 3rd ser., 32 (1975): 55-88.

--- *The European and the Indian: Essays on the Ethnohistory of Colonial North America*. New York, Oxford: Oxford University Press, 1981.

--- "The Power of Print in the Eastern Woodlands." *William and Mary Quarterly*, 3rd ser., 44/2 (1987): 301-9.

---*Beyond 1492: Encounters in Colonial North America*. New York, Oxford: Oxford University Press, 1992

Babha, Homi K. "Representation and the Colonial Text." In: F. Gloversmith. *The Theory of Reading*. Brighton: Harvester, 1984: 93-122.

--- , ed. *Nation and Narration*. London: Routledge, 1990.

--- *The Location of Culture*. London: Routledge, 1994.

Bailyn, Bernard. *Voyagers to the West*. New York: Knopf, 1986.

--- *The Peopling of British North America*. New York: Knopf, 1986.

Barbour, Philip L. *The Jamestown Voyages under the First Charter.* Cambridge: Hakluyt Society, 1969.

--- ed. *The Complete Works of Captain John Smith.* 3 vols. Chapel Hill, NC: University of North Carolina Press, 1986.

Barker, Francis et al., eds. *Literature and Power in the Seventeenth Century.* Colchester: University of Essex, 1981.

--- et al., eds. *Europe and Its Others.* Colchester: University of Essex, 1985.

--- , Peter Hulme, Margaret Iversen, eds. *Cannibalism and the Colonial World.* Cambridge: Cambridge University Press, 1998.

Bataille, Gretchen M., ed. *Native American Representations: First Encounters, Distorted Images and Literary Appropriations.* Lincoln, NE: University of Nebraska Press, 2001.

Baudet, Henri. *Paradise on Earth. Some Thoughts on European Images of Non-European Man.* Transl. Elizabeth Wentholt. New Haven and London: Yale University Press, 1965.

Bellin, Joshua David. *The Demon of the Continent: Indians and the Shaping of American Literature.* Philadelphia: University of Pennsylvania Press, 2001.

Bercovitch, Sacvan. *The Puritan Origins of the American Self.* New Haven, London: Yale University Press, 1975.

Billings, Warren M., ed. *The Old Dominion in the Seventeenth Century: A Documentary History of Virginia*: Chapel Hill, NC: University of North Carolina Press, 1975.

Bitterli, Urs. *Die Entdeckung Amerikas. Von Kolumbus bis Alexander von Humboldt.* München: Beck, 1992.

--- *Cultures in Conflict. Encounters between European and Non-European Cultures, 1492-1800.* Stanford: Stanford University Press, 1998.

Brasser, T. J. C. "The Coastal Algonkians: People of the First Frontiers." In Eleanor Burke Leacock and Nancy Oestreich Lurie, eds. *North American Indians in Historical Perspective.* New York: Random House, 1971: 64-91.

Brettell, Caroline B. "Introduction: Travel Literature, Ethnography, and Ethnohistory." In: *Ethnohistory*, Vol. 33, No. 2 (May 1986), 127-138.

Brown, Sharon Rogers. *American Travel Narratives as a Literary Genre From 1542 to 1832. The Art of a Perpetual Journey.* Lewiston, NY: Mellen, 1993.

Brumm, Ursula. *Geschichte und Wildnis in der amerikanischen Literatur*. Berlin: E. Schmidt, 1980.

Bucher, Bernadette. *Icon and Conquest: A Structural Analysis of the Illustrations of de Bry's Great Voyages*. Chicago: University of Chicago Press, 1981.

Campbell, Mary B. *The Witness and the Other World: Exotic European Travel Writing, 400-1600*. Ithaca, NY: Cornell University Press, 1988.

--- *Wonder and Science: Imagining Worlds in Early Modern Europe*. Ithaca, NY: Cornell University Press, 2002.

--- "Travel Writing and Its Theory". In: Peter Hulme and Tim Youngs, eds. *The Cambridge Companion to Travel Writing*. Cambridge: Cambridge University Press, 2002: 261-278.

Canny, Nicholas and Anthony Pagden, eds. *Colonial Identity in the Atlantic World, 1500-1800*. Princeton, NJ: Princeton University Press, 1987.

--- *Europeans on the Move. Studies on European Migration, 1500-1800*. Oxford: Clarendon, 1994.

--- "Writing Atlantic History; or, Reconfiguring the History of Colonial British America." In: *Journal of American History* 86 (1999): 1093-1114.

Canup, John. "Cotton Mather and Criolian Degeneracy." In: *Early American Literature* 24 (1989): 20-34.

--- *Out of the Wilderness: The Emergence of an American Identity in Colonial New England*. Middletown, CT: Wesleyan University Press, 1990.

Casper, Scott E., ed. *Perspectives of American Book History*. Washington, D.C.: Library of Congress, 2002.

Chambers, Ross. "Strolling, Touring, Cruising: Counter-Disciplinary Narrative and the Literature of Travel." In: James Phelan and Peter Rabinowitz, eds. *Understanding Narrative*. Columbus, OH: Ohio State University Press, 1994: 17-42.

Chard, Chloe and Helen Langdon. *Transports: Travel, Pleasure and Imaginative Geography, 1600-1830*. New Haven: Yale University Press, 1996.

Cheyfitz, Eric. "Tarzan of the Apes: US Foreign Policy in the Twentieth Century." *American Literary History*, 1 /2 (1989): 339-360.

Cole, Garold L. *Travels in America: From the Voyages of Discovery to the Present. An Annotated Bibliography of Travel Articles in Periodicals, 1955-1980*. Norman: University of Oklahoma Press, 1984.

Conroy, Jane, ed. *Cross-Cultural Travel*. New York: Peter Lang, 2003.

Crane, Werner W. *The Southern Frontier, 1670-1732*. Reprint. Westport, CT: Greenwood Press, 1979.

Craven, Wesley Frank. *The Colonies in Transition, 1660-1713*. New York: Harper&Row, 1968.

--- *The Southern Colonies in the Seventeenth Century, 1607-1689*. Baton Rouge: Louisiana State University Press, 1975.

Cumming, William P., et al. *The Exploration of North America, 1630-1776*. London: Elek, 1974.

Crosby, Alfred W. "Virgin Soil Epidemics as a Factor in the Aboriginal Depopulation of North America." *William and Mary Quarterly*, 3rd ser., 33 (1976): 289-299.

Danforth, Susan. *Encountering the New World, 1493-1800*. Providence, RI: John Carter Brown Library, 1991.

Dietsche, Petra. *Das Erstaunen über das Fremde. Vier literaturwissenschaftliche Studien zum Problem des Verstehens und der Darstellung fremder Kulturen*. Frankfurt: Peter Lang, 1984.

Doggett, Rachel, ed. *New World of Wonders: European Images of the Americas, 1492-1700*. Seattle: University of Washington Press, 1992.

Dussel, Enrique D. *The Invention of the Americas: Eclipse of the "Other" and the Myth of Modernity*. New York: Continuum, 1995.

Elliott, Emory, ed. *American Colonial Writers*. 2 vols., 1606-1781. Detroit: Gale, 1984.

--- , ed. *Columbia Literary History of the United States*. New York, London: Columbia Press, 1988.

Elliott, John Huxtable. *The Old World and the New, 1492-1650*. Cambridge: Cambridge University Press, 1970.

--- "Renaissance Europe and America: A Blunted Impact?" In: *First Images of America. The Impact of the New World on the Old*, ed. Fredi Chiappelli. Berkeley, CA: University of California Press, 1976. Vol. I, 11-26.

Ellul, Jacques. *Propaganda. The Formation of Men's Attitudes*. New York: Vintage Books, 1973.

Elsner, Ja`s and Joan Pau Rubiés, eds. *Voyages and Visions: Towards a Cultural History of Travel*. London: Reaktion Books, 1999.

Enders, Andrea. "Fremde Menschen in fremder Natur. Formen der Vereinnahmung einer Neuen Welt in romanischen Reiseberichten des 16. Jahrhunderts." In: *Fremderfahrung in Texten des Spätmittelalters und der frühen Neuzeit*, ed. Günther Berger und Stephan Kohl. Trier: Wissenschaftlicher Verlag Trier, 1993: 103-150.

Fausz, J. Frederick and John Kukla. "A Letter of Advice to the Governor of Virginia." *William and Mary Quarterly*, 3rd ser., 34 (1977): 104-129.

Franklin, Wayne. *Discoverers, Explorers, Settlers: The Diligent Writers of Early America.* Chicago: University of Chicago Press, 1978.

Fuller, Mary C. *Voyages in Print: English Travel to America, 1576-1624.* Cambridge: Cambridge University Press, 1995.

Galinsky, Hans. "Exploring the Exploration Report and Its Image of the Overseas World." In: *Early American Literature* 12 (1977): 5-24.

--- *Geschichte amerikanischer Kolonialliteratur.* Vol. I:1542-1676. Darmstadt: Wissenschaftliche Buchgesellschaft, 1991.

Geertz, Clifford. *The Interpretation of Culture. Selected Essays.* New York: Basic Books, 1973.

--- "Boundaries of Narrative." In: *New Literary History* VIII (1976): 1-13.

--- *Narrative Discourse.* Ithaca, NY: Cornell University Press, 1990.

Gilbert, Helen and Anna Johnston, eds. *In Transit. Travel, Text, Empire.* New York: Peter Lang, 2002.

Gilmore, Michael T., ed. *Early American Literature.* Englewood Cliffs, NJ: Prentice-Hall, 1980.

Gombrich, Ernst H. *Art and Illusion.* New York: Pantheon, 1960.

--- *The Image and the Eye: Further Studies in the Psychology of Pictorial Representation.* London: Phaidon, 1998.

Goodman, Nelson. *Ways of Worldmaking.* Indianapolis: Hackett, 1978.

Grabbe, Hans-Jürgen, ed. *Colonial Encounters.* Heidelberg: Winter, 2003.

Greenblatt, Stephen. "Invisible Bullets: Renaissance Authority and its Subversion: Henry IV and Henry V." In: *Political Shakespeare.* Ed. Jonathan Dollimore and Alan Sinfield. Ithaca, NY and London: Cornell University Press, 1985: 18-47.

--- *Marvelous Possessions: The Wonder of the New World.* Chicago: University of Chicago Press, 1991.

--- , ed. *New World Encounters.* Berkeley: University of California Press, 1993.

Greene, Jack P. and J.R. Pole, eds. *Colonial British America: Essays in the New History of the Early Modern Era.* Baltimore: Johns Hopkins University Press, 1984.

--- *Imperatives, Behaviors and Identities: Essays in Early American Cultural History*. Charlottesville, VA: University Press of Virginia, 1992.

--- *The Intellectual Construction of America: Exceptionalism and Identity from 1492 to 1800*. Chapel Hill, NC: University of North Carolina Press, 1993.

--- *Interpreting Early America: Historiographical Essays*. Charlottesville: University of Virginia Press, 1996.

Gunn, Giles B., ed. *Early American Writing*. New York: Penguin, 1994.

Gura, Philip F. "The Study of Colonial American Literature, 1966-1987." *William and Mary Quarterly*, 3rd ser., 45 (1988): 305-41.

Hadfield, Andrew. "Writing the New World: More 'Invisible Bullets'." *Literature and History* 2:2, 2nd series (1991): 3-19.

--- *Literature, Travel, and Colonial Writing in the English Renaissance, 1545-1625*. Oxford: Clarendon Press, 1998.

---, ed. *Amazons, Savages and Machiavels (1530-1630)*. Oxford: Oxford University Press, 2001.

Harbsmeier, Michael. "Writing and the Other: Traveller's Literacy, or Towards an Archaeology of Orality." In: Karen Schousboe and Michael T. Larsen, eds. *Literacy and Society*. Copenhagen: Akademisk Forlag, 1989: 197-228.

Hegeman, S. "Native American 'Texts' and the Problem of Authenticity." *American Quarterly*, 42/2 (1989): 265-83.

Helms, Mary W. *Ulysses' Sail: An Ethnographic Odyssey of Power, Knowledge, and Geographical Distance*. Princeton, NJ: Princeton University Press, 1988.

Henretta, James A., and Gregory Nobles. *Evolution and Revolution: American Society, 1600-1820*. Lexington, MA: Heath, 1987.

Herget, Winfried and Karl Ortseifen, eds. *The Transit of Civilization from Europe to North America.* Essays in Honor of Hans Galinsky. Tübingen: Narr, 1986.

Hogden, M. T. *Early Anthropology in the 16th and 17th Centuries*. Philadelphia: University of Pennsylvania Press, 1964.

Honour, Hugh. *The New Golden Land*. London: Lane, 1975.

--- *The European Vision of America*. Cleveland, OH: Cleveland Museum of Art, 1975.

Hulme, Peter. *Colonial Encounters*. London: Methuen, 1986.

--- et al., eds. *Cannibalism and the Colonial World*. Cambridge: Cambridge University Press, 1998.

--- and Tim Youngs, eds. *The Cambridge Companion to Travel Writing*. Cambridge: Cambridge University Press, 2002.

Hulton, Paul."Images of the New World: Jacques Le Moyne de Morgues and John White." In: *The Westward Enterprise: English Activities in Ireland, the Atlantic, and America, 1480-1650*. Ed. Kenneth R. Andrews. Liverpool: Liverpool University Press, 1978: 195-214.

--- *America 1585: The Complete Drawings of John White*. London: British Museum Publications, 1984.

Jameson, Fredric. *The Political Unconscious: Narrative as a Socially Symbolic Act*. Ithaca, NY: Cornell University Press, 1981.

Jehlen, Myra."History Before the Fact; or, Captain John Smith's Unfinished Symphony." *Critical Inquiry* 19 (1993): 677-692.

--- "The Literature of Colonization." In: *Cambridge History of American Literature*. Ed. Sacvan Bercovitch. Cambridge: Cambridge University Press, 1994: 13-169.

--- , and Michael Warner, eds. *The English Literatures of America: 1500-1800*. New York: Routledge, 1997.

Jennings, Francis. *The Invasion of America: Indians, Colonialism, and the Cant of Conquest*. Chapel Hill, NC: University of North Carolina Press, 1975.

Jones, Howard Mumford. "The Colonial Impulse: An Analysis of the Promotion Literature of Colonization." *Proceedings of the American Philosophical Society*, 90 (1946): 131-61.

--- *O Strange New World. American Culture: The Formative Years*. New York: Viking Press, 1964.

Jordan, Winthrop. *White over Black: American Attitudes towards the Negro, 1550-1812*. New York: Norton, 1977.

Kalb, Gertrud. *Bildungsreise und literarischer Reisebericht. Studien zur englischen Literatur (1700-1850)*. Nürnberg: Carl, 1981.

Kittay, Jeffrey, ed. *Towards a Theory of Description*. (Yale French Studies, 61) New Haven: Yale University Press, 1980.

Kolodny, Annette. *The Lay of the Land. Metaphor as Experience*. Chapel Hill, NC: University of North Carolina Press, 1975.

--- *The Land Before Her: Fantasy and Experience of the American Frontiers, 1630-1860*. Chapel Hill, NC: University of North Carolina Press, 1984.

Korte, Barbara. "Der Reisebericht aus anglistischer Sicht: Stand, Tendenzen und Desiderate seiner literaturwissenschaftlichen Erforschung." *Zeitschrift für Anglistik und Amerikanistik*, 42 (1994): 364-372.

--- *English Travel Writing: From Pilgrimages to Postcolonial Explorations*. Basingstoke: Macmillan, 2000.

Kupperman, Karen Ordahl. "English Perceptions of Treachery, 1583-1640: The Case of the American 'Savages'." *Historical Journal* XX (1977): 263-287.

--- "Death and Apathy in Early Jamestown." *Journal of American History*, 66.1 (June 1979): 24-40.

--- *Settling with the Indians: The Meeting of English and Indian Cultures in America, 1580-1640*. Totowa, NJ: Rowman and Littlefield, 1980.

--- "The Puzzle of the American Climate in the Early Colonial Period." *American Historical Review* 87 (1982): 1265-68.

--- *Roanoke: The Abandoned Colony*. Totowa, NJ: Rowman&Allanheld, 1984.

--- *North America and the Beginnings of European Colonization*. Washington, DC: American Historical Association, 1992.

--- *Providence Island, 1630-1641: The Other Puritan Colony*. Cambridge: Cambridge University Press, 1993.

--- , ed. *America in European Consciousness, 1493-1750*. Chapel Hill, NC: University of North Carolina Press, 1995.

--- *Indians and English: Facing Off in Early America*. Ithaca, NY: Cornell University Press, 2000.

Leacock, Eleanor Burke and Nancy Oestreich Lurie, eds. *North American Indians in Historical Perspective*. New York: Random House, 1971.

Leed, Eric J. *Die Erfahrung der Ferne: Reisen von Gilgamesch bis zum Tourismus unserer Tage*. Frankfurt a. M.: Campus; 1993.

Lefler, Hugh T. "Promotional Literature of the Southern Colonies." *Journal of Southern History*, 33 (1967): 3-25.

Lestringant, Frank. *Mapping the Renaissance World: The Geographical Imagination in the Age of Discovery*. Oxford: Polity Press, 1994.

Levenson, Jay A, ed. *Circa 1492. Art in the Age of Exploration*. National Gallery of Art Exhibition Catalogue. Washington, DC: National Gallery of Art, 1991; New Haven and London: Yale University Press, 1991.

Levernier, James A. and Douglas Wilmes, eds. *American Writers before 1800*. Westport, CT: Greenwood Press, 1983.

Looby, Christopher. *Voicing America: Language, Literary Form, and the Origins of the United States*. Chicago: University of Chicago Press, 1995.

Lurie, Nancy Oestreich. "Indian Cultural Adjustment to European Civilization." In: James Morton Smith, ed. *Seventeenth-Century America. Essays in Colonial History*. Chapel Hill, NC: University of North Carolina Press, 1959: 33-60.

Mackenthun, Gesa. *Metaphors of Dispossession: American Beginnings and the Translation of Empire*. Norman: University of Oklahoma Press, 1996.

Marshall, Peter J. and Glyndwr Williams. *The Great Map of Mankind: Perceptions of New Worlds in the Age of Enlightenment*. Cambridge, MA: Harvard University Press, 1982.

McGhee, Robert. *The Arctic Voyages of Martin Frobisher*. Seattle: University of Washington Press, 2001.

Meinig, Donald W. *The Shaping of America: A Geographical Perspective on 500 Years of History*. Vol. 1, Atlantic America, 1492-1800. New Haven, CT: Yale University Press, 1986.

Merrens, Roy H. "The Physical Environment of Early America: Images and Image Makers in Colonial South Carolina." *Geographical Review*, 59 (1969): 530-556.

--- and George D. Terry. "Dying in Paradise: Malaria, Mortality, and the Perceptual Environment in Colonial South Carolina." *Journal of Southern History*, 50 (1984): 533-550.

Mezciems, Jenny. "'Tis not to Divert the Reader': Moral and Literary Determinants in Some Early Travel Narratives." *Prose Studies*, 5:1 (May 1982): 1-19.

Miller, Perry. *The New England Mind from Colony to Province*. Cambridge, MA: Harvard University Press, 1953.

--- *Errand Into the Wilderness*. Cambridge, MA: Belknap Press, 12th printing, 1996.

Morrison, Samuel Elliott. *The European Discovery of America: The Northern Voyages 500-1600*. New York: Oxford University Press, 1971.

Murray, David. *Forked Tongues: Speech, Writing, and Representation in North American Indian Texts*. Bloomington: Indiana University Press, 1991.

Myers, Robin and Michael Harris, eds. *Journeys through the Market: Travel, Travellers, and the Book Trade*. Folkestone: St. Paul's Bibliographies, 1999.

Nash, Gary. "The Image of the Indian in the Southern Colonial Mind." *William and Mary Quarterly*, 3rd ser., 29 (1972): 222-223.

O'Gorman, Edmundo. *The Invention of America*. Bloomington: Indiana University Press, 1961.

Page, Evelyn. *American Genesis: Pre-Colonial Writing in the North*. Boston, Gambit: 1973.

Pagden, Anthony. *European Encounters with the New World. From Renaissance to Romanticism*. New Haven, CT: Yale University Press, 1993.

--- "The Impact of the New World on the Old: The History of an Idea." *Renaissance and Modern Studies* XXX: 1-11.

Parker, John. *Books to Build an Empire: A Bibliographical History of British Overseas Interests to 1620*. Amsterdam: Israel, 1965.

Payne, Anthony. "'Strange, remote, and farre distant countreys': The Travel Books of Richard Hakluyt." In: Michael Harris and Robin Myers, eds. *Journeys through the Market: Travel, Travellers, and the Book Trade*. New Castle, DE: Oak Knoll Press, 1999, 1-37.

Pearce, Roy H. *Savagism and Civilization*. London: University of California Press, 1988.

Pennington, Loren E. "The Amerindian in English Promotional Literature, 1575-1625." In: Kenneth R. Andrews, ed. *The Westward Enterprise: English Activities in Ireland, the Atlanic, and America, 1480-1650*. Liverpool: Liverpool University Press, 1978.

Penrose, Boies. *Travel and Discovery in the Renaissance, 1420-1620*. Cambridge, MA: Harvard University Press, 1952.

Porter, Harry C. *The Inconstant Savage. England and the North American Indian, 1500-1660*. London: Duckworth, 1979.

Pratt, Marie Louise. *Imperial Eyes: Travel Writing and Transculturation*. London: Routledge, 1992.

Quinn, David B. *The Roanoke Voyages 1584-1590. Documents to Illustrate the English Voyages to North America Under the Patent Granted to Walter Raleigh in 1584*. London: Hakluyt Society, 1955.

--- *England and the Discovery of America, 1481-1620*. London: Allen&Unwin, 1974.

--- *New American World: A Documentary History of North America to 1612*, 5 vols. New York: Arno Press and Hector Bye, 1979.

--- *Set Fair for Roanoke: A Documentary History of North America to 1612.* 5 vols. Chapel Hill, NC: University of North Carolina Press, 1985.

--- *European Approaches to North America, 1450-1640.* Aldershot, VT: Ashgate, 1998.

Raban, Jonathan. *Coasting.* London: Picador, 1987.

Richter, Daniel K. *Facing East From Indian Country: A Native History of Early North America.* Cambridge, MA and London: Harvard University Press, 2001.

Romm, James S. *The Edges of the Earth in Ancient Thought: Geography, Exploration and Fiction.* Princeton, NJ: Princeton University Press, 1992.

Ronda, James P. "'We Are Well As We Are': An Indian Critique of Seventeenth-Century Christian Missions." *William and Mary Quarterly*, 3rd ser., 34 (1977): 66-82.

Rubiés, Joan Pau. "Instructions for Travelers: Teaching the Eye to See." *History and Anthropology* 9 (1996): 139-190.

--- "Futility in the New World: Narratives of Travel in Sixteenth-Century America." In: Ja`s Elsner and Joan Pau Rubiés, eds. *Voyages and Visions: Towards a Cultural History of Travel.* London: Reaktion Books, 1999: 74-100.

--- "Travel Writing and Ethnography." In: Peter Hulme and Tim Youngs, eds. *The Cambridge Companion to Travel Writing.* Cambridge: Cambridge University Press, 2002: 242-260.

Ryan, Michael T. "Assimilating New Worlds in the 16th and 17th Centuries." In: *Comparative Studies in Society and History* 21 (1981), 519-38.

Said, Edward. *Orientalism.* London: Routledge&Kegan, 1978.

--- *Culture and Imperialism.* New York: Random House, 1993.

Salisbury, Neil. *Manitou and Providence: Indians, Europeans, and the Making of New England, 1500-1643.* New York: Oxford University Press, 1982.

--- *The Indians of New England: A Critical Bibliography.* Bloomington: Indiana University Press, 1982.

--- "The Indians' Old World: Native Americans and the Coming of Europeans." *William and Mary Quarterly*, 3rd ser., 53 (1996): 435-458.

Savage, Henry Jr. *Discovering America, 1700-1875.* New York: Harper&Row, 1979.

Scanlan, Thomas. *Colonial Writing and the New World 1583-1671: Allegories of Desire.* Cambridge: Cambridge University Press, 1999.

Seed, Patricia. "Taking Possession and Reading Texts: Establishing the Authority of Overseas Empires." In: *William and Mary Quarterly*, 3rd ser., 49 (1992), 183-209.

--- *Ceremonies of Possession in Europe's Conquest of the New World, 1492-1640*. New York: Cambridge University Press, 1995.

Seelye, John. *Prophetic Waters: The River in Early American Life and Literature*. New York: Oxford University Press, 1977.

Sheehan, Bernard W. *Savagism and Civility: Indians and Englishmen in Colonial Virginia*. Cambridge: Cambridge University Press, 1980.

Sherman, William H. "Stirrings and Searchings (1500-1720)." In: Peter Hulme and Tim Youngs, eds. *The Cambridge Companion to Travel Writing*. Cambridge: Cambridge University Press, 2002: 17-36.

Slotkin, Richard. *Regeneration Through Violence: The Mythology of the American Frontier, 1600-1860*. Middletown, CT: Wesleyan University Press, 1973.

Smith, James Morton, ed. *Seventeenth-Century America: Essays in Colonial History*. Chapel Hill, NC: University of North Carolina Press, 1959.

Spengemann, William. *A New World of Words: Redefining Early American Literature*. New Haven, CT: Yale University Press, 1994.

Stagl, Justin. *A History of Curiosity: The Theory of Travel, 1550-1800*. Chur: Harwood Academic Publishers, 1995.

Strelka, Joseph. "Der literarische Reisebericht." In: *Prosakunst ohne Erzählen: Die Gattung der nicht-fiktionalen Kunstprosa*. Ed. Klaus Weissenberger. Tübingen: Niemeyer, 1985: 169-184.

Thwaites, Reuben Gold. *The Jesuit Relations and Allied Documents: Travels and Explorations of the Jesuit Missionaries in New France, 1610-1791*. Cleveland, OH: Burrows, 1970 [microfilm edition].

Todorov, Tzvetan. *The Conquest of America: The Question of the Other*. Transl. by Richard Howard. New York: Harper&Row, 1984.

--- "The Journey and Its Narratives." In: *Transports: Travel, Pleasure, and Imaginative Geography, 1600-1830*. Ed. Chloe Chard and Helen Langdon. New Haven and London: Yale University Press, 1996: 287-296.

Vaughan, Alden T. "'Expulsion of the Savages': English Policy and the Virginia Massacre of 1622." *William and Mary Quarterly*, 3rd ser., 35 (1978): 57-84.

--- *New England Encounters: Indians and Euroamericans, ca. 1600-1850: Essays Drawn from the New England Quarterly*. Boston, MA: Northeastern University Press, 1999.

Viviès, Jean. *English Travel Narratives in the 18th Century*. Transl. Claire Davidson. Aldershot: Ashgate, 2002.

Washburn, Wilcomb E. "The Moral and Legal Justifications for Dispossessing the Indians." In: *Seventeenth-Century America. Essays in Colonial History*, ed. James Morton Smith. Chapel Hill, NC: University of North Carolina Press, 1959: 15-32.

Westrem, Scott D. *Discovering New Worlds: Essays on Medieval Exploration and Imagination*. New York, London: Garland, 1991.

White, Hayden. "The Value of Narrativity in the Representation of Reality." *Critical Inquiry* 7.1 (1980): 5-27.

--- *Tropics of Discourse*. Baltimore: Johns Hopkins University Press, 1984.

--- *The Content of the Form: Narrative Discourse and Historical Representation*. Baltimore: Johns Hopkins University Press, 1987.

Wright, Louis B. *The Elizabethans' America*. London: Arnold, 1965.

Young, Alexander. *Chronicles of the Pilgrim Fathers*. Boston, 1841.

Zuckerman, Michael. "The Fabrication of Identity in Early America." *William and Mary Quarterly*, 3rd ser., 34 (1977): 183-214.

American Culture

herausgegeben von
Norbert Finzsch, Bettina Friedl,
Hans-Peter Rodenberg und Joseph C. Schöpp

Band 1 Carsten Springer: Crises: The Works of Paul Auster. 2001.

Band 2 Carsten Blatt: Wege aus dem Krieg. Strategien literarischer Verarbeitung des Vietnam-Traumas in den Romanen von Tim O'Brien. 2001.

Band 3 Lars Schroeder: Slave to the Body. Black Bodies, White No-Bodies, and the Regulative Dualism of Body-Politics in Old South. 2003.

Band 4 Larissa Bendel: *The requirements of our life is the form of our art*. Autobiographik von Frauen der Beat Generation. 2005.

Band 5 Maike Kolbeck: From Word to Land. Early English Reports from North America as World-making Texts. 2008.

www.peterlang.de